NUMEROLOGY UNVEILED

THE MAIA METHOD

VOLUME TWO

How to live the ideal relationship with your lover,
your child or your professional partner

All calculations explained in this book can be
done for free, by going to our website
www.numerology-unveiled.com

Numerology Charts & Resources
including our free tool for calculations
www.online-numerology.com

Our powerful online Numerology Software
www.numeyoga.pro
Learn more about sidereal and karmic astrology
www.nostredame.com
Discover our online Astrology Software
www.astrozeus.pro

Michel Pirmaïer is the creator of the Maia method.
Method registered by Michel Pirmaïer and Wilfrid Pochat at the I.N.P.I. (France)
© 2011 Nostredame Éditions – Annecy (France) for the original French version
© 2016 Wilfrid Pochat & Michel Pirmaïer – Nostredame Publishing - Annecy (France) for the English/US version

Wilfrid Pochat & Michel Pirmaïer

NUMEROLOGY UNVEILED

VOLUME TWO

How to live the ideal relationship with your lover, your child or your professional partner

Nostredame Publishing

Translated from French by
Françoise Cadoux

Special thanks to
Chantal Anders
for her final read-through

To Valérie…

Introduction

"All lies in numbers."

Pythagoras

In our first volume, "The Unveiled Numerology", we had announced there would be a sequel. So we have kept our promise and here is the second volume. Essentially this book is meant to be practical, easy to read and easy to work with. The first volume aimed to lay out the metaphysical grounds of numerology and define the Maia method, as discovered by Michel. The second volume aims to highlight the symbolism and the energy of the numbers which enable us to comprehend how the relationships between two persons unfold and what is truly at stake.

To start with, it is obviously agreed that we do not live alone and that a relationship with another person takes on a particular dimension. Relationships undoubtedly drive us to question ourselves. As a matter of fact, discovering who the "Other One" is (the 2) enables one to discover oneself, in a process of individualization (the 1). This explains why, in a metaphysical perspective, 1 and 2 were created simultaneously. 2 does not stem from the addition 1+1. In numerology, 1+1=1. As an image, if you add white to white, you will get white. To create life, two different energies must be blended together. The energies of duality are represented by 1 and 2.

One cannot deny that the first embodied soul we meet on this earth (or should we say "meet again") is our mother. The bond with this feminine entity is so crucial that it determines our very existence and what we will make of it. This is why our mother's physical, mental and moral composition is such an important element when establishing a numerological chart. The Maia method, which is extensively expanded upon in our first volume, is based on this principle. Chapter II goes over the foundations of this method once more, thus enabling us to achieve a reliable numerological reading of who we truly are and how we relate to our close circle of friends and loved ones.

Our first maternal encounter deeply impacts our life. As we grow, we all need a certain amount of time to be able to unravel and distinguish what is genuinely ours from what we have inherited. We are certainly a part of our ancestral lineage and genetics, but we also need to discover what our true inner nature is. A spiritual path can enable us to differentiate from what belongs to us, to what belongs to our families or to past lives. Our incarnation in a tridimensional space requires that we understand that which can be coined as a "differentiation" process.

Any incarnated soul in search of their true nature must learn how to let go of all the things that do not belong to them. A great deal of information is passed on by other people through our lineage (family beliefs, stories and secrets ...etc). We take them on, even though they do not belong to us. They remain in our subconscious until we realize they are not ours. This process started at a very early stage, when we were babies. At that time, we were unable to filter, untangle and differentiate what belonged where. All the information we needed to grow up in this world has been transmitted to us through different actors in our close or less close surroundings: parents, siblings, relatives, teachers, the media and so on ... Nevertheless, we can wonder if that is all there is to it. This is why it is essential to analyze who we truly are, so as to be able to identify our deep inner nature and differentiate it from the package we have received at birth through our family background and culture. Where are we coming from, and why? What is our true mission in this incarnation? What are our genuine attributes? These are the questions that general sciences attempt to tackle, often failing to provide appropriate answers. In turn, esoteric sciences deal with the more subtle and relevant elements of answers that this book precisely strives to accomplish.

Numerology enables us to analyze how the different actors in our lives behave and why. By unveiling our actors' costumes, we appear as we truly are. Through a benevolent and yet adamant outlook, numerology thus reveals our deep nature, as well as the nature of the relationships we engage in. It helps us to understand why particular relationships emphasize particular positive or negative features. It points out the reasons why we react so dramatically when we are confronted with specific situations or persons. It so happens that what we most dislike about ourselves is very often highlighted by specific events in our lives. In other words, life often manifests and acts out precisely what we struggle to conceal, whether it is conscious or not. We have all been through situations in which we suddenly lost control, due to trivial triggering factors. It is OK as long as we use this opportunity as a safeguard or as a mirror in which we can observe the unfolding processes at work. But the positive realization we might obtain out of this event will only be achieved if we are true to ourselves, and above all, non-judgmental.

In order to launch a thorough and accurate numerological study of how two persons relate to each other, it is essential to identify a series of markers and to establish a hierarchy among them according to their relative importance. Keeping in mind that numbers are expressed throughout a wide range of meaningful significance, the main danger for the numerologists, lies in the risk of getting lost in the process of differentiating the most substantial elements from the less important elements. Taking into account the intensity of the different markers makes it possible for the numerologist to give value to the most essential indicators while leaving behind the least represented features. Such hierarchy prevents the numerologist from saying everything, anything and the exact opposite at the same time. This being said, entire books could be written based only on the minor features of numerological charts, for even minor indicators are interesting.

We will study how to work out the most meaningful markers (called "signifiers"), such as the Life Path, the Expression Number or the Aspiration Number.

In this second volume, we will analyze how the most meaningful indicators inter-react with one another, like astrologists use with the different aspects of the planets to read charts as accurately as possible. Furthermore, we also provide the advanced readers with a gripping investigation steeped in the basis of the most significant numbers (chapter IX). The definition of the aspects between numbers might seem slightly contrived, but this has been done intentionally, thus enabling to further emphasize the advantages and drawbacks of certain associations. As we examine them more expansively, we will see how numerology enables us to underline how we work in the presence of our given partners, no matter what their social background, age or gender may be.

Through the interactions of the most meaningful markers, we have chosen to study three different types of relationships: the parent/child relationships, the love and sex relationships and the socio-professional relationships.

Michel has already extensively expanded upon the links between astrology and numerology. To articulate these different aspects, we have therefore based our analysis on his wide experience and craft. One of the main difficulties we have encountered is that all meaningful indicators had to be given their full and complete definitions: true inner nature, expression, aspiration of the soul, potential... It might be useful here to point out that the numerological analysis of a Life Path 1 with a Life Path 4 is different from the interaction between an Active Number 1 and an Active Number 4.

What's more, we have tested our findings on our close circle of relatives, friends and even celebrities, so as to verify the foundations of our statements; because we hold the view that everything must be checked through practice.

We did not want to offer a mere sub-standard +/- chart, which would have resulted in over-simplifying the complex realities of our relationships. Understanding the link between two numbers, reflecting the bond between two persons, is far more interesting. Simple can also be subtle.

The science of numbers can definitely enable us to develop more harmony in our relationships with other people, by underlining the possible traps we should try to avoid. Wanting to be free involves getting to know oneself deeply. Getting to know oneself deeply entails being able to enhance the positive aspects of our personalities while subduing the negative ones.

These very choices are part of a new social paradigm, in keeping with the new energies at work in the world (as we write these lines). A new mode of expression and communication is being born, coming from the heart, and not the intellectual mind. It is therefore not at all surprising that the feminine principle Yin is returning to the full. And yet, it is not doing so at the expense of the masculine principle Yang. It is high time that the masculine principle actually surrenders the prominent position it has held for too long, thus becoming a complementary balance to the feminine principle, rather than an opposing one. At last, as Prince Charming takes a step back, Sleeping Beauty is waking up and gaining back the power she should never have lost in the first place (but that is another story...)

We all yearn to meet the ideal partner who will help us face life's hardships more easily. We feel stronger when we are two, provided we get along well...

All things considered, in our relationships, we all strive to reach the same goal. How can I acknowledge, accept and take into account the differences between the I and the Other One, without giving up who I am, and staying true to my own Self? This is precisely how this very book was written, by Michel and myself. Exploring this issue enabled us to both come up with this second volume. All in all, considering the topic of our work, how could it *not* have been written by two people?

CHAPTER I

The Hidden face behind each Number

"The Pythagoreans claim that all lies in numbers, and the perfect number is Ten. Ten is obtained by adding up the first four figures in order; this is why Ten is called Tetrachtys."

Photius library (9th century BC)

Both scientific and metaphysical aspects reside in numerology. Simple mathematical operations are needed to get accurate results. Numerology mainly uses additions, although subtractions and theosophical reductions are used as well. This latter process consists in adding up all the figures which make up a number superior to 9, until a single-digit figure is eventually obtained (from 1 to 9). One rule must be abided by: the numbers 11 and 22 should never be reduced.

Example: $39 \rightarrow 3 + 9 = 12$ (the result is superior to 9, therefore must be further reduced) $12 \rightarrow 1 + 2 = 3$.

Numerology consists in interpreting the different combinations which stem from the addition of various numbers. For instance, if you add up 1+2, the result is not a mere addition. What we are in presence of here is a different entity altogether, stemming from the alchemy of two different numbers. As such, the 3 resulting from 1+2 embodies a different energy, which is overshadowed by the duality of 1 and 2. All of these notions have been expanded upon in the first volume of "The Unveiled Numerology", and a wide and accurate overview of the qualities of every number has been given.

The arithmological approach of numbers mainly comes from the teachings of Pythagoras and his disciples. These teachings were given approximately 2,500 years ago.

This world has been created so that new and diverse possibilities could be experimented and other universes be created. The world acts as a resourceful playground for the "creative energies of the universe", as coined by Edgar Cayce, which has enabled them to create countless experiences and endless futures. Such experiments unfold in a concrete world, in which four principles rule:

- The principle of individualization. The mind is separated from the All by the ego, so as to experiment the dynamics of separation. Thus the 1.

- The principle of duality. The separation gave rise to a differentiation process. I discover that the other one is not me and that the other one is also entitled to his/her own individuality. Thus the 2.

- The principle of space. This is what de facto separates the two distinctive and individual entities. Thus the 3.

- The principle of time. Because going from one entity to another is not instantaneous, it takes time. Thus the 4.

All the other numbers come from the addition or the combination of these four simple single-digit figures. Please note that multiplications are never used in numerology.

Suppose you only have one ingredient (1, 2, 3 or 4). Whether it is added up or multiplied does not change anything, it stays as it is. In other words, suppose you are making carrot soup. To do that, you only use carrots. You can add or multiply carrots as much as you want, yet your soup will taste only of carrots. But suppose you add another ingredient? The taste then will obviously change. Metaphorically speaking, we bathe in a soup of numbers!

If you add the four principles at work in this world (1 + 2 + 3 + 4), you get 10, which, through a theosophical reduction, further gives the principle of Unity. (1+0=1). How about that, for magic?

The simple numbers

The single-digit numbers which precede the Unity (10).

0

In numerology, "zero" embodies a very particular energy. It bears potential. It may have different meanings:

Examples:

1) If you have no letters worth 8 (H, Q, Z in English for instance), the intensity of the letter 8 is worth 0, which actually means that 8 is missing.

2) If a number finishes with 0, it strengthens the potential of the number once it has been reduced. $30 \rightarrow 3 + 0 = 3$.

1
Fire

1 is the first principle, the individualization. It is fulfilled by itself alone. It experiences freedom. The ego prevails, whereas the expression of feelings is less important. It endeavors to achieve and face adversity. It thrives on forcing destiny and overcoming limits. It impulses, initiates, boosts and shows the way. It is yearning for acknowledgment and recognition of each and every one of its deeds.

"Ones" are convinced they are righteously right, no matter what. Whether people agree with them or not doesn't matter to them. Disagreements only make them stronger and more determined. They can be dry, harsh and adamant. They need to be aware they are their own worst enemy. If they keep arguing and bursting into fits of anger, they will eventually burn out. There is nothing they enjoy more than attempting to assert their views, convince people and urge them to do things their way. They are direct, somewhat aggressive and their straightforwardness may upset the people around them.

"Ones" are flamboyant and fiery beings. But they can also be naive, for they overestimate their power. Yet, their conspicuous sense of honor can lead them to behave in extremely generous ways. They would never ever hit an enemy who has fallen down, for example. But they tend to forget that life is more than just a battleground. They must become aware of this fact as soon as possible, otherwise they may suffer severe backlash and get badly hurt.

They are of course very warm-hearted beings, which is not surprising, given their very nature!

2
Water

With 2 comes the awareness of duality. I am not the only one, the other one exists, I must compromise. Like the unborn child in the mother's womb who depends on his/her mother to have a body, "Twos" are fully aware that they must rely on other people. Their deep inner nature is one of great sensitivity, which can be extreme, and which enables them to take into account who the other one is. Ones are the active components, whereas Twos are the reactive components. Their evolution and direction they take in their destiny are intimately linked to their capacity to master their emotions. This is a crucial issue they must deal with, unless they want to slowly drift away on stormy oceans and eventually drown.

They tend to delegate and let other people decide for them, hoping to get some advantages and benefits. They aim to escape what they can't face, and give endless love and affection. By doing so, they expect other people to do the same for them. And this does not always happen! They are the perfect spouses, mates, associates and collaborators.

"Twos" are very moved by children, animals, and any suffering beings. They are devoted people who are dedicated to the well-being of those around them and give a lot to their little world. It is very useful to take note of their advice, for they often have immediate deep intuitions.

They must refrain from becoming over-sensitive. Their tendency to whine might eventually become toxic for them and, what's more, make their loved ones flee. They need to get rid of this way of being; otherwise they may end up alone. And they can't stand being alone! In case of repeated failure, they might develop a certain form of cynical self-deprecation, which can eventually ruin their own life as well as that of their loved ones.

They are very intuitive, which is not surprising, given their aquatic nature!

3
Air

"Threes" represent space, and the distance there is between the self and the other one. Threes are created when the umbilical cord is cut, between the mother and the child. It is generally agreed that nature hates void, therefore Threes will strive to make up for that all lifelong. They are adamant in making themselves heard. They are intent on bridging the gaps of silence which they struggle so hard with and find difficult to accept.

They are active, dynamic and need a lot of space to act, move around and express themselves. They are driven by an urge to communicate. They may not easily accept being contradicted when their close circle of friends and loved ones disagree with them. They must avoid controversy if they don't want to be upset. If they lose their freedom of expression, they are likely to fall into depression or indulge in gossip and provocation. They must take care not to be blown away like feathers in the wind.

They are two-sided and can display either one or the ther personality. People usually don't know which way Threes are going, for Threes never show their emotions. They can say one thing and then the exact opposite, which is very uncomfortable for their loved ones. They are young spirits who always have the last word, but never want to get involved in anything in a lasting way. They always keep a door open, just in case they need to escape. They tend to over-simplify things, which may make them appear shallow and not committed enough.

They are skilled at graphic arts. They are motivated by speech and movement, which is not surprising, given their airy nature!

4
Earth

"Fours" are stabilizers. They are deeply grounded and are the foundations. After « Threes » who strive to invade any vacant space, the world needs to be structured and « Fours » are here especially for this purpose.

Of course, this process needs time; nothing can be built just by snapping one's fingers. Fortunately, Fours have a lot of time. They are deeply aware that organizing and setting things up require time. In order to master the laws that structure matter, they use patience, persistence and consistence. If these requirements are not met, Fours feel deeply frustrated. It is generally agreed that everything comes in time, and Fours are intent on proving this methodically. This being said, Fours are rooted in this world in such a way that might prevent them from following their spontaneous impulses.

While "Fours" are skilled with matter and time, they nevertheless tend to be too slow and rigid. If not careful they are liable to turn into inert, cold statues. They must learn how to express what they feel and think. They also need to refrain from thinking too much and act more, carrying out their plans.

They are grounded in patience and caution, which is not surprising, given their earthly nature!

5
Ether
(1 + 4) or (2 + 3)

What's special about « Fives » is that they combine the four previous principles, because they can either be created out of 1 + 4 or 2 + 3. This particular new energy embodies an entity which is able to use the first 4 principles so as to explore the world. As a metaphor, Fives are like thumbs that are able to use all other four fingers to satisfy their need for discovery. As a matter of fact, dealing with the world does involve a certain form of awareness, doesn't it? And perhaps they want to experiment that which attracts them.

We have five senses, and Fives use all of them to explore and perceive what is around them. "Fives" are curious about everything and strive to push their own limits even further in order to gain knowledge. They constantly try to widen their vital space, which they consider too small for them. This being said, they are liable to scatter their energy around and waste it. This is the main danger they face. Not only are they longing for adventure and discoveries, they also love to show their independence. This might trigger excessive excitability within them, and rebelliousness against the established order. In keeping with our metaphor, isn't the thumb somehow opposed to the other fingers?

"Fives" are original and this is how they regard themselves. They hate nothing more than being compared to other people. They want to be the only ones. They are deeply independent loners, who, paradoxically enough can't cope without their friends. Avant-garde domains are open to them.

They are made to explore immense (outer) spaces, which is not surprising, given their "etheric" nature!

6
(1 + 2 + 3) or (2 + 4)

"Sixes" symbolize perfection, in that they are *the* first perfect number [1], and the only one among the nine single-digit numbers. It is therefore not surprising that they are constantly searching for perfection. They thrive on detail and accuracy, and love carefully achieved tasks. Their sense of organization leaves no room for chance. Before they undertake any type of enterprise, they will think over it again and again, plan and prepare each and every step. They struggle to be in control over all aspects of their lives. Sounds tiring, doesn't it? As a matter of fact, they can become extremely tired mentally speaking, especially if they don't calm down and stop focusing on what they are dissatisfied about and that which isn't good enough. They never get involved without measuring the possible consequences of their deeds, for they hate it when things are rough or botched as they want everything to be perfectly planned. They are very committed in what they do and will always try to respect their obligations.

Their ideal world includes their close circle of friends and loved ones as well, because they need to live among their peers, to whom they apply the same scrupulous rules as for themselves. They love to welcome and host their guests, giving them the very best.

"Sixes" must learn how to relax, and accept what they regard as tacky or vile. If not, they can become cold towards others. They should refrain from asserting their opinions too loudly, and judging the world around them. Their excessive mental activity can trigger all sorts of illnesses. They can break free of this, by letting go of their judgmental mind. Nevertheless, despite their natural reserve, they are deeply humane and ethical. They are skilled at many diverse activities, such as singing, writing, commerce and specialized technologies.

---

[1] To be perfect, a number must be equal to the sum of its proper divisors (except that of itself). The first perfect number is 6, because of the sum of its proper divisors 1+2+3=6.

The next perfect number is 28 (1+2+4+7+14).

Note: To create 6 from the four principles/numbers, 2 is always required. Ex: 1 + **2** + 3 or **2** + 4. This explains why Sixes rely on the other (2).

7
(1 + 2 + 4) or (3 + 4)

"Sevens" are the expression of ideals, commitment and vocation. They are driven by their quest for the absolute. They need their lives to be meaningful and want their resolve to be honored. They are curious about everything and are constantly looking for new fields of research. They are enamored by an idealized view of the world, in which they play a prominent role. They need to know that God has given them a mission... and if the contract was signed by His/Her hand, then even better!

They are charismatic individuals, in search of icons and idols. The depth of their inner life urges them to constantly push back their limits, overcome obstacles and get involved in exploring the world around them. Their commitments are straightforward and unidirectional. They are often too direct and blunt, and find it difficult to accept failures and change. When they promise something, they expect other people to do the same. If others don't keep their promises, they feel betrayed. Although they find it difficult to find the right words and tone to express their inner self, they can expand in length upon their feelings (paradoxically enough); and when they do so are skilled orators. They can also be very good actors, which is why one should not take what they say for granted. Their skills in drama can open a lot of doors for them and they sure know how to make use of them.

Sevens never act lightly, for they always strive to protect their own. If you belong to their close circle of friends or loved ones, you will benefit greatly from their generosity. If not, you will obtain nothing at all. They act tactful and never obtrusive when they try to protect their loved ones. Although they are idealistic, they do have a deep sense of reality as they have a need to live comfortably. It is difficult not to be under the spell of their tactful and charming ways. They know it and must not abuse it, or it might lead into serious backlash. If they don't want to end up bitter and alone (and they hate being alone!), they must learn to take other people's advice into account, although they find this difficult. They can easily indulge in gossip and arguments. They love books. They can also be deceitful and make up a lot of stories. The areas they are skilled in are so numerous that it is impossible to note them all. They are able to specialize in just about anything.

Note: Sevens always require a Four, to be created out of the four principles/numbers. 1 + 2 + 4 or 3 + 4.

8
(1 + 3 + 4)

"Eights" are the archetypes of the karmic numbers, inasmuch as they are based on the sexual nature of humans. Their energy is considerable as it is the energy of sexuality, power and domination. This number embodies the primary energy (nicknamed "the primary soup", by some scientists) at work in the world from the beginning of life. Creation also means destruction, for both are intimately linked. Here, there is no discussion, no compromise. Two extremes are together. As a matter of fact, this aspect can be seen in its very calligraphy: two earths/two circles sit one on top of the other which represents the infinite. Draw a big 8 on the ground: wherever you walk on the line, you will end up where you started. Life is made of such winding loops, ups and downs.

The mechanisms which urge Eights to explore the world are mysterious. They themselves find it hard to define what motivates them. They aim to take pleasure in each and every thing of this earthly existence, and yet they struggle to keep away from these very pleasures, always attempting to justify themselves. This is why they act covertly. They would like to master all aspects of life, but they do not want to be the center of attention. They actually loathe nothing more than when people are being intrusive and invade their privacy, lest people discover their little indiscretions...

It is generally agreed that the aims justify the means, which is exactly what Eights think. This being said, Eights are likely to face many dangers. If they don't try to behave more justly, trouble is to be expected. Because they are never afraid of hazards, they are capable of persistently falling into deep traps. Moreover, they can be naive and gullible, which further enhances the risks. They might want to analyze things more deeply, or they may end up getting trapped in their own ploys. If they are ever abused in any way, their revenge can be terrible!

Provided they manage to find a way towards the light, they have the ability to become saints. They are generous, helpful and understanding.

Note: Eights are created out of the principles/numbers 1 + 3 + 4 with 2 being absent. Conversely, they combine the active energies of 1 and 3 with the structure of 4.

9
(2 + 3 + 4)

« Nines » are deeply mystical beings. This number is the last of the single-digit numbers and bears the weight of all the others, as if it had reached the end of a cycle. Nines benefit from the accumulated experience and they are fully aware that this world is not only material. Their intuitive knowledge and their natural empathy enable them to have access to the so-called spiritual world, and thereby take them away from the material aspect of life. They are intuitive and very compassionate. Relentless energy flows through them and they don't really know what to do with it, at least at first. As time goes by, experience will enable them to better master their emotions rather than drowning in them. They are like very sensitive sponges and therefore find it difficult to create their own personality, in that they tend to absorb or copy what they perceive around them. Their deep faith and connection with the invisible drive them to accept life as it comes. They consider they are guided and there is nothing anyone can do about it.

Nines are helpful and attentive to other people's suffering and yet they tend to flee from what makes them suffer. They might feel like running away as soon as clouds appear in their sky and they know trouble is on its way. They only go for the essential in life. They are likely to be a little lazy and not very organized. They like to take their time and not be rushed. They know how to seize opportunities and are able to adjust to just any type of circumstances. They are very flexible with their loved ones' demands and people appreciate them for their kindness. They do not have a big ego, and therefore they are not moved by banal flattery, although they enjoy feeling loved. They are tremendously romantic and sentimental. They will have to learn how to be more disciplined and have a healthy lifestyle, as they have a tendency to carelessly let everything go and deteriorate. Such negligence might then lead them to having big physiological problems. They are often afraid and yet this very fear can spur them to break free from lethargy and daydreaming. In short, their fear can be a stimulating incentive.

Master Numbers

11

"Elevens" belong to the master numbers. They should never be reduced to obtain 2. When you are working out numbers, if you get 11 after a theosophical reduction, leave it as such. You do reduce for instance a 12, 12 → 3 (1 + 2), but you cannot reduce an 11, which is made up of two 1's, that is to say twice the same principle. The same intangible rule also applies to 22.

This being said, certain specific instances can result in either an 11 energy or a 2 energy. But we will see now that this does not come from the fact that 11 has been reduced to a 2. It actually comes from the fact that one of the calculations has resulted in a sub-number 20, which has then been reduced to 2. The signifier is then 11/2.

Here is an example of a calculation of a Life Path (the number linked with our date of birth).

Let's take the case of a person born on October 16, 1965.

1) In a line, the addition of day, month and year:

```
16+10+1965 = 1+6+1+1+9+6+5 = 29
29 → 2+9 = 11.
```

29 is the sub-number of the master number 11.

2) In a column, the addition of day, month and year.
```
       16
+      10
+  1965
------
   1991 → 1+9+9+1 = 20 → 2
```

20 is the sub-number of 2.

3) In a column, the addition of day, month and year, after being reduced.

$$16 \rightarrow 1+6 = 7$$
$$10 \rightarrow 1+0 = 1$$
$$1965 \rightarrow 1+9+6+5 = 21 \rightarrow 2+1 = 3$$

$$7+1+3 = 11$$

Directly master number 11

See how these three different calculation methods have resulted in different results. The first calculation results in 11 stemming from sub-number 29. The second calculation results in 2, stemming from sub-number 20. The third directly results in master number 11. It is therefore essential to do the three different calculations, so as to discover that this particular Life Path is colored by both 11 and 2.

Let's repeat once more, because this is a crucial key to understanding what numerology is about: this 2 in our example doesn't come from the addition 1+1, but from the sub-number 20 found through different calculation methods. Yes, there are Life Paths 11 and Life Paths 11/2.

Elevens embody twice the same principle, i.e. twice 1. They thereby have all the features of 1 (*refer to corresponding paragraph*), but with a certain form of duality. This triggers an unquenchable thirst for action and relentless exploration of all sorts of unknown universes. This may develop into indecision and a waste of energy. They are not capable of making choices, wanting to see and experience all. They struggle to leave their mark for other people to follow, though they'd actually be very proud if they had followers.

As we have previously seen when we worked out the life path, the fact that 2 and 11 are side by side means that relationships are crucial. These individuals need to be connected with others. Their need to share is linked to their intense sentimentality, which may lead them to either slow down or speed up their momentum, especially when they feel obstacles are preventing them from doing what they want. They are prompted by good intentions and feel that they have the right to do what they do. However, they might

32

prove to be blunt and adamant in their ways, and are not always understood and accepted by their loved ones. In other words, they are hypersensitive individuals. Although patience is not a key component of their personality, they must understand that the world was not created in one day. Even God needed 6...

Elevens can be very open to the world of computer sciences, any new technologies, and esoteric studies.

They always attempt to add a collective dimension to their actions. They embody rediscovered Unity: (10) + 1. They can be good guides. "I (1) know how to find unity (10)". Elevens can either be fools or gurus. They are motivated by their expansive enthusiasm, but they must be careful not to get lost on the way as they need to keep their focus.

Whereas "Elevens" can stem from double-digit sub-numbers (29 → 2+9, 38 → 3+8, 47 → 4+7...), « Twenty-twos » never stem from any reduced sub-numbers [2]. They directly come from an addition. This master number can never be reduced to 4. As a rule, two identical figures should never be added up in numerology. If a 4 is present, it means that, in the calculation method used to obtain 22 (in a life path for example) there was another sub-number which resulted in 4 when reduced (ex: 13, 31, 40...). In this particular case, we say that a 4 is side by side with a 22. The corresponding abbreviation reads 22/4 in numerological charts.

Example of a person born on January 28, 1955.

1) In a line addition of day, month, year:

```
28+01+1955 = 2+8+1+1+9+5+5 = 31
31 → 3+1 = 4
```

31 is the sub-number of 4.

2) In a column addition of day, month, year.

```
      28
+     01
+   1955
   ------
   1984 → 1+9+8+4 = 22
```

This particular calculation method results in the master number 22, which should NOT be reduced.

---

[2] The first sub-number of 22 is 499. It is impossible to come up with such a result in any other numerological calculations.

3) In a column addition of reduced day, month and year.

```
28 → 2+8 = 10 → 1+0 = 1
01 → 1
1955 → 1+9+5+5 = 20 → 2+0 = 2

1+1+2 = 4
```

This person's Life Path is 22/4.

Once again, the 4 doesn't come from adding up 2+2 in master number 22, but because it was highlighted in the previous calculations methods.

Actually, pure Life Paths 22 (without any 4 in any calculation methods) are rare. But they do exist and we have encountered some.

"Twenty-twos" are long term builders. They have long planned projects and can be very patient about carrying them out. They are persistent and consistent. They are also very good at resisting outside pressure, particularly the social pressure of our modern rat race.

Twenty-twos hate being rushed and will do anything they can to avoid being pushed around. They can appear extremely slow and nonchalant, unmoved by everyday concerns. This doesn't come from the fact that they are insensitive, it is just that they do not understand why everyone is running around worrying over what they see as petty concerns. They are like philosophers who have already lived so many lives that nothing really influences them. They consider everything as being natural and normal, with nothing to worry or be fussed about. This attitude may not be understood by their loved ones, who blame them for never doing anything. They ARE substantially static and unshakable. They look absent-minded. Although they would never fight to have their views agreed on, they do find it hard to accept that other people disagree with them, for their ego is prominent. They are neither particularly happy, nor enthusiastic individuals. Therefore their seriousness can become a weight for those around them. They fail to understand that life is also made up of lightness and spontaneous fun. Because they regard this aspect as childish or tacky, they'd rather return to their cherished solitude.

33
A very special case...

Thirty-three is in all likelihood the ultimate master number. It is colored by a new type of energy, slowly spreading around the earth. Its energetic frequency is very high and will undoubtedly and substantially impact the structure of our matter in evolution, which is growing in higher vibrations. Here we are in the presence of a Christ-like energy, connected with the heart. Emanating from the heart, this energy opens up vast fields of superior experimentation. These individuals embody awareness, compassion, unconditional love, perfection and creation.

This number is still very mysterious, for it does not yet impact directly our space/time. Therefore, for the time being, we will associate it with 6. When you are setting up a numerological chart, you might want to write 33/6 in the corresponding space, and not just 6. Its first sub-number is 6999!

Thirty-threes convey a personal and special touch to Sixes: they are deeply connected to perfectionism, harmony and extreme dedication.

This being said, it is not considered as a master number as a whole. We will therefore regard it as 6, when we come across it.

Actually, unlike 11 and 22 which come from the only created numbers (1 and 2), 3 is already a combination of the two different energies embodied by 1 and 2. This is why 33 can't have the same status of the master numbers 11 or 22, numerologically speaking.

Sub-numbers

In numerology, numbers are divided up into three categories, simple numbers (from 1 to 9), Master numbers (11, 22), and all the other numbers, which are called sub-numbers. In other words, all the numbers you obtain when you add up the letters of a first name, last name or date of birth are actually sub-numbers, except for 11 and 22, or a resulting simple number (1 to 9).

This is why, when the addition results in a number superior to 9 other than 11 or 22, you have a sub-number which requires to be reduced until you obtain a number between 1 and 9, or a master number 11 or 22.

Examples taking into account the value of each letter, according to the English alphabet:

1	2	3	4	5	6	7	8	9
A	B	C	D	E	F	G	H	I
J	K (11)	L	M	N	O	P	Q	R
S	T	U	V (22)	W	X	Y	Z	

```
Peter
75259 → 7+5+2+5+9 = 28
28 → 2+8 = 10 → 1+0 = 1
```

Peter is worth 1. This 1 comes from 28. You will therefore write 28/1 in your chart.

```
Charlotte
381936225 → 3+8+1+9+3+6+2+2+5 = 39
39 → 3+9 = 12 → 1+2 = 3
```

Charlotte is worth 3. This 3 comes from 39. You will therefore write 39/3 in your chart.

As a metaphor, the definition and interpretation of sub-numbers are similar to a palette of colors that a painter would use to obtain different shades. The wide range of colors is obtained through subtle blending. If you mix a blue with a yellow, you will get green. This green is neither a blue nor a yellow, and yet it features both of these initial colors. This can be compared to how the combination of numbers works.

Sub-numbers are crucial in the interpretation of numerology readings. They enable us to bring precious hues to each of the numbers and master numbers obtained after having been reduced, thus emphasizing essential accuracy to deepen our analysis.

Further elements of information can be found in the last chapter of the present book, dealing with thorough explanations on how such a subtle alchemy works.

CHAPTER II

How to discover the ideal partner with the Maia method

"Mom, is there anything I own that isn't yours?"

Emile Zola

In our tridimensional world, the only possible way we have to express our individuality (1) is through being born. Paradoxically enough, seeking who we truly are can only be done through the other (2). The initial and only way we are given at birth to do this, is to meet the other through our mother. There is no other alternative; the first person we meet is our mother. Throughout our life, we will meet numerous other people along the way

But the very first encounter is with our mother, which leaves the first profound imprint on our consciousness at all levels. The period during which the fetus is in the maternal womb is crucial. The fetus is in total fusion with the mother's environment, soaking up her love, as well as her culture, thoughts and emotions of the moment.

Within this range of different factors, one is particularly significant, and this is language, as it determines our possibilities of communication with the world. We first of all soak in the language spoken by our mother during her pregnancy, which in most cases happens to be the language spoken in the country where we are to be born, even though there are many exceptions. We, numerologists, believe that this does not result from chance, inasmuch as souls do choose their languages when they decide to incarnate. Languages convey the fruit of the collective experiences, karmas, cultures and histories of the countries they embody. When we receive a body, we also receive a language. The language is passed on from one generation to the next, along with the rest of the "package" we take on as a heritage: family memories, secrets, representations, conscious and subconscious beliefs and myths. Languages are the vehicle through which all the experiences of life are transmitted, whether they are personal or social. By absorbing the heritage we receive, we also absorb its spoken word.

Languages embody the collective consciousness of given cultures of people. Numerology considers that the essence of a language can therefore be identified. As essential oils can be extracted from plants through specific techniques, the essential features of a language can be extracted through numerological tools. These tools are namely the letters of the alphabet and their connections with one another and numbers. Numerology enables a subtle process through which values are given to letters, according to the place they have in the alphabet. In English and French, the first letter is A, it has therefore been given the value 1, and B is worth 2 etc... Refer to the corresponding chart at the end of the previous chapter or in appendix 2 at the end of this book.

To put it in a nutshell, two factors are absolutely crucial at birth and will determine our life: our biological heritage and the energies conveyed by our mother tongue.

Women have already had all their eggs from when they were born, or more accurately they've had all the oocytes which were to become eggs. In other words, the oocyte which would later turn into an egg, be fertilized and then become "me" was already present in the mother's body, from her very first breath. This very special part of her which was to become "me", this "would- be me", had been sitting there, inside my mother, all this time! No wonder the bond with my mother is so intimate and powerful, whether I like it or not...

This is NOT the case with my father, given the manufacturing process of spermatozoon, including the one which is going to become "me".

Our mother was given a family name and first names at birth. Each of these names has a particular vibration. Although we do not necessarily share her first names, which are exclusively hers, we do share the resonance of her family's last name, that is to say her maiden name. We share its features which embody our ancestral lineage and all the history of our family. This is the reason why, in order to draw birth charts, numerology must take into account the mothers' maiden names, which are the precious links between generations.

The genetic heritage of the mother is within the real biological mother's egg. This is why the fact of having been born from a surrogate mother is irrelevant in numerology. Scientifically speaking, the genes of surrogate mothers do not influence the initial genes. The natural biological mother's genes received the family heritage and these are therefore the genes we will consider in our numerological chart studies.

This has been widely expanded upon in our first volume of « The unveiled numerology ». The Maia method consists in taking into account the mother's maiden name; instead of the last name we have been given at birth (bearing in mind that these names might be identical, in certain cases).

To sum up, to discover your true personality, you must take into account the following components: all of your first names, your date of birth and your mother's maiden name. Through our different investigations and research, we are now able to draw the conclusion that the alphabet which must be considered is the one which was used to establish the birth certificate. There is nevertheless one important exception: in case the official alphabet does not correspond to the mother tongue we have been exposed to during the first years of our life, only the mother tongue's alphabet should be considered.

Example: A person born in Austin (Texas USA), with a birth certificate established in English, from an Spanish mother who was speaking Spanish at home, must use the Spanish alphabet to draw his/her numerological chart. Suppose this person studies English at school and thereby becomes bilingual: the social personality of the given person will be studied according to the English alphabet, although his/her deep, inner nature is expressed through the Spanish alphabet.

Let us regard alphabets. Alphabets have evolved and have been altered over time. This is not surprising, in that they embody the collective consciousness of societies which are in constant transformation. One does not exist without the other. The alphabetical order of the letters follows the collective consciousness of a people, a culture, a country, a nation etc. Except for languages which benefit from relatively stable alphabets, such as French or English for example, who have not been altered for over a century, it is necessary to take into account the evolutions of alphabets. It can be noticed that the creation of the European Union has triggered a standardization of European alphabets. Whether this results in an impoverishment of specific languages or not remains to be seen. This process also stems from a will to communicate with a common language, thus giving rise to more integration. The Tower of Babel is collapsing.

Keep in mind that numerologists should take in consideration the alphabet in use at the time of birth. Portugal has added the 3 letters the Portuguese alphabet was missing, so as to have the same letters as in French or English. In 1994, Spain deleted the letters CH and LL and considers since then that CH is a C followed by a H, and LL is L, followed by another L. This must be taken into consideration for the persons born after January 1st, 1994.

People originating from Russian, Ukrainian or Serbian languages, or any languages written in Cyrillic, must consider the letter/number correspondence in the Cyrillic alphabet. This principle applies for any alphabetical language.

Furthermore, another consideration should be added. Numerologists should consider the first and middle names of the persons in the order they were given at birth. The hierarchy of the first names is not random. The expression of the first name is different from the expression of the second first name, also called middle name, (if there is one), and so on.

To conclude, we can say in summary that the numerological Maia method is based on:

- The mothers' maiden names (and NOT the last name she might have adopted when she married, nor the last name she might have received, after a possible legitimization).

- All the first and middle names declared on the birth certificate, in that order.

- The date of birth (numerology does not need the time nor the place of birth, unlike astrology).

If you have any doubts over your genuine identity, we recommend you ask for a copy of your birth certificate, as well as of your biological mother's. Everything you require to set up your numerological chart is on this certificate. You might even discover bits of information you were unaware of: You might have been registered at birth under your mother's maiden name, until a "father's" name was added on later for various reasons (late acknowledgement from the father, legitimization from a stepfather ... etc). This is exactly what happened to Michel and I, as a matter of fact.

Of course you are free to choose, compare and test other numerological methods. Testing other classical methods, such as the French or the American methods, might enable you to come up with different results, or not. You will then be able to choose the results you find the most relevant. Surprisingly enough, we have observed that, even though different methods are used, the results do not vary much. As a matter of fact, the mother's maiden name might turn out to give the same numerological result as if the "classical" family last name (usually passed on by the father) had been used.

Example: Let's consider the Expression Number of Laurence Pascale Musial, whose mother's maiden name was Martin.

The value of all the letters must be added.

Let's first use the Maia method, with all first and middle names and the mother's maiden name.

```
Laurence Pascale Martin
31395535 7113135 419295
```

The value of all the added letters is 85. This number must then be reduced, to obtain a number between 1 and 9 (except if we get 11 or 22). The final result is 4.

$$85 \rightarrow 8+5 = 13 \rightarrow 1+3 = 4$$

Now let's use the American method, with all the first/middle names and the person's family name received at birth (last name):

```
Laurence Pascale Musial
31395535 7113135 431913
```

We now have 76, which must then be reduced to ... 4

$$76 \rightarrow 7+6 = 13 \rightarrow 1+3 = 4$$

In our example, either of these methods results in the same Expression Number 4, because Martin and Musial are both reduced to 3.

This being said, most of the time, the results are different.

5 keys to compare two individuals

In our essay, we have emphasized 5 numerological features. At the beginning of each chapter, we explain how to calculate them accurately, with corresponding examples. At the end of this book, you might want to have a look at a summary of all the different calculations, which you may photocopy. You can also work out all your calculations with the help of our on-line software: www.online-numerology.com

You can also work out the calculations through a simplified version of our on-line application, available for free at: www.numerology-unveiled.com

An easy way for calculating the 5 indicators which are:

- **The Life Path** (resulting from the person's date of birth). The Life Path features the deep nature of the person. Because it brings into play how two individuals get along, it will therefore be highly highlighted in our summary. It also reveals our potential destiny, thereby underlining the nature of the relationships we share with the people in our life on earth.

- **The Expression Number** (resulting from the letters of the mother's maiden name and the letters of all the person's first/middle names). This number features the personality and emphasizes how the individuals express themselves. It also enables us to understand how to harmonize ways of expressing, which thread together our desires and possibilities.

- **The Soul Aspiration Number** (resulting from the vowels in the mother's maiden name and in all the person's first names). Whether we want it or not, we all have a soul, whose deep motivations must be perceived, if we want to understand how it influences our communication.

- **The Potential or Realization Number** (resulting from the consonants in the mother's maiden name and in all the person's first/middle names). It features our potential power. We all have an infinite potential, waiting for us to allow it to develop, from possibilities to achievements.

- **The Active Number** (resulting from all the letters of the person's first names, without taking into consideration the mother's maiden name). It embodies the spark, the dynamic, the energy that urges us to act in such or such way. It is highly unpredictable, in that it is fueled by instincts, more than by reason.

Our book attempts to define the above five indicators, as accurately as possible, keeping in mind that it is almost impossible to reach a tailor-made definition for each specific case. The personality features are described in a global way, as archetypes (sometimes almost as caricatures), for they do not take into account the sub-numbers, for instance. It is your role and responsibility, dear readers, to explore and dwell on all the possible components (sub-numbers), so as to come up with refined, subtle and detailed findings from the numerological charts. It is essential to analyze all the different factors which are revealed through your calculations.

For example, when attempting to work out how a 3 and a 7 get along, we reason as if every individual was made up of only one number! This is of course never the case as we are defined by all of the numbers. Number 8 might be absent from a specific chart (i.e. there isn't any letter worth 8), but the number 8 can be nevertheless present in the sub-number 18, which had resulted in 9. In other words, everything is a matter of proportion. Some numbers come up more often than others, which mean that they are more meaningful than others. It is also crucial to keep this in mind.

Studies usually emphasize at least two essential numbers, but in some cases, there are three or four. They embody so to say the pillars of the construction, and the analysis is therefore based on them. Let's take the example of a person whose Life Path is 3, Expression is 3, Aspiration is 6 and Potential also 6. All that refers to 3 and 6 is obviously highlighted.

When a certain number comes up with prevailing frequency in a study, in other words when different calculations result in the same numbers, these numbers ought to be analyzed with very special care. For instance, a chart in which the person whose Life Path is 8 and Aspiration also 8, is with a partner whose life Path is 7 and Aspiration also 7, will echo very strongly what those two numbers symbolize.

A great many factors must be taken into account when setting up charts, enabling you to bring more subtle shades and more accurate precisions regarding the person's personality. Numerous books could be written, to deal with all the range of possibilities of the analysis. Hopefully, such tremendous work will be undertaken one day and more books written.

Numerological studies and charts set ups can lead numerologists to all sorts of dead-ends and overblown information. The most common trap is entering a maze of hypothetical explanations. It is necessary to prioritize factors, so as to sort out the essential from the incidental. This is the reason why the numbers which come up more frequently must be emphasized, unlike the less representative numbers. Another trap numerologists should not fall into is to analyze numbers bluntly, thereby forgetting the phases

48

which led to their results, that is to say leaving the sub-numbers behind. Studying a Life Path only through the general and general explanations is over simplifying numerological analysis. A 17/8 Life Path is not a 26/8 Life Path.

When studying how two people might get along, numerology reveals a curious and amusing outcome. A sort of echo is at work between the different features of the charts. To make a long story short, a person whose Aspiration is 6, is very likely to meet partners with a Life Path 6, which is most logical, when you think of it. We could give you many such examples. But one thing remains certain. When partners refuse to acknowledge one another, conflicts arise. Time is sometimes needed before the partners discover, recognize and truly accept what has brought them together. Compare different numerological charts and discover the interactions at work. It's fun and inspiring! Our relationships are embedded in deep and complex dynamics. There must be some kind of great architect at the root of all this, don't you think?!

CHAPTER III

How to understand numbers

"Knowing oneself allows to know others too, for in each individual dwells the entire mankind."

Michel Eyquem de Montaigne

This chapter is devoted to expanding on all the aspects which have been introduced in the first volume of *The unveiled numerology*. We will now go through them with extra details. In order to achieve this, three types of relationships have been selected, which come from the structures of our society.

- Parent/child relationships. This is the very first relationship we experience in our early life that begins within our mother's womb. We are likely to come across these dynamics again further on in our life, through any type of hierarchical relationship, such as master/ disciple, boss/employee and so on.
- Couple relationships. This type of relationship includes intimacy and sexuality.
- Socio-professional relationships, based on partnerships.

The people we meet along the way come into our lives for a reason. There is no such thing as chance. Relationships are part of a meaningful design. As in a piece of music, the chords played between people do not necessarily sound harmonious. Of course, some are sweet, while others are less sweet. And yet, realizing you are out of tune might drive you to intensify a particular aspect you need to work on. Difficult beginnings in relationships can be compared with the moments before a philharmonic concert begin, when the musicians of the orchestra are tuning their individual instruments: it sounds dreadful! Indeed, attempting to understand why such numerological sounds exist will enable us to gain leverage on how to work on our relationships so as to turn down the volume of our egos. Living through our hearts, instead of through our egos, will make our symphonies sound a lot nicer.

Besides, a completely harmonious life would lead to a form of immobility and comfort which would stop self-questioning and growth. Questioning the reasons why conflicts may arise enables us to evolve and grow, once the struggles have been settled.

This is the reason why we will be emphasizing the antagonisms in relationships, so as to be able to identify the possible sources of conflicts, thus bringing about an awareness that is helpful and healing.

1 with 1

General aspect: It's either everything or nothing, inasmuch as the exchanges in this type of relationship are mostly based on egos. The relationship works as long as the individuals have similar objectives. If this is not the case, authority and personality conflicts are to be expected. This association is based on intelligence.

Parent 1 and child 1: Children 1 admire their Parent 1 and tend to identify with them. Yet, becoming free from parental authority will prove difficult. Parent 1's dynamic energy benefits children 1 as long as they don't perceive such as oppression, which would then stir up rebellion.

In our male-dominated societies as we know them, fathers are often 1, whereas mothers are 2.

Associates 1: Both partners have a strong common will for innovating, pioneering and researching. Success is to be expected. Even though they each want to have things their own way, they are sincere and honest enough to give their business first priority. However, they need to be surrounded by skilled and trustworthy collaborators if they don't want things to get out of control.

1 in love with another 1: It is a passionate relationship, in which sex plays a prevailing role. Both partners are out to explore the universe of bliss... as well as the universe of arguments!

1 with 2

General aspect: Strength vs. softness. The association 1 + 2 refers to the issue of expression (3). It is a dominating-dominated relationship, but numerous antagonisms may be overcome through dialogue and communication. Provided one of them plays their part and accepts their partner's part, the couple is happy. Twos are searching for One's strength of character. And Ones appreciate Two's listening abilities.

Parent 1 with child 2: The parent will have to prove patient and not fly off the handle as soon as the child gets into a fit. The parent needs to weigh up and understand the child's difficulties, without urging her/him to have to be the best in any discipline.

Parent 2 with child 1: Even if the child appreciates being protected at times, the child will eventually find such too intrusive. This will lead her/him to escape from the family nest as soon as possible.

Associates 1 and 2: Twos will be skilled at taking care of the project's structure and at meeting with all the associated partners. Ones want things to happen fast and will strive at making the project work, regardless of how the means are obtained in order to reach the goal. They should be particularly careful how the work is shared, so that neither of them feels left behind, as they have very different ways of implementing their ideas. They might each feel that the other doesn't achieve enough. This misunderstanding stems from the fact that they do not realize how much their partner does.

Love relationship between 1 and 2: Ones live out of passion and strong emotions. Their vitality must find a way to express itself. This is why they will find it hard to get along with Twos. As long as Ones bring Twos what they need, i.e. protection and comfort, Twos will be able to cope with the outgoing and excessive Ones. But will Ones be able to put up with Twos' capriciousness? If Twos let Ones the freedom to explore other horizons, the relationship is possible. Yet, other conflicts may arise, regarding children's education.

1 with 3

General aspect: In the long run, the association of King 1 and Joker 3 leads nowhere and generates difficult relations. Ones are touchy and brilliant, whereas Threes are critical, logical and keep questioning everything. Threes need to communicate and analyze, and are likely to suffer from Ones' authority and impulsiveness.

Parent 1 with child 3: The parent must keep explaining again and again the reasons for his/her actions. Unless a constant dialogue is maintained, the child will tend to do exactly the opposite of what he/she is asked.

Parent 3 with child 1: The child will be happy to have a parent who is able to explain the consequences of the actions he/she is attempting to experience. The parent should be particularly careful not to curb the child's impulses by giving too much advice. In case where the child's creativity is hampered, instant and impulsive reactions are to be expected.

Associates 1 and 3: This association is particularly auspicious if each associate brings the other what they lack. Threes are critical and judgmental; which is why they need Ones' natural impulsive instinct. Ones tend to start everything and finish nothing. They therefore need Threes' discipline and logic.

Love relationship between 1 and 3: Love usually entails tenderness and sweet feelings... and this is not Ones' and Threes' cup of tea. The relationship is more likely to be based on mutual respect and intense communication which may lead to conflict. Long discussions by the fireplace are likely to be on the agenda. However, their effusiveness and way of communicating may be more sportive than intimate; as neither is romantic nor emotionally expressive.

1 with 4

General aspect: The association (1 + 4) is surprising, out of the norm and unpredictable in its outcome (5); as they don't live life the same way. Ones are impulsive and quick-witted whereas Fours are obstinate and pragmatic. They need to agree on strong common aims, and share the tasks required in order to reach their goals. They need to know each other extremely well and learn to accept their major differences regarding their views on life.

Parent 1 with child 4: The energy spent by the parent and the ambition they project onto their offspring might not turn out as expected. The child possesses significant apathy and yearns for peace and quiet. This is not likely to please the parent's fervor and demands. The parent should therefore learn how to be patient and tolerant, instead of getting angry and frustrated.

Parent 4 with child 1: The parent will be of benefit to the child as long as he/she teaches his/her offspring patience and persistence. This being said, the child might not find the parent's explanations very clear and may not feel much supported, even though there are no particular obstacles preventing the child's need to create and develop.

Associates 1 and 4: The creative meets the hard-worker. This might be an excellent partnership, provided both of them stick to what they know. Yet, a great deal of imagination will be required to understand each other. Ones will need to curb their dissatisfaction and be more patient, while Fours will need to be less sensitive when their feelings are hurt.

Love relationship between 1 and 4: This partnership is strange, in that they have completely different ways of operating. Provided they succeed in making a real effort to maintain dialogue and understanding, there will be no problems. Ones will need to curb their appetite and Fours will need to be shaken up a little. Ones really love Fours' sensuality and appetite for life, while Fours will find Ones stimulating.

1 with 5

General aspect: They get along well. While conflicts over personality and ego are not absent, they both admire and understand each other. They have a lot in common. Nevertheless, Ones might feel thwarted when Fives make fun of their arrogance. Humor, curiosity and playful activities lie at the heart of their relationship.

Parent 1 with child 5: Nice fireworks at home! In such conditions the parent might want to curb the child's extravagance and idealistic ways. Both of them are very outgoing and need to communicate and be constantly on the move. Numerous angry and strong reactions are to be expected.

Parent 5 with child 1: The parent is very open-minded, liberal and communicative. Yet, this might not be enough for this child to feel supported and guided as he/she needs. The parent thinks that experimenting freely is best for his/her child, but this particular child needs more structure and discipline.

Associates 1 and 5: The partnership is very positive, but can also be explosive. Both have strong egos and will try to dominate, even though they don't do so in the same ways. Ones will need to be less directive and Fives will need to narrow down their field of experimentation and curb their urge for freedom. This association is not always peaceful, but these two intelligent beings can bring a lot to each other.

Love relationship between 1 and 5: This might not be a lasting relationship. This type of association relies more on friendship than deep love. Of course, they may want to move in together, but they need to keep their freedom. In the long run, Ones are likely to suffer more, because their natural warmth will not be reciprocated by Fives.

1 with 6

General aspect: The master vs. the servant. As long as Ones serve Sixes' aspirations, everything will be fine. If not, the relationship will be impossible if Ones can't meet Sixes' requirements, namely love, respect, life's principles and protection. Likewise, if Sixes do not bring Ones the acknowledgment they seek, the outcome will be difficult. Who is eventually more dependent on the other and who needs the other the most?

Parent 1 with child 6: The parent brings a great deal to the child in terms of how to find motivation, how to take a hold of life and reach expected excellence. Little by little, the child will gain more confidence, feel less guilty about his/her failures and be less self-judgmental. In turn, the parent will appreciate the child's natural ability to serve, be responsible and sociable.

Parent 6 with child 1: The parent is able to teach the child how to be responsible, more single-minded, and above all, how to complete the projects once they are started. The parent teaches the child rigorousness, method and efficiency, even though the child tends to be exasperated by all these things.

Associates 1 and 6: The spirit of initiative here is associated with efficient methods, which inevitably leads to fruitful creations. In spite of being very critical, Sixes are able to compromise and are ready to set up and organize the ideas that Ones have come up with. Ones will feel supported, although they may also feel hurt.

Love relationship between 1 and 6: Ones are able to surprise and inspire their partners, for Sixes are very sensitive and in need of communication. This being said, they will have to be persistent, because Sixes are easily disappointed, in that their rational and critical mind is always lurking nearby. Passion is what brings them together, although it might not last due to Ones' strong ego.

1 with 7

General aspect: Passion and love. They share the same objectives, ideals and ambition. They are very much attuned to each other. Sevens admire Ones' sense of creativity and enterprise, and Ones truly appreciate Sevens' advice, insights, depth and devotion.

Parent 1 and child 7: The parent will be able to encourage the child's dynamic energy and development. The child will be supported in his/her ability to try things out and succeed. This being said, the parent must pay particular attention to give thorough explanations, because this particular child needs to learn and understand everything through his/her mental capacity.

Parent 7 and child 1: This parent gives his/her child faith, confidence and hope. The parent will inspire the child with a vision of life that is useful for the child's sense of initiative. Adversely, the child might find that his/her parent "preaches" too much, but on the whole, the lesson will be well learned.

Associates 1 and 7: This is one of the most productive, fruitful and efficient associations there are! Charismatic and creative Ones meet methodical and safe Sevens, who are able to establish the necessary safeguards: what promise! They benefit each other a lot. Even though the essence of their ambitions is different, their goals are similar.

Love relationship between 1 and 7: Their passion enables them to express beautiful feelings, which manifests as common desire to fulfill each other. Sevens need role models and Ones are ideal for this. Ones need not fear Sevens, who are entirely devoted to them. Moreover, Ones know how to get in touch with Sevens' inner emotions so as to transcend them. The relationship is steeped in mutual fascination.

1 with 8

General aspect: They can get along fine, provided one does not overshadow the other. Yet, this association is likely to turn into a masochistic relationship, leading either to construction or destruction. They have significant admiration and fascination for each other. Ones must make sure they show enough respect to their partners, and refrain from boasting and taking advantage of Eights' gullibility. If not, Eights will retaliate fiercely. Eights should come out in the open and refrain from keeping things secret.

Parent 1 with child 8: The parent will be able to motivate their child to want to succeed, feel alive and experience the whole range of his/her abilities, even if it does not look to be so. These children might prefer a certain form of obscurity which is the opposite of their parent's brighter ways. Such children's psychological make up of secret and covert ways is ingrained, and yet, they are very much aware of their parent's drive for success. As a matter of fact, their parent will above all teach them how to be less gullible.

Parent 8 with child 1: The child may feel as if he/she was not supported and guided enough. This parent wants to make the child understand that all you need to do, if you want to succeed, is to put in motion that which motivates you. Under such circumstances, the child is likely to develop the impression that the parent is not caring enough nor entirely present. However, this will not prevent the child from experimenting by him/herself. The parent may want to teach the child how to be more tactful... but will they accept such?

Associates 1 and 8: This association is positive, as long as they respect each other enough. They are both out for success, but how they get there is different. They can bring each other what they themselves lack. As a matter of fact, one is skilled at expressing things, whereas the other is skilled at hiding them. If they manage to get along, they can be invincible, for they are extremely resistant and both of them strive for power.

Love relationship between 1 and 8: Exploring all pleasures of the senses, from the authorized to the forbidden... What a show! Both of them are determined to enjoy life, without inhibitions and taboos. Yet, they both have strong egos and this is why conflicts are to be expected.

1 with 9

General aspect: Action vs. contemplation. They will get along beautifully, in terms of delight and sensuality. Nines provide a haven of peace and calm. Will Ones be able to appreciate this aspect? They are so restless that they very well may not, although they do bring a great deal of energy to the couple. This being said,

Nines truly understand Ones' personality, while Ones do not understand Nines. Ones fail to perceive how deep Nines can be. Nines, in turn, see how vain Ones can sometimes be. Music will definitely benefit the relationship and enable the partners to be more attuned to each other.

Parent 1 with child 9: No matter how hard the parent might try to energize the child and drive him/her to be more alive and eager; he/she will face strong resistance from the child. This is liable to give rise to exasperation. They do not operate the same way nor live on the same planet. The child finds his/her parent much too intrusive and dominating, which is why he/she will retreat during childhood into his/her own, private world, thereby obliging the parent to be more patient and cooperative.

Parent 9 and child 1: As dynamic and disruptive as this child may be, he/she will definitely appreciate the parent's sweet love and care, even if he/she does not feel supported enough, as a general rule. Yet, this will not bring about any open conflicts, for the parent proves very understanding and loving, and is therefore likely to accept just about anything from his/her child.

Associates 1 and 9: Although Nines are completely and unconditionally devoted to Ones' projects, this association does not necessarily result in a happy outcome. Indeed, two very different universes meet here. Nines are sustained by peace and calm, and they cannot be bothered by Ones' drive for power. Adversely, Ones tend to find that Nines distance themselves from essential priorities and goals in life.

Love relationship between 1 and 9: Ones are responsive to their partners' sweet and peaceful outlook. For them, Nines provide a haven of calm and quiet, after long and hazardous struggles. But, after the calm, they may well become bored. In turn, Nines freely accept Ones' vitality, for they know when to withdraw, so as to be able to return to their peace and tranquility. Likewise, they can't deal with open conflict, which is why they must take care not to succumb to masochistic relationships.

1 with 11

General aspect: Who will rule? Their dialogue is honest, sincere and constructive. In any case, this is a must for them. They desperately need mutual acknowledgment. If this doesn't happen, conflict is to be expected. Elevens need to overcome their arrogance and accept that they need Ones. In turn, Ones must learn to respect Elevens' vital need for space, spirituality and their sense of ideals, as idealistic as they may seem. Ones act according to their own inner selves. Elevens act according to the people around them, as if they are giving out signals to be followed.

Parent 1 with child 11: Family life may not be very quiet. The parent is a good teacher for the child, showing possible ways towards success. But the child may not listen, for he/she is very idealistic. The parent's goals seem miles away from that of the child's, who may not be ready to give up his/her friends and dreams, for the harsh realities of life.

Parent 11 with child 1: The child may look upon the parent as some kind of firework or extravagant being. In any case, the child will find it difficult to deal with this parent, even though he/she recognizes the parent's open-mindedness and rich approach to innovation. All in all, the child will benefit from the parent's sense of adventure.

Associates 1 and 11: In spite of their intelligence and drive for mutual well-being, the relationship between them may well give rise to numerous conflicts. They must learn to be more patient, open-minded and flexible so as to find common ground. Although they can both prove extremely innovative and pioneering, both of them lack persistence in the long run.

Love relationship between 1 and 11: The relationship features a strong sense of adventure, innovation, discovery and unique experimentation. Proving faithful to one another is not a virtue they possess. This is why they need to find a common passion if they want their relationship to develop in a lasting way.

1 with 22

General aspect: The King vs. the Republic. How can they be joined? Twenty-twos are serious and dogmatic, whereas Ones are utterly pragmatic and can set any principle aside, in order to reach their goals. This is the reason why they oppose each other. Ones need to make room for society's demands and let go of their self-centered interests for that of the collective.

Parent 1 with child 22: The child reacts to the parent's authority, and hates being pushed to do something when he/she doesn't feel like it. Nevertheless, such a parent is a good advisor and pioneer for the child, who will learn how to integrate this, as time goes by.

Parent 22 and child 1: The child may find the parent cumbersome, uptight and rigid. The child develops the feeling that his/her parent is restricting possible fields of discovery, is preventing him/her from truly expressing him/herself. In any case, the child does not feel supported enough. However, the parent IS there and deeply cares. But the parent's quietness is liable to come across as a lack of enthusiasm, to this particularly active and lively child.

Associates 1 and 22: In such a relationship, the common interest must be very wide-ranged and shared by both, if they want to work in harmony. In which case, Twenty-twos will prove faithful allies for their boisterous partners, thus enabling them to achieve their projects. Adversely, in case Twenty-twos fail to accept Ones' authority and spirit of initiative, the relationship might very well go down the drain.

Love relationship between 1 and 22: The relationship is only possible if Ones accept to stay at home more and pay extra attention to their partner; and less to their personal goals and business. Although they are not devoid of earthly appetites, they seldom enjoy them.

2 with 2

General aspect: This is a peaceful association, sustained by calm and quiet understanding, although it might lead to a certain lack of motivation. While this is not a very dynamic combination it does allow for material growth.

Parent 2 with child 2: Emotions prevail. Attachments are prominent. The umbilical cord is difficult to cut, emancipation is slow. No conflict here, only intense emotional exchanges.

Associates 2 and 2: Is this a real association or is this the perfect association for a social business or social activity? Dependency is strong, with neither partner trying to overshadow the other. This being said, this partnership reinforces a certain lack of dynamic energy and may result in an absence of decision making.

2 in love with another 2: The relationship may be strong. Procreation might be the purpose of such a union. Yet, a kind of apathy or inertia might make the relationship wither in the long run, even though everything in the beginning seems fine. They will have to take care that the daily grind doesn't take over, and to be open to having fun. Otherwise their melancholy mood swings will overshadow their dialogue.

2 with 3

General aspect: Respect prevails between both parties. Mutual acceptation and understanding are present. Communications are fruitful. Outlooks on life are similar. Twos bring Threes comfort, security and peace while Threes respond with intellectual stimulation and organizing a pleasant life for Twos... as long as Twos' emotions get along with Threes' brains...

Parent 2 with child 3: A gap is likely to appear, between this emotional parent and this child whose brain is always active. They do understand each other, which is not in question. Rather that the parent may not be able to meet the needs of the child's constant inquiring mind. This in turn might drive the child to feel frustrated.

Parent 3 with child 2: This parent cannot refrain from over-analyzing the child's emotional and psychic patterns. However, he/she will definitely help the child to fulfill him/her self intellectually, by teaching him/her how to be logical and rigorous. Do be careful about the child's possible quick-tempered reactions in case of misunderstandings or too much criticism.

Associates 2 and 3: Does air get along with water? In such a partnership, Threes struggle to organize and plan whatever is necessary so that their common projects can operate smoothly, when Twos never actually asked for this to be done. The association can work, provided their project is based on a complementary exchange, rather than an intensity brought about by two similar types of energies.

Love relationship between 2 and 3: The relationship can prove extremely positive, for neither of them tries to harm the other person. Twos appreciate Threes' sense of organization, but they dislike their criticisms. In daily life, this is a partnership based on logic and comfort, thus helping avoid life's hardships and accidents. This being said, a passionate symbiotic relationship is not on the agenda.

2 with 4

General aspect: This is a down-to-earth encounter of two beings whose ways are complementary to each the other. Fours bring material security and comfort to Twos who reassure them in turn. They both share common interests in family concerns and the acquisition of goods. The relationship is lasting and constructive. They are a classic traditional couple.

Parent 2 with child 4: This is the ideal relationship between a protective parent who takes care of the child's well-being. The child is happy and curious about life's pleasures. Every time the parent comes up with new ideas to make life easier, the child will love it. Nevertheless, the child might develop a certain indolence and reserve.

Parent 4 with child 2: The parent is pragmatic and not as prone to emotional unrest as the child, which will definitely help their offspring to be more stable. This parent is calm and quiet, which makes the child feel safe. However, the parent is possessive to such a point that the child might be prevented from developing his/her own way.

Associates 2 and 4: Such an association might very well stem from creative and artistic dynamics. In these domains, Twos and Fours are a fruitful and productive team. Yet, they may lack ambition.

Love relationship between 2 and 4: Fours are protective and sensual, and therefore get along very well with Twos, who are extremely sensitive. Their love relationship is likely to be intense and sustained by their quest for earthly pleasures. They enjoy the hedonistic pleasures of life and will look to live their union privately in their own nice environment away from the crowd.

2 with 5

General aspect: They are mutually attracted and drawn to each other like magnets. While they are not insensitive to each other's charm, the relationship has difficulty settling down in the long term. This is a tumultuous relationship. Twos struggle tremendously hard to accept Fives' eccentricity while, adversely, Fives tend to get bored with Twos' traditional outlook. This being said, children are liable to bring them together, even though they don't hold similar views on education.

Parent 2 with child 5: The spirit of independence in this child triggers a need for freedom from an early age, which is not part of the parent's plan. The child's excessive unrest and thirst to discover the world will often frighten the parent. Such a child finds it difficult to accept that the world may not be as infinite as he/she thought it was. Yet, they will learn to get along in the long run.

Parent 5 with child 2: The child will definitely benefit from this parent's original, liberal, open-minded views. For starters, it will never be a problem to invite friends over. Such a parent is able to help the child discover the world safely, according to his/her own pace. This being said, the child will have to learn to come out of his/her excessive emotional states, otherwise the parent will become very annoyed.

Associates 2 and 5: There is a need for both to have specific and well-defined tasks that are complementary to each the other. If this is not the case, the association will not work. Twos will only be able to give advice to their partners through patience, compromise and dialogue, while Fives can be terribly impatient, unpredictable and curt, especially when their dreams are at stake.

Love relationship between 2 and 5: Twos are conciliatory and conservative. They readily accept Fives' lively mischievousness, but they must put up with Fives' friends as well. In addition, Fives' spirit of adventure and discovery is not liable to suit quiet Twos.

2 with 6

General aspect: The relationship brings about productive harmony. Their views on life are similar, as well as the way in which each of them operate. Support, ethics and family matters prevail. Yet, they might tend to close themselves off into their little world or to forget themselves. They share the same points of views regarding their roles in society.

Parent 2 with child 6: The environment is very comfortable for this child who particularly appreciates a balanced and peaceful surrounding. He/she who loves human relationships will feel protected, supported and loved. But with the coming of age, he/she might start to find it difficult to understand and accept the ups and downs of a parent who does not always control their emotions and fears. This is liable to trigger a great deal of fear. In turn, the child will definitely benefit from the parent who finds their child very easy going, devoted and attentive.

Parent 6 and child 2: Such a parent is surprisingly skilled at organizing, planning and managing the child's education in a way that fulfills him/her. This being said, he/she is extremely demanding and finds it difficult to accept the child's whims. He/she expects the child to meet their requirements and comply with what he/she is told. Nevertheless, harmony will come about, as the child understands that the parent is not trying to deprive him/her of anything.

Associates 2 and 6: This association is one of harmony. Sixes are skilled at planning, organizing and strive for perfection. This helps compensate Twos' minor insufficiencies without any problems. For both of them, human relationships are tremendously important. They both lay great emphasis on the quality of the human relationship, which is why they will manage to overcome certain mishaps. They are both attached to efficiency and security.

Love relationship between 2 and 6: No particular conflicts are expected, as Sixes are determined to meet Twos' desires for harmony and tranquility. Such a way of communicating emphasizes tender and sweet relationships, as long as Twos succeed in coping with Sixes' criticisms. Education and children are favored. Both of them are cautious as they strive not to hurt each another. Yet, they must pay particular attention not to keep things secret and unsaid. Dialogue is essential, inasmuch as Twos may feel that Sixes are intellectually superior to them.

2 with 7

General aspect: A harmonious relationship with regards to home, family and love partnership matters. However, the outlook is not that promising, as far as common business or artistic goals are concerned. Twos are not particularly interested in developing higher forms of culture. They don't need to feel they belong to any kind of elite groups. This is liable to displease Sevens, who get bored easily and wish nothing more than to teach their partners something. Here, Sevens have found the ideal disciples. In turn, Twos are liable to find that Sevens are being too intrusive, too complicated and not present enough in their everyday life. Yet as there is no overt conflict, all in all the relationship is favorable.

Parent 2 with child 7: This child particularly appreciates this parent 2 who is able to bring him/her protection, tenderness and a sense of safety. The child will be aware of domestic tasks and community concerns at a very early age. Yet the child might feel he/she is being over-protected, and as a result prevented from trying out new experiences and adventures. In the long run, an indelible trace will be left on the child who will in turn prove extremely protective towards his/her ageing parent.

Parent 7 with child 2: Such a parent is very idealistic. As such, he/she is attached to group life and family concerns and will therefore make sure that his/her children will be given protection and safety, but also a taste for curiosity and adventure in the wild world. He/she will give excellent advice. However, the relationship might turn out to be awkward, in that the parent may neither understand nor accept the child's shy and introverted behaviors. Yet, this difficulty will never give rise to any serious conflict, for the parent is tremendously aware of the child's acute sensitivity.

Associates 2 and 7: Flamboyant Sevens have found their ideal and perfect partner, except for one little problem: they might tend to find them too stay-at-home and not daunting enough. This being said, they manage to find common ground, in order to be together and cooperate. Sevens will just have to curb their critical views while Twos must refrain from hypersensitivity and becoming swamped by their own emotions. Sevens will be able to plan and protect, so as to make common projects operate and run smoothly and successfully. Artistic matters are particularly favored.

Love relationship between 2 and 7: Very fine prospects. Both of them share the same tastes for romanticism, expressing their feelings and showing their affection. Yet, they must make sure to keep their feet on the ground and not get carried away. They wish for a peaceful and comfortable little nest where they can enjoy their love life away from the crowd.

2 with 8

General aspect: The relationship will remain harmonious as long as Eights are able to keep the secret parts of their life quiet. Material aspects are favored, inasmuch as Eights are amazingly skilled at making money and thus generating a certain form of prosperity. Twos are attracted to Eights' wanton sexuality. Moreover, their taste for privacy suits Eights' need for secrecy. But Twos expect Eights to use their natural authority in favor of a group, and not themselves.

Parent 2 and child 8: The parent greatly helps the child, through his/her human qualities. Yet in spite of this, the child's mysterious world will remain secret for a long time and remain out of the parent's reach. Strong opposition must be expected, in that they have very different ways of operating. The child feels over-protected and needs more space to breathe. Adversely, the parent does not understand this need and is likely to suffer from what he/she sees as a lack of gratitude from the child for all he/she has been given.

Parent 8 and child 2: This child needs relationships, feeling and protection. But it is very likely that he/she will not receive them from this parent who is unable to be more present and attentive. This will trigger a great deal of frustration and anger in the child's heart, resulting in the child holding long grudges against his/her parent. Eights appear cold and hard in Twos' sweet eyes. Such a parent does not harm the child intentionally; it's just that he/she does not understand that some people require more spontaneous and sensitive expression.

Associates 2 and 8: There is strong antagonism. A considerable effort is needed to understand each other and get along well. While they are both very interested in the outcome and possible benefits of their common projects, they do not share the same views as how to get there. Twos usually show great care and respect for other people, so are liable to feel upset with the dodgy methods used by Eights in order to reach their goals. This being said, financial aspects are favored.

Love relationship between 2 and 8: They are extremely attracted to one another, although they do not operate in the same way at all. Eights are blunt and rough when it comes to expressing their feelings and desires, including their sexual needs, which Twos might not appreciate very much. As a matter of fact, Twos' deepest desire is to create a family, whereas Eights' most profound desire is to quench their longing for pleasure. As a result, Twos might never truly know the deep, inner nature and identity of their partner who is worlds apart from them. Nevertheless, as long as Twos can be content with the comfort and safety that Eights can provide them, they will be able to accept Eights' eccentricities, even if their principles of life are toppled.

2 with 9

General aspect: Conflicts must be expected, between the very traditional Twos and deeply mystical Nines. This being said, a certain form of harmony can be reached as far as humanitarian concerns. Twos have great potential for associating and cooperating, which fits perfectly with Nines who have the wonderful potential for giving and supporting others. However, Nines tend to want to escape from life's limits and restraints, whereas Twos are deeply attentive to managing everyday life.

Parent 2 with child 9: In this particular case, the relationship looks slightly too smooth to be true. Both of them want to protect themselves from the harmful effects of the outside world which they consider extremely aggressive. By doing so, they tend to close themselves off and become isolated. They both lack initiative and awareness. However, the relationship does not give rise to any major conflict for Two's sweet tenderness is always present. Yet this does not allow a clear break from the umbilical cord.

Parent 9 with child 2: Although the parent over-protects the child, he/she also behaves in such a distant way that the child is liable to become very frustrated and upset. The parent conveys two contradictory messages. On the one hand: "Do whatever you want, whenever you want" and on the other "Be still, do not move" This does not contribute to a solid framework for the child's sense of safety. Sincere dialogues and genuine exchanges are missing, not because there isn't enough love, but because there might be too much! When you want to avoid conflict at any costs, things are kept secret and deep emotions aren't shared. Resentment then builds up and one becomes out of touch with reality.

Associates 2 and 9: This association emphasizes altruistic common projects in which duty is highlighted. Local business is favored as well. What will be difficult, is finding the right means to reach their goals in a lasting way. Everything will depend on the human element of this association. They therefore must learn how to implement their ideas realistically and lastingly.

Love relationship between 2 and 9: The relationship is sustained by harmony, sensitivity and sweet exchanges. Such an association favors romance and honeymoons. There is no major antagonism, as both of them try to make life easier for their partner. Nines, when in love, can prove surprisingly attentive and delicate towards Twos who look to merge and fuse with another. Yet, they must be careful not to indulge in any emotional games. The relationship will favor children, school matters, and education as a whole.

2 with 11

General aspect: This association can either be very fortunate or go all amiss. It will be positive provided both accept each other's personality without ulterior motives. Otherwise the association is impossible. Whatever the case, this is a highly original partnership, although laborious. Twos are skilled at adjusting to Elevens' peculiar ways, but the opposite may not be true, unless Elevens manage to find other means to express themselves, outside the scope of Twos'.

Parent 2 and child 11: This particular parent is extremely worried as to whether he/she will be able to calm his/her child down and curb a little of their excessive energy and eccentricities. The relationship may be awkward, in that the parent's peace and quiet is liable to be disrupted. Although the child is receptive to the parent's warmth and protection, he/she needs to break away and open up to new adventurous horizons. This might not be possible with such a parent who is over-protective and cautious. This being said, both of them will have very fruitful discussions.

Parent 11 and child 2: The child needs to feel safe and protected. Such a requirement is not likely to be met by this liberal parent. There is a huge gap between a free-minded parent who does not lay great emphasis on emotions and feelings, and a child who is starving for affection and emotional exchanges. This particular parent aims to develop the child's self-sufficiency, quick decision-making processes and critical mind. And this particular child might not understand this type of language, for what he/she mostly needs is attention and care. This will result in a great deal of frustration, as the childish ways of the offspring will upset this parent who lacks patience.

Associates 2 and 11: Both of them will need a great deal of patience and understanding if they want to get along, so that their skills can operate on a common basis. Twos are able to prove easy, flexible and understanding, just enough to adjust to boisterous Elevens. The opposite though may not be true. While elevens are far from being insensitive and closed to their emotions, they do not express their feelings in the same ways as Twos do. Elevens tend to be too curt, with their short explanations and aggressive ways. They have so much energy that they are likely to tip Twos over.

Love relationship between 2 and 11: Apart from a possible and fleeting moment of passion, they will need to make great and countless efforts to understand each other in a way that would enable them to walk through life together. As long as Elevens manage to bring safety and comfort, it is possible common ground can be found. But will Elevens prove patient and understanding enough? As a matter of fact, the very opposite might occur: Elevens might eventually get tired of Twos' constant worries and emotional excesses.[3]

2 with 22

General aspect: They have interests in common. They both share the same drive to build something stable and they behave as if they had signed a contract in this regard. Twenty-twos make Twos feel safe and Twos respond with sweet love and care. The partnership is lasting and the association outlook is very auspicious. This could be the ideal couple, for they both strive to strike a balance between their personalities. Twenty-twos build the house, whereas Twos decorate it and bring life to it. Twos will eventually be able to soften up and gentle Twenty-twos who can be a bit austere and rugged at times.

Parent 2 and child 22: In this relationship there is neither conflict nor aggression. There is no need for the parent to coerce his/her mind structure or lifestyle unto the child, for the child already accepts what the parent believes and behaves like the parent in a natural way. All the parent has to do is emphasize kindness and benevolence. Even if the child does not show his/her gratefulness straight away, he/she is nevertheless very appreciative of the kind and benevolent atmosphere. On the other hand, the child will miss out on situations where he/she must face obstacles. He/she is searching for this kind of confrontation, so as to use his/her aptitude for facing difficult challenges. But this particular parent may not be able to create and offer such situations.

---

[3] This might nevertheless not be quite so conspicuous. For example, in the case of number 20 being present along with the sub-numbers of 11 (29, 38, 47...), 11 would then be an 11/2.

Moreover, both of them must pay attention not to fall into depressive pessimistic thinking.

Parent 22 and child 2: This parent has his feet firmly placed on the ground, although he/she can be rigid at times. He/she will unwillingly teach his/her child how to fight and to be fearless when facing adversity. Yet, the child is liable to suffer from not feeling loved or cherished enough. The parent's mere presence is not enough for this child. This being said, they both bring a lot to each other: the first through strength and the latter through affection. The child will be grateful to his/her parent provided Twenty-twos succeed in moderating his/her way of being. If this is not the case, a gap is liable to widen between the parent and child.

Associates 2 and 22: In this association, Twenty-twos act as the pillars Twos can consistently rely on. This makes the partnership feel safe and sound. Twos can definitely trust their partners to implement what they have launched and bring it to fruition in the long run. In turn, Twos are faithful allies and will not hesitate from taking on subordinate tasks, for this trait of character is part of their nature and they view their 22 partner as trustworthy. They communicate quick and efficiently, neither being prone to longwinded or endless discussions.

Love relationship between 2 and 22: The outlook is extremely positive, in that both of them profoundly agree on family matters, home organization and environment. Yet, although they are very much attracted to each other, they may not want to express their feelings out loud. The relationship is likely to last as it is one that is based on sensuousness, well-being and the shared pleasures of life.

3 with 3

General aspect: Castor and Pollux. Complicity, verbal communication, creativity. A harmonious and understanding relationship. Youthful personality. An association that sometimes lacks maturity. A lot of movement. A sincere quest for harmony and alliance.

Parent 3 and child 3: This relationship features a great deal of exchanges and discussions, as well as a kind of brotherly partnership. The child yearns to discover and understand the world around him/her and this longing for explanations will be quenched. As far as the parent is concerned, while he/she will be bewildered at the child's early maturity and curiosity, he will easily meet the child's needs. However, frequent questioning and endless criticisms must also be expected.

Action is what drives both of them to act, thus emphasizing outings and social life, which brings them together. In this type of relationship, the parent acts as an elder brother or sister, more than as an actual father or mother.

Associates 3 and 3: Their relationship is grounded in communication and dialogue. They have a lot to exchange with one another. If things operate smoothly, everything will go fine. But as soon as worries come about, conflicts are to be expected, as they both hold the other partner responsible for any problems. They must learn how to be more organized and structured, and to plan ahead before undertaking any projects together.

3 in love with another 3: This is a relationship steeped in brotherly love and devoid of passionate sentiments. Of course, they have a lot to say and exchange with one another, at times too much, but their rapport is based on intellect rather than emotional feelings. They can spend long evenings talking endlessly about the state of the world and their relationship, but they will never become Karma Sutra fans!

3 with 4

General aspect: A practical spirit of organization prevails here. This association particularly favors socio-professional business partnerships. Sentimental feelings and love life are less favored. Fours find Threes too brainy and excitable, while Threes blame Fours for not being active enough.

Parent 3 and child 4: The parent tends to explain too much how the world operates, to a child who is not very open to this type of intellectual discussion. This being said, the relationship might very well be constructive as the child is very down-to-earth and is able to differentiate that which is important from what is not. The parent must learn how to be more pragmatic and less theoretical, if he/she wants the child to understand.

Parent 4 and child 3: The child is liable to feel frustrated with this parent who does not express him/herself enough. The child wants and needs more details, explanations and further knowledge. He/she will either have to be very patient, or to find this elsewhere. The parent, in turn, will find it terribly difficult to fathom why this child needs to analyze things so much. They will not share many warm exchanges of affection, as they do not convey their love and care in the same way. In spite all of this the parent will succeed in teaching the child a hands-on know-how, so as to learn how to make things happen.

Associates 3 and 4: Provided one partner takes care of the communication and the public relations while the other partner handles the organization and implements the structure, everything will run fine for a long time. Threes may want to curb their critical mind and to calm down a little. Fours may want to be more open-minded and show less resistance to the constant movement set forth by energetic Threes.

Love relationship between 3 and 4: How can Fours and Threes get along well? Fours are searching for peaceful and quiet pleasures in life, whereas Threes are never satisfied and keep looking for more explanations and analyses. How can Threes accept

Fours' persistent silence, let alone their discretion and inertia? One thing is sure: the relationship will be awkward. However, Fours can teach Threes how to enjoy life's down-to-earth pleasures and Threes can teach Fours how to break out of their old ways. However this might be difficult to accomplish.

3 with 5

General aspect: Dynamism and stimulation. There is a mutual taste for new explorations and discoveries. Both share outdoor interests. However, peaceful family matters are not favored. How the mind and the psyche operate is what brings them together. Rivalry is frequent, inasmuch as Threes blame Fives for being too idealistic, while Fives blame Threes for not thinking enough by themselves. Such an association usually generates nervousness.

Parent 3 and child 5: There is nothing more exciting for this parent than to feel like hosting a little genius at home! Exchanges are numerous and positive, as well as the urge for discovery. Yet, the idealistic ways of this child may disturb this rational parent. This being said, the child is independent and aware, and will therefore quickly learn how to listen to their parent's good advice, provided the latter refrains from criticizing too much. If not, the child will most certainly thwart his/her parent's plans, which he/she regards as hindering. If this occurs, the parent might not understand nor accept the child's thirst for independence, which would be considered a terrible flaw for this so-called open-minded parent.

Parent 5 and child 3: The child will have to learn how to take care of him/herself at an early age and implement the principles of life stemming from his/her analytical spirit, because the parent will give him/her significant space to do so. However, this child does need structure and guidance, for he/she thrives on explanations. The father or the mother certainly has all the necessary abilities to respond to the child's constant questioning, but only up to a certain point. As a matter of fact, the parent will try to make the child understand that he/she must find out the answers by him/herself through his/her own experience, and not through his/her permanent thinking.

Associates 3 and 5: This association promises dynamic and even explosive prospects. They can bring a great deal to each other, for both are intelligent enough to understand each other well and curb their antagonisms. However, certain violent arguments must be expected, unless they succeed in calming their nervousness and quick temper. If they do manage to get along, they will accomplish great things together.

Love relationship between 3 and 5: Fives need adventure and new experiences. Their thirst for discovery does not necessarily suit Threes however; whose life's principles are completely different. Threes are open to fun, of course, but in a much quieter and less excessive way. Such a union is possible, but it will be a brotherly partnership. Threes must learn how to criticize their partners less, if they want to hold on to them. In turn, Fives need to learn how to be more patient and show more willingness to keep up with their partners' complicated, distressed psyche.

3 with 6

General aspect: Run after me, I want to catch you! As ambiguous as it seems, commitment is possible, but never total. The duality featured in both numbers is expressed through this particular association. Something is missing. Although they do get along well in their communication and exchanges, the association is not very constructive as it lacks safe stability.

Parent 3 and child 6: If the child does not reject, nor disapprove his/her parent's way of educating them, the child will nevertheless truly understand his/her parent's meandering psyche, for they are indeed terribly confused. Although the child shares similar points of view, he/she requires more hands-on activities, and not intellectual games. They both operate with the same outlook, but the child's structure is one that is more grounded and demands application and accomplishment. The child is liable to feel very disturbed by the parent's nervousness. While the parent is able to give sensible advice, he/she must subdue his/her critical mind, so that the child's feelings don't get hurt.

Parent 6 and child 3: This particular parent is able to instill the child with a taste for exchange, well-achieved tasks and organization skills. He/she is good at pacifying the child's energetic unrest. He/she will teach the offspring how to be less self-judgmental and how to forgive him/herself for what is considered wrong. In other words, the child will be taught persistence and will significantly benefit from this parent's qualities.

Associates 3 and 6: They can bring each other a great deal, provided they succeed in not constantly criticizing each other. This association also emphasizes perfection and a sense of accomplished tasks, therefore aiming at excellence. Yet if their outlook about the analysis of a project differs, they will strongly disagree and fail to get along.

Love relationship between 3 and 6: These two ways of expression might not be particularly suited; in that both of them see in the other person what he/she does not wish to see and admit within him/herself. The prospects however are not totally out of reach. If they manage to find common ground they can agree on, they will then have enough resources to create an environment of mutual respect in which a lasting relationship can develop. As far as sex is concerned, intense prowess must not be expected, as they must first learn how to overcome their shyness and worry. As long as they remain stressed about outer concerns, they will be unable to enjoy their sexual relations together.

3 with 7

General aspect: The extravert vs. the introvert. Getting along is possible, as far as common objectives are concerned, but it can be awkward. Conflicts are likely to arise, due to the opposition between Sevens' faith and deep inner beliefs and Threes' excessively rational mental mind. Sevens blame Threes for their lack of idealism, while Threes blame Sevens for their lack of realism. However, teaching and knowledge are benefited through this association. As a matter of fact, both of them have the same objective; it is simply that their methods and means are different.

Parent 3 and child 7: The child may find that the parent lacks a certain depth, in that the parent expands at length on useless explanations, does not follow his /her deep motivations and places too much emphasis on analyses. As a matter of fact, this particular parent gives too much priority to side issues and outside concerns, instead of to the deep inner emotions that the child prefers. Even so, studies and education are benefited from on the whole. Numerous exchanges can take place between them as they bring a lot to each other. Particularly that which the other one lacks, i.e. the parent will teach the child how to express his/her deep feelings more and live according to them, while the child will teach the parent how to focus more on what works and less on what does not.

Parent 6 and child 3: This particular parent is able to give the child a taste for exchange, well-achieved tasks and a sense of organization. He/she is also good at pacifying the child's energetic unrest. He/she will teach the offspring how to be less self-judgmental and to forgive him/herself for what is considered as wrong. In other words, the child will be taught persistence and will significantly benefit from this parent.

Associates 3 and 7: They can benefit each other a great deal, for Sevens highly appreciate Threes' meticulous sense of detail, while Threes particularly appreciate Sevens' ability to give life to their ideas. They are both attached to perfection and yet, they do not operate similarly. Threes might prove too critical and too focused on current worries, whereas Sevens are driven beyond this towards larger and wider ambitious views. As a result, Sevens are liable to be blunt and acerbic towards their partner, whom they consider too materialistic and not visionary enough. Adversely, Threes are liable to find Sevens too idealistic, unrealistic and not focused enough on the actual implementation of their projects.

Love relationship between 3 and 7: In spite of their differences, they are extremely attracted to one another, in such a way that leads to harmony and a truly loving relationship. Both of them are curious by nature as they love to exchange, talk and communicate. Sevens are able to soothe Threes and through romanticism are able to break through their psychological armor. Nevertheless, Sevens must be careful not to cut themselves off from the outside world and pay more attention to their partner, for they do tend to lose touch with reality. They are here but not here sometimes not being genuinely present, which terribly annoys Threes.

3 with 8

General aspect: Is this truly possible? As a matter of fact, it is, provided both of them make the effort to be more mature, so as to accept each other's differences. In this case, the relationship will definitely be a special and creative one. If this is not the case, the honest, upstanding and sociable Threes won't adapt well to Eights' secret excesses and their rigid ways. Conversely, Eights are likely to consider Threes as shallow, not complex enough and too easy to see through.

Parent 3 and child 8: In this particular scenario, the parent must learn how to curb his/her sharp criticisms as well as subdue his/her hyperactivity, because, at any rate, it will have very little impact on the child's deep nature. The child actually behaves as if he/she was naturally impervious to such behaviors. His/her inner nature is sustained by feelings, energy and contact with the invisible and   as such, therefore opposes the parent's more materialistic outlook. This does not mean that the child is unaware of the parent's sensible advice, just that this particular child is mature enough to know what is right from wrong. On the other hand, the parent is likely to be frustrated, for he/she feels that he/she cannot enter the child's secret world.

Parent 8 and child 3: The parent will enable the child to explore and discover a world of sensation and feeling, despite the fact that this particular child is more compelled by what is rational and of knowledge than by sentiment. The mother or the father is open-minded enough to let the child express what he/she likes or dislikes.

As a matter of fact, this particular parent is patient when being questioned, disproved and misunderstood. On the other hand, what the parent must avoid is giving way to anger and quick-tempered reactions when annoyed by the child. This child is very able in pointing out the parent's contradictions and will have no qualms in rubbing it in their face. Certain tensions are to be expected.

Associates 3 and 8: As long as Threes manage to accept Eights' apparent unrest and their difficulty in having a rational dialogue, everything will go just fine. However this remains to be seen, as getting along under such conditions is certainly not easy. Threes endeavor to organize, plan and give shape to things, while attempting to protect themselves from possible hardships. Quite unlike Eights who cannot be bothered. In fact, Eights can only focus on current benefits and they will develop any kind of contacts, even if they are unaware whether these contacts are useful or not in the long run. Such a partnership is however feasible, provided both of them keep to his/her own respective tasks.

Love relationship between 3 and 8: Eights will be able to make Threes discover an entirely new world, one they had no idea existed or one they have had a tendency to reject. If Threes come to accept this challenge, everything is possible. If this is not the case, massive misunderstandings will come about.

Eights actually live through their senses. They yearn for enjoyment and satisfaction without limits or restraint. Threes hold opposite views: they cannot refrain from criticizing that which does not fall in with their puritan outlook. Despite the odds and unavoidable arguments, they may learn to love each other. Eights will at the very least manage to help uptight Threes loosen up, who will, in turn teach Eights honesty and a sense of limits.

3 with 9

General aspect: The couple is peaceful and constructive though they don't live in the same sphere. Threes' minds do not operate like Nines' minds do and yet, they are very attracted to one another and this results in a harmonious relationship. Their differences do not give rise to antagonism. Both of them are interested in exploring the processes of the mind, but they go about it through different ways. There is mutual respect. In addition, Threes are very social beings and this will inspire Nines' way of living.

Parent 3 and child 9: The parent will enable the child to explore all sorts of new horizons. The child never actually asked for such and he/she might not want to commit to all these new prospects, perhaps finding it difficult to choose which domain suits him/her best. Both of them enjoy dialogue, although their ways of expressing themselves are radically different. The parent strives to be rational, accurate and efficient whereas the child tends to embellish, create and daydream a lot. The child's inertia and apathy may make the parent even more critical. The parent will have to learn to be more patient and lenient, while the child will need to learn to be more precise, orderly and efficient.

Parent 9 and child 3: The parent takes life on the bright side and tends to easily accept temporary difficulties and mishaps in the way Destiny leads our lives. The parent does not ponder over the why and how, which does not suit the child at all who requires structure in order to compare and understand. This is why the Three child might not be satisfied with his/her education that he/she may consider as not supportive and structured enough. There is a great struggle between this fatalistic parent and this child who is the opposite.

Associates 3 and 9: Threes are steeped in order and discipline and this is why they have a hard time with Nines, who tend to be sluggish and prefer to flee when faced with something they don't like. Nines yearn for calm and serenity, whereas Threes are restless, structured and rigorous. Yet, both of them are attached to the idea of service and commitment, although they do not immerse themselves in the same way. Nines take things as they come, and manage to adjust to the events as they unfold. Threes endeavor to control things in such a way that they can master it, struggling to prevent problems from happening again. Yet, if they are able to get along and accept their differences association is bound to be extremely profitable. Nines need to stop worrying about being criticized and Threes will have to accept his/her partner's global vision, human qualities and even his/her apparent disorder.

Love relationship between 3 and 9: If such a relationship occurs, it will be grounded in mutual desire to understand one another with a willingness to devote oneself to the other. Nines are romantic and sentimental; and have a divine idealistic view of love. They will succeed in giving a more human touch to Threes who can seem cold and distant, despite the deep feelings they have and are unable to express out loud due to feeling impeded by their obsession for perfection. As soon as Threes understand it is not necessary to shape and structure everything and that you can also let go and enjoy the present, they will then relax and accept being led into a world of senses where the analytical mind does not prevail. If Threes fail to understand and realize this, the relationship will not be viable.

3 with 11

General aspect: Passion, fireworks, explosion. Threes are propelled by Elevens, while keeping a critical eye on his/her actions, which is liable to hurt Elevens' feelings. This being said, they are successful when investigating or setting up new common projects. Neither family life nor intimacy is favored. Each individual needs to temper their passion.

Parent 3 and child 11: The relationship can prove extremely positive, in that this child has a tremendous need to be taken care of, structured and supported. The child loves nothing more than when his/her parent shows interest in what he/she does and supports his/her goals, aspirations, desires and urges. Everything is fine, as long as the parent doesn't pay much attention to the child's quick-tempered and possibly angry reactions, and lets him/her have their space and freedom. In the case where the parent is too critical, the child may think of ways of how to escape from this cumbersome presence. Both of them are smart, bright and respect each other. This is why they should be able to come to a mutual agreement. The parent is in a position to teach the child that something greater exists out there, beyond our petty egos.

Parent 11 and child 3: This parent appears to be somewhat liberal and carefree. He/she isn't used to expending much effort or speculation on organization and the meaning of life. Yet this child does require more precise structure, which the parent may not succeed at giving. However, he/she will manage to open up new fields of investigation for this child so that he/she can discover other realms, beyond the restrictive, intellectual mind. The relationship is far from being perfect, particularly if the parent is unable to refrain from impatience and exasperation when facing the child's criticisms. But the child definitely yearns for the knowledge this particular parent can pass on, and will, therefore, come to accept the learning his/her parent is ready to convey, even if it is a little disturbing.

Associates 3 and 11: Two very excited beings are brought here together. Elevens set to conquer the world and will not be slowed down by any obstacles. Threes are unhappy until they have planned and organized the world around them to perfection, or at least to their own idea of perfection. This is why it can be said that while their destination is the same, they do not take the same route to get there. However, as odd as it may seem, they can contribute so much to each other. Threes' famous organization skills will enable Elevens to construct their world into solid form, even if it means losing some of their precious freedom. As a result, conflict and arguments are likely to take place. However, each is intelligent enough to rise above their antagonisms, so as to resume their favorite activity: pursuing enriching conversations and exchanges over varied subjects.

Love relationship between 3 and 11: The most profound exchanges between these two occur through discussion, explanation and analysis. Both try to talk the partner into accepting their respective views. They both struggle to prove to the other one how strong and skilled they are, as if this was the basis for a true loving relationship. As long as they remain on the same wave length, tuned to the same vibration level, everything is just fine. But as soon as a little something goes wrong, everything goes wrong and the relationship immediately collapses. They have forgotten that a relationship is made up of shared feelings and subtle energy, and not merely intellectual ideas. They tend to behave like brother and sister rather than lovers and friends. It is easy to know when there is a problem as they will they stop talking altogether.

3 with 22

General aspect: The outlook is mixed. While technical and pragmatic matters are emphasized, feelings and sensitivity are left behind. Threes might put up with Twenty-twos' tendency to comply, but they cannot stand their pessimism. In addition, Threes are likely to deeply disturb Twenty-twos' quest for peace and discretion even though Threes could serve as the ideal spokespersons on behalf of their partners.

Parent 3 with child 22: Threes' famous skills of organization, planning and detail will enable the child to develop and give structure to what he/she needs. As a matter of fact, the child has found a perfect role model to help achieve the vision of life he/she has while ensuring no obstacles get in the way. In turn, this demanding parent will be highly satisfied with the child's sincere, honest, righteous and methodical behavior. However, there may be a risk of complying too much with the rules, to the point where pessimistic views are liable to arise. This being said, education, profession and life's accomplishments are favored.

Parent 22 and child 3: The child might be disturbed by the parent's lack of presence. The child wants more explanations and dialogue. While the parent does a great deal to provide the child with a sense of well-being, he/she does not care much for talking. This being said, the parent's pragmatic outlook and his/her exceptional strength of character combine to provide great protection to the child, even if certain deeper philosophical aspects may be missing from the relationship. The child is in constant demand of finding answers to his/her questions on the meaning of life, and this might very well exasperate the parent who doesn't normally take these issues into account. Nevertheless, the child will always be able to rely on this parent, who has the ability to face life's hardships without pondering over existential questions.

Associates 3 and 22: This association can prove to be extremely positive in the long run, in that Twenty-twos have the strength and ability to face adversity, which is the perfect soothing antidote to Threes anxieties and worries. Conversely, Threes are very skilled at organizing, which will enable the partner to accomplish his/her projects. All that is serious and efficient is highlighted. Everything will be carried out according to plan. However, Twenty-twos must learn how to give their associates more explanation as to what they are up to, which will reassure and comfort Threes who have an great need to be informed and kept up to date. Twenty-twos are never overwhelmed by their emotions and will therefore not be overly distressed by Threes' criticisms, unless they get fed up with Threes' longwinded verbal explanations.

Love relationship between 3 and 22: They have found the perfect partner, as both of them appreciate a shared, simple love life in the countryside or quiet place where they can raise their many children. Their common centers of interest (their children, food, pets and home), lie at the very heart of their exchanges and concern. Romance comes after, or doesn't come at all. Carnal pleasures are not on the agenda. And yet, they both have powerful earthly appetites (especially during Threes' younger years) and they are determined to satisfy them. All they need to do is refrain from sinking into a dull and tedious routine.

4 with 4

General aspect: Their motto is "let's hide and live happily ever after". This association looks monotonous and discreet from the outside, but enables a significant increase in material wealth. There is a shared quest for nature and a peaceful constructive life. Well-being is highly sought. The values of work are also emphasized. Principles. Persistence. Focus on the small things, instead of embracing larger perspectives.

Parent 4 and child 4: They are in tune with each other as far as their projects, desire for peace and calm are concerned. Yet, they are determined to enjoy all sorts of pleasures in life, particularly material ones. The parent is liable to urge the child to live in a pragmatic way, to carry out hands-on projects and to focus on what is essential. The parent will not push the child to overcome any limits, as he/she does not do this to him him/her self. The parent will teach the child how to go about life in a down-to-earth way, so as to achieve perceptible results. Even though conflict is not to be expected, a lot of unsaid issues can develop. It also must be noted that the parent may wish the child to make up for the successes he/she did not obtain in his/her own life. The child is liable to inherit the family company and take the business over. The parent will be intent on passing on his hereditary values and principles.

Associates 4: Here are two workaholics, who are persistent and determined in carrying out their projects. They do not slow one another down because their outlook is very similar. What they pursue is peace of heart. They are attached to a certain routine, act with regularity and know how to share the work that needs to be done, thereby doubling their work strength. Both of them are hedonistic. This is why, along with their genuine and powerful determination as far as work is concerned, they are also able to relax and unwind and can be inclined to laziness. As a matter of fact, they might need to make an effort to not let this sort of lethargy settle in, which would then be difficult to come out of.

4 in love with another 4: They are both driven by their thirst for pleasure and entertainment, which is why they get along so well. Yet, their shy and discreet nature might hinder spontaneous expression of their desires. They would like to be surrounded by beauty and harmony, but in an unobtrusive way. They will definitely fulfill their desire in making their home cozy, using their artistic senses. This being said, they are likely to indulge in a monotonous routine. To avoid this from happening, they should express and share their deep, inner emotions. They also need to be wary of being too possessive.

4 with 5

General aspect: How can quiet Fours live in harmony with boisterous Fives and their relentless urge to explore new things? How can Fives put up with slow and rigid Fours? Fours' material aspirations just cannot match Fives' thirst for discovery. They will only be able to get along at the expense of mutual compromise and sacrifice. Provided they find such common ground, the association will result in a combination between adventure and the methodical.

Parent 4 and child 5: This boisterous and disruptive child will definitely disturb the legendary quiet parent. The former wants to possess the ones he/she loves and therefore will be upset by this child who loves nothing more than taking off on adventures far away from his/her familiar home. The parent will have to learn to understand that he/she should not curb the child's spontaneous and uncontrollable urges, but rather give him/her wise advice instead. In other words, the parent must learn to listen to the child more. As soon as the parent attempts to be too protective or possessive, the child will inevitably be driven to flee and oppose what oppresses him/her, so as to lead his/her life as he/she wishes. All this is done without any intention of hurting anyone.

Parent 5 and child 4: This boisterous parent is very open-minded and refuses to be trapped into any preconceived ideas. He/she will teach his/her child how to overcome his/her limits and go beyond his/her quest for comfort. This way of behaving may prove a little too much for the child who requires more quiet bearings. The parent must learn more patience with the child and not get upset with his/her slow way of understanding things. This might prove to be difficult for this impatient parent to handle.

Associates 4 and 5: They do not operate in the same ways and this is why they are liable to disagree on many issues. Fours are slow and this deeply frustrates Fives who are fast and bright. Fives know how to explore and discover, but they do not know how to give structure to things. As a result, they must find partners who are able to structure the material aspects of their projects and preserve them well. Adversely, Fours must refrain from fretting whenever Fives unwillingly push them around a little too much. Fives relentless nervousness can make the otherwise reserved Fours fly off the handle.

Love relationship between 4 and 5: Such a relationship is not completely incompatible, in that they bring each other the right specific experience the other one needs. As adventurous (often broke!) and attracted by new horizons as Fives may be, they do enjoy returning to quiet Fours who offer them a haven of peace. They are also attracted by Fours' sense of pleasure and enjoyment of life. Conversely, if Fours manage to accept boisterous Fives and leave them their freedom and space, they are likely to be amused by their natural ability of adding spice to life. Fours may not appreciate when their partners become restless and tiring, but they will definitely enjoy their sense of humor and joyousness. Fours will attempt to bring more consistency to Five.

4 with 6

General aspect: They share common interests, such as the need to build something together and achieve fulfillment. There are no apparent antagonisms. They share a quest for harmony and mutual consent. They also share a taste for the arts, aesthetics in general, well-being, a good quiet life and tradition. Family matters are favored as is common material aspirations.

Parent 4 and child 6: The parent is liable to bring a certain comfort and peace of mind to this child who needs to be reassured and supported. Gentle mutual understanding is found here. There are no apparent conflicts. The parent enjoys life's pleasures and will be able to teach the child how to make his/her own choices, so as to live the life he/she needs to feel happy. The child searches for perfection and ideal relationships. He/she will find his parent is able to listen to each and every small thing. The parent is certainly easy going and flexible, but he/she should nevertheless teach the child that perfection does not exist, that mistakes are opportunities to learn more and that one should be satisfied with what one has.

Parent 6 and child 4: This particular parent is attached to human relationships and he/she is a perfectionist who will not be at peace until he/she succeeds in teaching the child how to overcome limits and be more persistent when facing obstacles. The child has a tendency to give up and needs to be taught how to make more effort: this is essential for his/her development. Although he/she has a real ability to work well, he/she tends to be satisfied with too little. It will not be easy to convince him/her that he/she has the means to attain more accurate, efficient and ambitious goals.

Associates 4 and 6: This association is very constructive in the long run. Both of them strive to shape and structure things, so as to set things up in a safe and lasting way. Fours are no example of order and perfection of course, but Sixes are - and will therefore be able to implement projects and organize structures. By acting in such a way, Sixes will eventually overcome their partners' carefree attitude and inertia. Fours will not be particularly upset when Sixes criticize them. On the contrary, they will be able to teach Sixes how to take things more lightly and worry less about what they regard as trivial imperfections. However, Fours will definitely have to cope with criticism and being shaken out of their little habits.

Love relationship between 4 and 6: With such a companion, Fours will be able to fully live up to their passion and earthly appetites. These appetites are equally shared by Sixes, even though their sense of perfection might prevent them from expressing all their desires. The relationship can be lasting, as long as Sixes do not attempt to structure every single thing. If they do, Fours are liable to close themselves off. Sixes hate lack of order, while Fours cope with it very well. This being said, home improvement and well-being are favored. Both of them endeavor to avoid anything that disturbs the peace and quiet they seek.

4 with 7

General aspect: Here we have matter and spirit. Although they are worlds apart, they are able to get along, provided they respect each other's personalities. Sevens very much admire Fours´ abilities for designing projects and carrying them out, which makes Fours feel more confident. Fours could do with a little more of Sevens´ faith and trust in their endeavors, in whatever domain is concerned. The marriage of the material and the spiritual blends well together, resulting in lasting peace and harmony.

Parent 4 and child 7: Although the parent attempts to bring stability and safety to the child, he/she may collide with the child´s dreams and ideals. Yet, the relationship remains positive, in that there is no underlying resentment. They both love, understand and respect one another. But there is a risk that the parent is likely to curb the child´s thirst for exploration, when he/she is only trying to prevent the child from getting hurt. The child is smart enough though to understand that the parent´s overprotectiveness is harmless. The child will be able to compromise and, later, to become free when the time comes. The parent must teach the child how to respect the environment in which he/she lives.

Parent 7 and child 4: The parent is determined to ensure the child studies successfully and achieves high-caliber goals. However, the parent will have to wait and be more realistic, as the child isn't interested in gaining knowledge. Unless the parent quickly acknowledges and accepts the child's way of being and how he/she works, the relationship might turn into a nightmare. This being said, the child will help the parent learn that things can be done in a much more practical and non-intellectual way.

Associates 4 and 7: This association looks difficult, in that Fours do not appreciate being pushed around. They need to do things in their own slow way. Sevens however will particularly appreciate their associate's stability, even while they resent Fours' lack of initiative and enterprise, and their difficulty in getting involved in new projects. If they succeed to understanding how they each operate, they will get along very well. Fours will bring a sense of cautiousness that Sevens need, while Sevens will drive Fours to step out of their routine and habitual setting.

Love relationship between 4 and 7: Idealistic Sevens might very well fall for Fours' natural and charming nature. They will particularly appreciate Fours' ability to take life as it comes, without giving too much thought. Fours actually attempt to protect themselves and consequently try to create a pleasant environment to live in. Sevens will be happy with that too, because they are aesthetically aware and love having a pleasant home. Nevertheless, Sevens also need to explore the world and commit to it. This is not particularly suited to Fours' cautious ways, which is why they will have to find common ground to agree on.

4 with 8

General aspect: They share a common taste for earthly pleasures and creativity. This association favors financial and material success. Yet, deep, dark, hidden instincts (such as jealousy or persecution paranoia) might give rise to significant conflict. In which case, the relationship may prove very destructive. Either all good, or all bad...

Parent 4 and child 8: The child requires structure and advice, even if he/she does not like it. But this particular parent is not likely to provide such, as he/she cannot fathom how the child's mysterious and enigmatic world operates. And yet, this child feels compelled to face life's harsh realities, and will do so even if this entails resorting to dodgy means. The parent on the other hand is not in touch with life's tough realities and will therefore be unable to pass on the required skills to the child. As a matter of fact, the parent will have to step out of his/her little comfortable world, in order to be able to help the child, which he/she will eventually do, because he/she is determined to be a good protector.

Parent 8 and child 4: In this relationship, the child desperately needs protection and above all, wants to avoid being hurt. Yet, the parent never worries about the vicissitudes of life and consequently is unable to meet the child´s needs. At first, the child will find it difficult to believe that he/she must live in such an unstructured world. He/she will just have to come to accept this and cope with it, by creating his own protective barriers that will enable him/her to live peacefully and in harmony. The parent is likely to rant at the child and have fits of anger for she/he either being too cautious, shy, and not brave enough, or for not being in touch with reality according to the parent´s beliefs. The parent will eventually succeed in teaching the child how to get by on his/her own, to face adversity and to revise his quiet ways.

Associates 4 and 8: Despite the fact that they operate in very different ways, they are both extremely attached to all kinds of material and financial benefits. They will therefore favor any projects that enable them to increase their wealth. Fours tend to hoard, while Eights tend to keep their eyes out for good poker-hand operations and risk. Provided they manage to blend their two very different approaches, they can go very far. If not, jealousies are liable to arise, as well as resentment and bitterness regarding conflicts of interests and possible corruption. Both of them are so tense when it comes to making money that neither of them agrees to give up what they own. Eights are very much attracted to mysteries. They are unpredictable by nature and are therefore likely to be irritated by Fours´ uptight and covert ways.

Love relationship between 4 and 8: In this case also, two highly opposed views on love are present, which albeit can prove very beneficial for both. Both of them appreciate the pleasures of life. Yet, Fours are cautious and shy, while Eights are outgoing and quick-tempered. Eights will therefore have to teach Fours how to disclose their secrets and move beyond their limits. In turn, Fours will have to teach Eights how to be more patient, soft and gentle, as well as how to control their deep impulses. In other words, Fours enjoy foreplay and must teach Eights how to give pleasure in that respect. Financial aspects are favored.

4 with 9

General aspect: This is a productive relationship which will be profitable in many areas. These two numbers are very much suited, in that they share a quest for harmony, peace and unity. They can bring each other a lot. When Nines feel worried and frightened by life, they will feel highly protected by Fours. Fours are not insensitive to Nines' spirituality and generosity.

Parent 4 and child 9: The parent would never interfere, intrude nor trespass into the child's quiet world. This is not a relationship based on order, discipline and organization, but rather one of human contact, exchanges of emotions and feelings. The relationship does not place emphasis on a structured and planned life. However, they do not dare to express their feelings for fear they might hurt the other person. They therefore fail to share their deep thoughts with one another; about their views on life in general and their personal relationships. This serious lack of communication might eventually give rise to a certain form of laxness.

Parent 9 and child 4: The parent is in search of peace and would never coerce the child to do anything. This is fine, but it can become extreme, in that the parent may fail to give the child any structure at all. And this child needs it. Unless the child is given some kind of framework, he/she will withdraw from human contact and from anything regarded as harmful. Tenderness, feelings and affection are certainly present, but this is not enough. The parent is so frightened to hurt the child's sensitivity that he/she may end up actually encouraging the child's inability to deal with the outside world. This being said, the parent will eventually succeed in prompting the child to pursue studies and to want to do something with his/her life, or at the very least to feel humanly and socially useful.

Associates 4 and 9: They will never manage to create an orderly, structured, planned and efficient partnership. They are not rigorous and effective enough to be reactive. As long as their association lasts and does not require accurate decision-making, everything will be fine. But if this is not the case, it will be awkward. Domains such as teaching, social work or local trading, are favored, whereas domains that entail high pressure and quick reaction are not favored at all.

Love relationship between 4 and 9: Romance is found here. A shared impulse to make each other happy brings them together. While there are no signs of aggression, there are a lot of un-expressed emotions and heavy silences. The relationship lacks dynamic energy and might lead to a certain form of routine, monotony and even boredom, which may prompt the feeling of not being able to control one's own destiny. Because of this they are vulnerable to having their space invaded by outsiders and freeloaders who are likely to take advantage of them, while bringing some spice to their boring lives. At least, this will drive them to realize how much they need to allow more spontaneity into their lives. Because they avoid getting involved with the varied everyday commitments of their own lives, they can resort to showing a great deal of interest in other people's adventures instead.

4 with 11

General aspect: Powerful intense opposition and antagonism. It is extremely difficult for these two to find common ground. The relationship will only work if Fours are willing to accept unconditionally Elevens' tyranny and independent action. Adversely, Elevens will need to wind down and cope with Fours' placid ways. Provided they manage this, the association is liable to be successful, particularly in professional matters.

Parent 4 and child 11: The parent is persistent, constant and overprotective, which does not encourage the child to embrace his/her unique and dynamic way of being. This particular child has a strong need to prove, to him/herself and the world what he/she is able to accomplish and achieve. From a very early age, he/she loves to discover, experiment and search for new horizons, and this will with no doubt frighten the parent as he/she just can't understand their child's outlook on life. The child relentlessly seeks to widen and deepen his/her fields of exploration, whereas the parent is determined to narrow them. This being said, the child will always be able to rely on his/her parent in times of hardship (and there will be quite a few of these!). The parent is reliable and always at hand to offer shelter for recharging batteries.

Parent 11 and child 4: This child needs calm and quiet, but will have to give in to the parent's wishes, willingly or unwillingly. The parent will in no way be moved by the child's protests and cries. The child will just have to comply, no matter what. Yet, he/she will definitely benefit from the parent's adamant urging to step out of one's comfort zone and reassuring routine and overcome his/her innate shyness and fears. Nevertheless, a great deal of misunderstanding can be expected. As a matter of fact, misunderstandings are likely to increase throughout the course of life, as the child deeply resents the parent's seemingly deaf attitude and lack of respect that began in early childhood.

Associates 4 and 11: This association is difficult, yet it can work providing certain conditions are met. If Elevens succeed in convincing Fours of the significance of their initiative while understanding how Fours operate, that is to say if they come to accept their partner's slow natural way, they can get along fine. But this might prove awkward, in that Elevens will have to be patient and persistent. Adversely, Fours will have to accept to step out of their comfort zone and cozy environment. Yet, the relationship may prove very satisfying in the long run, because Elevens do need Fours to give shape and structure to their projects. Time is Fours' friend, but Elevens' foe.

Love relationship between 4 and 11: A tumultuous relationship. Elevens are liable to take advantage of Fours' ability to create an enjoyable environment to live in, and at the same time, go and look for adventure elsewhere. Provided Fours do not feel they are missing out on something or that their familiar nest is being jeopardized, they can very well adjust to this situation. As a matter of fact, Fours enjoy taking part in a happy, dynamic, active environment, as long as it remains an enjoyable entertainment. But as soon as Elevens make decisions that are likely to impact Fours' peaceful world and comfortable material life, issues will develop.

4 with 22

General aspect: They generally agree on most things. Material and financial goals are reached. The pleasures of life are sought after. Peace, calm and retreat from mundane activities are favored. A return to nature is indicated and ancestral values are emphasized. While this association may not be the most original one, it is lasting and safe. There is however a tendency to be overprotective and isolate themselves.

Parent 4 and child 22: This parent will be delighted to have a child who not only doesn't disturb his/her tranquility but also has the strength, capacity and power to fulfill him/herself. The parent brings softness, warmth and feeling, even if long discussions by the fire are not on the agenda. What might happen instead is a role reversal, in which the child plays the protector towards his/her own parent, as the child's serious, strong solidity renders him/her mature from a very young age.

Parent 22 and child 4: The parent is caustic, austere and abrupt. As such, he/she will certainly not over-protect his/her offspring, nor even disturb their peace of mind. The parent will obviously however protect the child from potential dangers, providing what he/she needs in terms of food, shelter and education, keeping to the essential. The parent does not appreciate superfluous, childish, useless gadgets and therefore keeps to the fundamentals. Despite the fact that the relationship doesn't manifest outwards signs of affection, the child will nonetheless be thankful for having received a good education, as well as the discipline and structure.

Associates 4 and 22: The partnership is constructive, viable and lasting. However, it lacks imagination and dynamic energy. Efficiency is the key word here. However, elements such as animals, nature, certain social ambitions and public work are favored. Great breakthroughs and innovations are not to be expected, for neither of them is willing to go beyond the limits of their activities. In addition, they are not willing to call into question their habits, outlook and the ways in which they operate in life. Their business association is characterized by their seriousness and respectability.

Love relationship between 4 and 22: They are both characteristic, traditional and attached to established customs. They might prove a little too uptight, or nostalgic, depending on the circumstances. The couple appreciates material comfort and regular routine. Although they do enjoy this seemingly dull life, they suffer from not being able to express themselves deeply as they fear each other's judgment. Yet, they are perfectly able to enjoy life's pleasures together. As a matter of fact, their libertine outlook may help them overcome their shyness and leave their comfort zone. They are likely to bestow a long lineage, or dedicate themselves to the animal world or child care.

5 with 5

General aspect: They agree on most dynamics, but lack depth. A great deal of common values enables them to have exhilarating and expansive moments and share their experiences, but their general outlook doesn't allow them to carry out their projects objectively. They are altruistic. They find it difficult to know what belongs to true friendship and what belongs to true love. They attempt too many things at once and therefore their adventurous lives remain unstable and not productive enough. This is what you get when you are driven by non-stop adventure.

Parent 5 and child 5: The parent's open-minded, innovative and humanitarian views definitely get through to the child. Both of them respond to the unusual and that which lies beyond their familiar surroundings. They are determined to free themselves from any type of restraint. Although the parent does bring a lot to the child in terms of awareness and development, the relationship fails to provide structure and foundation. Leading an independent and free life is fine, as long as the parent succeeds in teaching the child how to set limits, which he/she may not necessarily have. Both of them can get into fits of anger, sometimes explosive ones. Both of them have a tendency to make their point by proving he/she is right, and struggles to force the other one to change his/her mind accordingly. This results in endless arguments. The relationship is more of friendship than familial. The child is liable to liberate him/herself and leave home from early.

Associates 5: The independent, rebellious, reactive and revolutionary nature of both of these beings does not fit into a traditional partnership. Even though humanitarian attitudes are present, and both of them are innovative, loving nothing more than experimenting new things, neither of them is likely to give in as they are intent on proving they are right. If they operate in fields such as show-business, human relationships and travel, they can bring each other a lot, thanks to their adventurous nature. However they must give each other space. As a matter of fact, they need to learn how to transcend their independent and free nature, so as to be able to work together, on common ground. They also need to refer to knowledgeable persons of good advice. They will eventually have to take the financial aspects of their partnership into consideration, for they both are very poor managers.

5 in love with another 5: This particular type of relationship is more based on friendship than true love. Their rapport is free, independent, and both intend to keep their private space and autonomy. As long as their daily life is adventurous and enables them to meet many new people, or launch a great number of projects, everything will go just fine. If not, they are likely to get bored quickly and fall into gloomy moods which will drive them to search new horizons. Theirs is a free, brotherly, universal love.

5 with 6

General aspect: They get along perfectly well. Sixes bring harmony and rigor to Fives who, in turn, bring excitement to Sixes' life. Yet, Fives may find it difficult putting up with Sixes' rigid principles. And Sixes may find it hard to cope with inconsistent Fives who tend to avoid responsibility.

Parent 5 and child 6: The child is fond of relationships and therefore appreciates the parent's innovative, open and brotherly views. Nevertheless, this particular child needs to be given a structure. The child needs time to polish up the projects he/she has become involved in. It is a question of acknowledging his/her skills and abilities. But the parent is not likely to recognize these particular skills and will therefore not be supportive enough. This relationship will eventually prompt the child to liberate him/herself at an early age. This will actually enable the child to strengthen his/her abilities to overcome inhibitions, without dwelling too much on failure. The parent doesn't usually spend much time worrying about why things may go wrong and will therefore not burden the child's psyche.

Parent 6 and child 5: The parent brings a great deal to the child in terms of structure, achievement and perfection, and most of all patience. Pursuing his/her quest for independence and freedom, the child may want to hasten things, carrying out several projects at once and therefore scattering his/her energy. The parent will teach him/her how to wind down, so as to be able to follow one goal at a time, and to continue to try again and again until what has been launched is completed. This is why the child is likely to be upset by this parent that he/she considers as too picky yet, as time goes by, he/she will eventually appreciate the need for perfection and the ability to question him/herself. They will develop a deep friendly relationship.

Associates 5 and 6: This is a paradoxical relationship, in which both individuals operate in very different ways. Fives thrive on adventure, new exhilarating projects, and love to overcome their limits and carry out their own experiments, without taking into account the possible consequences of their actions. This behavior is the total opposite of Sixes' views. For Sixes are accurate, efficient, and rigorous and never give up trying to succeed what they are involved in, until perfection is reached. If Fives learn how to be patient and refrain from criticizing their partners, while Sixes learn how to compromise and accept their partners' superficial ways, everything is feasible. If not, the partnership is likely to fail. Either way, provided they manage to find common ground, the mix between innovation and efficiency can bring about a significant outcome.

Love relationship between 5 and 6: The relationship is likely to be dynamic, boisterous, and even explosive at times. Yet, these two beings are driven by a true sense of brotherly spirit and agree on one significant point: the importance of human relationships. This being said, Fives can prove cynical and will not hesitate to make fun of their righteous and perfectionist partners. Sixes have a self-deprecating way and will therefore find it difficult to cope with Fives' sense of humor, particularly when Fives won't accept criticism. And yet, the relationship can work. With their intelligence, they are able to soften the tone in their communication and come to accept their different ways. In doing so, they can even find enjoyment and amusement in the process. The relationship is a game of challenge and continual seduction.

5 with 7

General aspect: Here we have rivalries, misunderstandings and two different ways of understanding independence. Sevens find it hard to understand Fives' expansive universe, whereas fives find it hard to understand Sevens' introverted universe. However, common ground can be found, provided they are driven by similar goals and take the time to communicate. Fives express themselves easily, while Sevens don't. Sevens are more profound and secretive.

Parent 5 and child 7: In this particular case, the parent is liberal, boisterous and open-minded. This will be quite disturbing for the child who is extremely curious, like the parent, but who doesn't involve him/herself in the same way the parent does. As a matter of fact, the child widely differs from the parent, with regard to his/her capacities of fathoming and exploring the world. His/her natural curiosity propels him/her to analyze and understand in a very set and focused way. The child can become deeply absorbed in what he/she considers as important or true and will not let go until he/she feels the question has been solved; whereas the parent is interested in everything, without dwelling too much on any particular thing. The parent continuously widens his/her field of experience and wishes only to stay free. This is precisely where misunderstandings might come up, between the child who needs slow and accurate facts and the parent who is quick and carefree. Yet, the parent will manage to meet the child's most pressing needs.

Parent 7 and child 5: This parent can do a lot for the child; not only does he/she enable the child to satisfy his need for adventure, but also pushes the child to discover things her/himself. What's more, the parent is able to canalize, structure and discipline the child, teaching him how not to scatter his energy. From the child's point of view, this may appear as coercive so as to hamper her/his plans. The parent is totally committed and single-minded, who may across to the child as being too dogmatic. The child, in turn, may appear to the parent as too carefree. The child's prompt angry outbursts are likely to upset the parent. The more the parent tries to control the child, the more the child will try to escape. The parent must accept that he/she can only educate the child as long as the child's privacy and freedom are respected. The parent will eventually come to accept that the child must learn by his/her own personal experiences.

Associates 5 and 7: This association may give rise to a deal of arguments. Fives' legendary impulsiveness and dynamic reactions may not get along with Sevens' inquisitive and suspicious nature, which often ends in pointless bickering. Sevens are introverted, whereas Fives are extroverted. And yet, the partnership may work, provided Sevens learn how to express themselves better, especially as far as their deep emotions are concerned. If Sevens communicate too superficially or too bluntly, they will hurt Fives' feelings, who are very easily hurt. In turn, Fives must learn patience and to refrain from reacting impulsively. As long as these conditions are met, they can contribute a lot to each other. Sevens are fine negotiators, accurate and reliable. Fives are open to the world, and always up for trying out all sorts of new experiences. They actually both enjoy traveling and are very curious about all sorts of new things which may prompt new projects. Provided both keep to his/her own domain, the partnership will work. If not, catastrophe can be expected.

Love relationship between 5 and 7: Fives are carefree. They are fond of adventure, friends, relationships, and new horizons. This does not suit Sevens at all. Although Sevens do have a sense of adventure, they would rather protect themselves from life's potential hardships, by building a peaceful haven through material and financial means. Fives are not bothered by material or financial comforts, which they can do without. They'd rather widen their scope of experience. If they are united by a bond of deep feeling, their love is possible. If not, Sevens' mercantile interests will end up making the relationship wither, for Fives are then likely to flee.

5 with 8

General aspect: Both of them are attracted to the dark side of the moon and mysteries in general. Both of them are mediums. They are also stimulated by all sorts of games in life. Yet, Fives can be disturbed by Eights' appetite for power. And Eights may find Fives' thirst for humanitarian values, freedom and exploration a little out of control.

Parent 5 and child 8: This is a very special relationship. The parent's open and outgoing behavior may seem to oppose the child's secret and covert ways. Although these worlds may appear as utterly different, they do meet together in one particular domain: the area of exploring what may seem invisible and unexplored at first glance. The parent is sharp and generous, and will definitely succeed in understanding the child. Both have access to mysteries and secrets, although the parent may be more equipped to give them shape and structure. The parent is idealistic, which will help open up the child's perceptions and awareness. The parent is likely to be surprised by the child's naïve and genuine candor, as well as his/her instinctive and spontaneous determination. Both of them are tempted to create imaginary worlds and should be careful to remain rooted in reality.

Parent 8 and child 5: The parent does not take the child's independent antics too seriously, because he/she is able to handle them. On the contrary, he/she may even find them amusing. In turn, the child loves the parent very much, because he/she is understanding and does not attempt to control and coerce. The child will come to understand that the parent does have authority and a strong personality. This relationship is steeped in respect and trust. As disruptive and restless as the child may be, he/she knows that he/she can rely on the parent, no matter what, and will not be judged. Their life can prove folkloric.

Associates 5 and 8: They will need a lot of time, patience, and understanding if they want to come to a common agreement, so as to follow the same path. Their ways of being are as opposed as night and day. This is why they must develop extraordinary capacities to adjust to each other, if they want to pursue common interests. Fives are restless, idealistic and free spirits. They cannot stand being restricted in their projects. They find it extremely difficult to cope with things they do not want and to focus on only one thing at a time. This might explain why they are not very good with money. This drastically opposes Eights, who are mainly motivated by one thing: financial well-being. Eights have a strong personality and are able to withstand hardships, as long as these contribute to material growth. Unlike Fives, Eights can be thirsty for power. What brings them together is their need for freedom and independence.

Love relationship between 5 and 8: Both of them have powerful and unpredictable personalities. They both intend to show how different they are and cannot stand being told what to do and say. In addition, both are attracted to new experiences, unusual sensations and excursions. As a matter of fact, this urge to live away from mainstream society and its values is precisely what brings them together. However, long lasting relationships, with children and family life, must not be expected. Being true to one another is not on the agenda either, although Fives seem to cope better in terms of open relationships, because they are more open minded and honest than Eights, who tend to do things secretly. This being said, if they are set on living a remarkable adventure, off the beaten track, they are well found.

5 with 9

General aspect: Agreement and mutual respect. They share a quest for an easy and comfortable life. They get along well, although things might remain unsaid due to fear of disappointing the other person and/or ruining the relationship. They do not regard each other as opponents. They both need to explore but they do so in different ways. They look to live in harmony, with the least possible conflict. Because they are deeply aware that compromise is required, they are able to enjoy the sweetness of life. Nines are diplomatic and consistent, which sooth and calm explosive Fives who realize Nines are not potential rivals.

Parent 5 and child 9: The child is deeply attached to peace and quiet and will therefore do everything possible to maintain such. This is why he/she would never ever try to confront this boisterous parent, although the parent uses all sorts of means to come to terms with the child's routine and habits. Yet, the child is aware of the parent's personal intentions and will therefore not take it too personally. The parent brings the child the very thing that he/she is also seeking, i.e. space and freedom. Nevertheless, the child might feel that he/she is not cared for enough, thus giving rise to feelings of anxiety. Feeling so unsecure might, over time, drive the child to blame the parent for being too liberal. The child does appreciate socializing, but not as much as the parent. In fact, the child tends to escape from reality and definitely needs to be drawn back to earth, which the parent might not be willing to do.

Parent 9 and child 5: The parent considers the child unpredictable, disruptive and explosive, and might just well resign from any responsibility. The relationship is not simple for the parent who needs, above all, peace and quiet. As a matter of fact, he/she will not hesitate to sacrifice him/herself for what he/she considers a good cause. The parent would rather not talk or disturb, and will refuse confrontation and arguments. And this is precisely what the child cannot fathom, as he/she will never refrain from expressing what he/she feels and thinks while rejecting what he/she dislikes. What's more, the child is very fond of experiencing all that is exorbitant and excessive. The parent is wise enough to allow what is tolerable, but will this be sufficient? The child knows he/she can always rely on the parent's understanding, helpful and caring ways. The child also knows that he/she will never be blamed for anything, nor forced to do anything. This being said, the child very much needs structure and discipline which will never happen with such a parent. This being said, their relationship is friendly and harmonious.

Associates 5 and 9: They are brought together by a common desire to live in an ideal world of ethical values. However, their relationship is not that simple, especially for Nines who would rather explore the realities of their psyche than that of the outside world. Adversely, Fives literally keep on moving and actually need to explore new horizons, through multiple and unforeseen experiences. Nines will patiently have to put up with their boisterous partners' antics. However, Fives might eventually get bored and tired of Nines, whom they regard as too fearful and not daring enough in their joint projects. This being said, Nines give good advice, though Fives are not always willing to listen. Neither of them intends to hurt the other person, on the contrary, but is this enough to build a partnership together? It is not that easy... Fives may prove too restless and do not hesitate to push others around, in order to have their way while Nines are running behind the scenes trying to make everybody happy.

Love relationship between 5 and 9: It is difficult to build safe foundations on sandy terrain. Nines need to feel financially safe in order to feel happy and this is not part of Fives' program! They do have a lot to give and share with each other as they love each other deeply and tenderly. And yet, one may wonder if their spiritual and humanitarian connection will be strong enough to deal with the social and environmental restraints they will have to face. As time goes by, they are likely to come to blame each other for not being realistic enough. The hazard they face is their difficulty in putting up with life's constraints and cumbersome duties.

5 with 11

General aspect: They can go very far together... as long as they don't kill each other! They can be very efficient when they act together as they are both willing to overcome their limits and aim to live beyond conventional social structures. This union is one of intelligence and understanding, but nevertheless, strong impulses are present. Who is likely to dominate the other? Such an association favors all sorts of different dynamics in varied domains. Fives' spirit of freedom must not be hampered by Elevens' drive for success.

Parent 5 and child 11: The parent brings a great deal to the child, by fostering his/her abilities to discover his/her environment. The parent teaches the child how to trust in his/her ability to experience on his/her own and thereby to rely on what he/she regards as true. Such a child needs to be left alone, so as to be able to test his/her own skills and assess his/her own abilities. Such a parent is ideal for this as he/she would never force the child to do anything. Yet, the child might end up feeling left behind, which might result in difficulties in making decisions and finding his/her own path. The parent's lack of authority is also likely to cause difficulty for the child learning how to be stable and settled.

Parent 11 and child 5: Although the parent is deeply open-minded, he/she is also extremely authoritative. The parent tends to drive the child to do certain things which he/she may not want to do. The child might easily rebel against the parent's authority, so as to assess where they stand. The relationship is therefore awkward and prone to numerous fits of anger. The parent does understand the child's restless urges to explore and discover, but he/she will not accept their excesses, as he /she considers that the child is taking things too far. This being said, they are able to agree on entertainment, which definitely soothes their relationship.

Two associates 5 and 11: Here we are in the presence of two pioneers who constantly challenge conventional and social rules. Both are extremely skilled at clearing the way, discovering and exploring, but they may be unrealistic with regards to the financial aspects of their projects. Material concerns are not their cups of tea. Indeed, they couldn't care less... Their relationship is likely to be punctuated by angry disagreements, yet their friendship and understanding are strong enough to enable them to return to common ground.

Love relationship between 5 and 11: They have been brought together by a mutual urge to exchange, share and undertake common projects. They can talk endlessly about the subjects they are interested in. All this does not bring them very far financially speaking, but money is not what they are after. They seek freedom and independence. They can go quite far together, as long as they maintain their individual space and privacy. Striking compromises will be necessary, though difficult. Such a relationship is actually more founded in deep friendship than passionate love. Elevens tend to use their natural authority to drive other people to accept their viewpoint, whereas Fives, who also teem with brilliant and new ideas, are more liberal in letting things be. Elevens might eventually feel left behind and excluded from Fives' scope and range of freedom, which is likely to result in growing tensions.

5 with 22

General aspect: The association is difficult, although mutual respect and understanding are present. Fives' exaggerated optimism regularly challenges Twenty-twos' deep pessimism. Both are attracted to earthly pleasures, but they experience them in different ways. They may share a common social goal and yet, we are in the presence of an idealistic liberal opposing a pragmatic conservative. Twenty-twos mainly want to achieve financial comfort and cannot understand Fives' deep desire for freedom.

Parent 5 and child 22: The parent may find the child is too serious, shy and rigid. The parent tries to respect the child's nature, but he/she cannot help getting upset and angry at this child who acts as if he/she understands all the parent's requirements, yet doesn't take them into account. The child proves to be mature and independent enough to stand on his own feet from an early age. The child does not need long speeches and explanations, but rather down-to-earth instructions. This is mainly why the parent, no matter how willing and understanding he/she may be, will have a hard time trying curbing his/her impatience and anger. The parent will have to learn to accept the child's introverted ways, if he/she wants them to have a harmonious relationship. The child's covert behavior collides with the parent's open-minded spirit. Yet, not everything is lost. In order to bring more harmony, the parent needs to rapidly understand the child's goals and views. They can understand each other and find common ground, particularly when it comes to facing obstacles. However, the child might suffer from a certain form of instability in the home.

Parent 22 and child 5: A serious parent, who gives priority to long-term development, and who will help the child build a solid foundation, to settle down and focus. However, the child will find it difficult to accept parental discipline, for this dramatically goes against his/her need for freedom and, as such, is considered a restrictive measure. This being said, the child will eventually realize that this benefits him/her in the long term and that he/she will even implement the parent's advice! Yet, this particular parent could be more communicative and provide more explanation. Instead, the parent often regards the child as tiring and time consuming, and therefore will have a difficult time putting up with him/her. The parent is skilled at coping with adversity and behaves as head of the clan, who gives strength to his tribe. This is definitely not the type of parent who will indulge in emotional and sentimental effusiveness with the child, nor anyone else for that matter.

Associates 5 and 22: Fives push and pull while Twenty-twos put on the brake. Twenty-twos aim to build things and therefore need stability. This can be a problem for Fives, who are constantly on the move and restlessly trying out new things. They just cannot make themselves understood to their partners, and feel that their wings are being clipped and their enthusiasm curbed. If they manage to find common ground to agree on, they will be able to achieve substantial success, as one will explore the environment while the other manages the running of the business. They are smart enough to understand this, and yet Fives' optimistic, over-reactive and rebellious spirit will definitely challenge Twenty-twos' pessimistic, anti-social conservatism.

Love relationship between 5 and 22: A great passion may be born between these two individuals. It will not necessarily be a long-term relationship though, for it will only last as long as they can stand being opposed, as far as their views on life are concerned. Fives are completely open-minded and will therefore challenge Twenty-twos' natural reserve. Twenty-twos can prove very judgmental towards Fives' constant antics and continual need for relationships. They do not feel it necessary to display their private lives and aspirations to the world, unlike Fives who need an audience. As long as they succeed in uniting against adversity and/or an occasional hostile environment, they will be able to understand and accept each other. If, however, their lives are only made up of daily routine, Fives will end up walking away. It must not be forgotten that Twenty-twos are proud and may not be able to accept that their love life is not perfect.

6 with 6

General aspect: A great deal of dialogue and exchange exists here. They also share a quest for harmony. Conjugal life is favored, as well as family, shared values and responsibilities. There is a common drive to structure, shape and embellish. Yet, they tend to criticize each other a little too much, and may not be able to reach a certain level of intimacy, out of fear of being too intrusive.

Parent 6 and child 6: The child was not asking for this much! Having a parent who supports the child's desire for perfection in doing things well: what more could one ask for? The relationship is positive, in that they both are very sociable individuals, despite the fact that the child is too self-critical with regards to him/herself and their imperfections. The child should not immediately take the parent's observations as criticism or judgment. The parent does his/her best to improve the child's abilities, but he/she may not be aware of the impact criticism has on the child's development. Moreover, the parent must also accept criticism by the child. As a matter of fact, they are both extremely observant and use such as a reason to point out what is wrong. Schooling and education are highlighted.

Associates 6: They bring each other a lot. This association is one of perfection with a shared desire to create the perfect collaboration. They can go very far together, as long as they refrain from criticizing every little detail in their partner and focus instead on their common goal. They help each other systematically and with ease, which enables them to carry out all sorts of projects. Their partnership emphasizes efficiency and accuracy, and might therefore prove a little too rigid. If they want to avoid becoming too uptight in their persistent desire for perfection, they should learn how to take things a little easier, to have more breaks, relax and enjoy life. They should under no circumstances let themselves become overworked to the point they are unable to enjoy their taste for the pleasures of life.

6 in love with another 6: Their relationship is rooted in mutual understanding and respect. Both of them strive for harmony and perfection in their lives. Nevertheless, they must try to overcome their natural shyness, which actually stems from their fear of imperfection, and can give way to criticism. They support each other and bring each other what is necessary for a happy, daily life. Material aspects are favored, as well as education, children and home. Both of them thrive on beauty, pleasure and enjoyment; which is why they would never miss an opportunity to appreciate the pleasures of life together. They need to be careful however of their tendency of always wanting more of the best and most perfect.

6 with 7

General aspect: The association proves awkward, in that they have different ways of regarding problems and details. Sixes fail to understand Sevens' ways of achieving their goals. Sevens might consider Sixes as too down-to-earth. Moreover, Sixes find it difficult to feel cherished and loved by Sevens, whose nature is extremely independent and introverted. Yet, they do share common interests, especially when dealing with their desire to bring harmony into their lives.

Parent 6 and child 7: The parent is structured and a perfectionist and therefore brings a great deal to the child, who needs to be reminded of more realistic points of view. The child actually lives in a fantasy world made up of dreams and imagination, and does not always appreciate the way his/her parent brings him/her back down to earth. Neither does the child appreciate his/her parent's criticisms. As he/she grows up, he/she tends to regard the parents' world as far too petty, precise and systematic. Yet, the child will eventually benefit from the parent's constant support as far as education, schooling and studies are concerned. Although the child is extremely attached to cleanliness, he/she is not, paradoxically enough, tidy. The parent will often point this out to the child.

Parent 7 and child 6: The parent brings a tremendous amount of imagination and fantasy to the child, who might prove a little too shy and serious. The child feels a prisoner to his/her constant thinking and worry about his presumed imperfections. This particular parent is able to sense the child's doubt and fear and will teach her/him how to take things a little more lightly and to shrug off his/her anxieties. The parent supports the child's education, well-being and fulfillment. What's more, the parent is sensitive to beauty and aims for a certain quality of life. S/he will teach the child how to develop his/her own taste. Yet, the parent should not feel bad, if the child criticizes him/her, because the child tends to express easily what s/he notices... and is often very observant!

Associates 6 and 7: Provided Sevens succeed in putting up with Sixes' criticisms and perfectionism, the relationship can prove particularly constructive. Sevens are skilled at aiming for attainable goals, while Sixes are good at planning, organizing and structuring the means to get there, thus shaping the project in the longer term. This can result in perfect efficiency. Sevens appreciate Sixes' ability to organize, while Sixes recognize Sevens' business sense. Yet, if they start criticizing each other, the relationship will immediately turn into confrontation and open conflict.

Love relationship between 6 and 7: The difficulty in maintaining harmony here may lie in the fact that both are extremely critical. Sevens are romantic and sentimental, and therefore need warmth. They might feel frustrated with their partner who is too shy and uptight. If they don't get what they want from Sixes, Sevens will tend to criticize them for this lack. Yet, they will eventually manage to seduce Sixes into creating a romantic atmosphere, so as to break the ice. This does not mean they are unable to live together, just that Sixes might feel annoyed by this overwhelming sentimental impetus. As a matter of fact, Sixes are not insensitive to affectionate intentions, but their desire for perfection takes precedence over romance. This being said, they are very sociable and sentimental souls, only more shy in manner. Sevens can be very offended by the way Sixes look down on everyone, including them. However, when it comes to children's education, there are no problems at all.

6 with 8

General aspect: A very constructive partnership with two extremely different worlds attracted to each other. Eights can rely on their partners' honesty, providing Sixes cope with Eights' secret nature. As a matter of fact, Sixes mustn't know everything about Eights; otherwise they will be shocked by what they discover. Sixes appreciate the material and financial comforts Eights' bring. When facing a problem, their strategies differ: Sixes will emphasize a methodical approach to manage the situation, whereas Eights will force their way through.

Parent 6 and child 8: The parent strives to give the child a strict education, teaching her/him how to organize and structure her/his life; most particularly how to be more rational because the child tends to be naive and too gullible. This being said, the child does not take the parent's advice well: s/he will rebel, get angry and close her/himself up into her/his secret world. Yet, the parent will find a way to approach the child, because s/he has a sharp eye and is able to investigate, identify what is wrong, and eventually connect to the child. This will benefit the child in the long run, even though s/he may not always appreciate it. The parent must refrain from constantly psychoanalyzing the child. The challenge lies in striking a balance, between letting the child express her/his spontaneity and giving her/him a framework to do so.

Parent 8 and child 6: In this particular case, the relationship is much more awkward, inasmuch as the child requires shaping her/his world in a rational and safe way, according to her/his own vision. And such a parent is not able to provide this, in that s/he is too irrational and nonchalant. Yet, the parent will definitely teach the child how to take life as it comes and not as you wish it to be, without being too rigid. The parent will therefore enable the child to let go and be less stressed when facing obstacles. However, the 6 child is everything but spontaneous. They plan, anticipate and calculate... things which the parent never does! Will the parent be able to teach the child how to simply enjoy life without analyzing?

Associates 6 and 8: The association is feasible, as long as Eights can cope with Sixes who keep criticizing and pointing out the very flaws and weaknesses that Eights possess. Eights are willing to use any which way to reach their goals (including the less recommendable means), whereas Sixes are genuinely attached to honesty and easily comply with rules and laws. Sixes hate nothing more than being blamed for something (they blame themselves enough already!), especially for their organization sense which Eights are likely to blame them for if Eights get upset. And yet, the association may work. Eights are outgoing and daring, and need to be structured by Sixes, who know how to manage their shared projects. Eights know how to seize opportunities, and will do so, unlike Sixes who are too shy and therefore often miss out on life and the realization of their goals.

Love relationships between 6 and 8: The difficulties here often stem from Sixes' desire for perfection, order, detail and rules. Sixes' sexuality is not easy-going, unlike Eights' who are always at ease, without any taboos, and will accept any venture, as long as it is an opportunity to enjoy pleasure. This does not mean Sixes are unable to let go, rather that they face a real challenge, in wanting to satisfy their partners' appetites. As a matter of fact, Eights do have an unquenchable thirst for pleasure, as their fields of experimentation are limitless, yet they are able to hide this aspect of themselves in an extremely covert way. Let's hope Sixes can teach them how to abide a little more by the rules. In addition, Sixes need things to be organized and clean, whereas Eights cannot be bothered. Two extremely different worlds meet here.

6 with 9

General aspect: Both of them feel they owe a great deal to society as a whole, yet they are not interested in each other's personal concerns. Of course, they are able to help each other, but the way they do so is very different. Sixes tend to blame Nines for daydreaming and being inconsistent, while Nines tend to be indifferent to Sixes' daily domestic concerns. Yet, they get along very well when doing charity work, because they are both driven by a desire to serve people.

Parent 6 and child 9: The parent has a lot of work with such a child, who is yearning for a quiet and harmonious life without taking any responsibilities for chores or any other obligations. The child can prove untidy and messy, which drives the parent crazy because s/he is attached to order and detail. Let's hope the parent succeeds in teaching the child to comply with rules and discipline, which is definitely not the child's cup of tea. Such a strict education will eventually bear fruit. The child is idealistic and struggles to avoid any form of conflict. S/he will end up calming the parent through his/her innate kindness and caring love.

Parent 9 and child 6: The parent is too soft and therefore accepts whatever the child does, including inappropriate behaviors stemming from the child's search for his/her identity. The parent understands the child's concerns and issues (especially her/his thirst of perfection), and thus responds with loving care. The parent manages to teach the child how to be more understanding and flexible. He/she is also able to soothe the child's fears, so as to make her/him less attached to her/his own image. Both are very interested in human relationships, but their approaches are different. The parent emphasizes her/his sensitivity, while the child affirms her/his persistence. This being said, the child feels a little left to his/her own devices. S/he will forgive the parent for this, which s/he considers as an imperfection and will accept it, as the parent never expresses aggression or objection.

Associates 6 and 9: As long as they dedicate themselves to humanitarian activities, social relationships and education at large, they can bring each other a lot. Sixes are born organizers and easily make up for Nines' lack of regularity and efficiency. However, Nines are idealistic visionaries and can therefore learn a lot from their partner, in terms of method and rigor. In turn, Sixes become more humane, through their understanding and flexible partner. Nevertheless, things are not easy. Nines tend to retreat from any sort of criticism and control, and might therefore be tempted to run away from Sixes and their cumbersome regulations. Sixes are likely to be exasperated with Nines' hypersensitivity, their tendency to always being late, disorganized and, let's face it, with Nines also being a mess.

Love relationship between 6 and 9: Sixes have nothing to fear from Nines who are entirely devoted to them and strive to please them at any cost. Yet, some issues may arise in their exchanges and discussions, for they do not operate in the same way. Nines hate nothing more than expressing their desires, leaving Sixes to guess what they are. On the other hand, Sixes keep pointing out what does not satisfy them with regard to their partner's behavior. They must therefore strike a balance between these two extremes. Although Sixes fail to recognize Nines' deep nature and therefore tend to consider them as unreliable, love is bound to win.

6 with 11

General aspect: The association will only be constructive providing one accepts being dominated by the other, i.e. in a hierarchical context. Sixes can bring a lot to Elevens, for instance: rigor, discipline, structure, project implementation ... And Elevens bring a lot to Sixes as well, for example in helping them open up to new possibilities. But watch out: As soon as Sixes start being critical or rigid, Elevens are liable to get very upset and angry.

Parent 6 and child 11: Here we have the ideal parent to discipline and structure the child, as well as teach her/him patience. This is not an easy task, for the child finds it difficult to accept any kind of limitation and can't stand being restricted in what s/he regards as her/his personal space. But the parent must not give up, because the child definitely needs to be taught how to think before acting. The child might not easily accept this, but s/he is likely to be grateful for such, as time goes by. Learning method and efficiency can be very useful. The relationship features a great deal of dialogue and exchanges.

Parent 11 and child 6: The parent is active, dynamic, enthusiastic, and yet the child does not regard these features as necessarily positive. The child needs most of all to be reassured and hates nothing more than being tossed around, without his/her bearings and knowing which foot to stand on. The parent tends to change her/his mind, desires and direction often, which makes the child feel nervous and unsafe. The child would like to have life explained slowly, little by little. But the parent is always in a hurry, and cannot be relied on for this. Much dialogue will take place between them, but the child cannot help feeling that the parent is superficial and artificial.

Associates 6 and 11: Guess who is getting ready to conquer the world, while the other one is busy with the packing...? Elevens are full of energy and need to discover and explore, but they're not very patient. This is why Sixes have a lot to do, if they want to teach their partner how to use caution and apply method. This is liable to trigger off many arguments, particularly in the case of Elevens, who have big egos and get very upset when criticized by Sixes. However, if they can get past their quarreling, they can bring each other a lot and achieve their common goals. Sixes know how to plan and organize their lives, and this could definitely benefit Elevens, even if they consider such a waste of time and energy...

Love relationship between 6 and 11: A tumultuous and chaotic relationship. They will need to make a great deal of effort if they want to get along. Sixes tend to plan and organize their lives according to their goals, unlike Elevens who just can't be bothered. However, they do share the quality of being humane for which Elevens appreciate and admire Sixes. Their relationship is based more on strong friendship, than wild passion. Both search for common ground to build their relationship. They will quickly learn how to respect each other's privacy and freedom, without being intrusive.

6 with 22

General aspect: The relationship is complementary with regards to serving their common goals. Both aim to create long term projects on solid foundations. Harmony and understanding is based on intelligence. They are methodic and efficient. Yet, they might lack imagination, fantasy and the spirit of adventure. Ideal though for setting up all kinds of shelters (for children, animals etc....)

Parent 6 and child 22: The child needs to grow up in a structured, safe, efficient and stable environment, where there is little room for doubt and uncertainty. Here the child has found the ideal parent, in that the parent is skilled at helping and supporting her/him to reach objectives. In turn, the parent has found the ideal child to educate and teach who is particularly sensitive to what the parent says and will consider the advice willingly. For example, the child is not particularly tidy, but will comply with the parent's discipline. And the parent loves being listened to and appreciates that the child follows the methods s/he suggested. However, expressing one's feelings in a demonstrative way is not on the agenda for either of them. A little more spontaneous fun would do them good.

Parent 22 and child 6: The parent can bring stability, comfort, peace and quiet in a safe environment...but the child needs to be advised and the parent is unable to explain things well enough. The parent is a pragmatic protector, and knows how to listen to the child, but is unable go into lengthy explanations to how the world works and why. Yet, the parent will eventually enable the child to relax more and take it easy. The child will definitely benefit from the parent's quiet way.

Associates 6 and 22: They have found themselves! Sixes' ability to organize things sets the perfect framework with Twenty-two's legendary stability. They bring each other a lot. Twenty-twos don't get offended when Sixes start criticizing them and they can even let Sixes carry out their common goals as far as implementation and method are concerned. In turn, Sixes completely trust Twenty-twos, who are truly reliable. Over time, they are likely to set up many projects together. They feel very close to one another, as they are able to bring to each other what the other is lacking. However, the relationship could do with a little more fantasy and fun.

Love relationship between 6 and 22: Stability and trust may very well compensate for the enthusiasm and passion they lack. They are very skilled at creating a nice and comfortable environment, so as to live peacefully and in harmony (in some cases away from society). They are not interested in maintaining boisterous friendships and would rather create a family and devote their lives to their children. Although their feelings do exist, it simply that they do not make a great show of demonstrating their love to the outside world. They share an affinity with the animal world.

7 with 7

General aspect: In order to get along well they must find a common ideal and goal in life. They need to feel devoted to a mission. They need to respect each other's independence and not tell each other tales. They share an interest in knowledge, teaching and travel, but find it difficult to express their deep selves. Both of them need to admire their partners in a way that allows them to acknowledge their own self through the other. In such a relationship, the fascination they feel for one another might either be beneficial, or lead to the non-recognition of their deep personalities. It's either all - or nothing.

Parent 7 and child 7: The relationship is harmonious, although it might result in a type of competition which stems from their unquenchable curiosity. The parent, as all 7 parents, emphasizes success through education and study, which suits the child perfectly. As a matter of fact, the child's desire to learn and develop her/his knowledge is strongly benefitted. Nevertheless, issues may arise, the moment the child's desires differ from what the parent has in mind for her/his offspring. While they both love to exchange their points of view regarding their interests, they might not always know how to go about presenting and explaining them. Due to fear of being judged, the child finds it particularly difficult to express her/his inner world.

Associates 7: The association is excellent, especially with regards to investments, investigations, education and any kind of projects based on faith and ideals. Both of them are able to maintain their respective interests and know how to keep in mind their objectives in every situation. They get along well, except maybe in instances of tense situations, in which their quarrelsome spirit may take over. This being said, they are both smart enough to take a step back, in order to preserve their interests. Putting two "gurus" together is not necessarily easy! They are both extremely curious and constantly search for new horizons, new perspectives and take advantage of every possibility for such.

7 in love with another 7: They are both romantic and very much in love. They will certainly give each other much support and help, while anticipating a bright and happy future. Their lives as a couple are as organized and comfortable as the house they live in. They want many children and endeavor to ensure their offspring's success. This all sounds wonderful, but problems may arise when financial issues come up. Their partnership encourages both to express their viewpoints and to live their deepest aspirations. They share a love of theater, teaching, travel and any gathering with those who share their ideas or faith.

7 with 8

General aspect: The relationship is a harmonious one, providing both are able to share their taste for mystery and secrets. They are brought together by a desire to enjoy life's pleasures (money, property, well-being, sexuality...). Eights are able to support Sevens' aspirations, while Sevens bring Eights dynamic energy, safety and the ability to visualize the future. In other words, Sevens aspire to live through their faith and hopes, whereas Eights are more attracted to immediate profit.

Parent 7 and child 8: The parent will need to use all of their understanding, depth of mind and intuition to enter the child's secret universe and guide her/him in life. The parent has wonderful qualities, but will require a great deal of patience in coming to terms with the child's subtle and mysterious dynamics. Although the child is a little naive and gullible, and therefore accepts easily the parent's advice and support, s/he cannot bear any intrusion on her/his privacy. This is why the parent must refrain from poking into their child's need for privacy. Nevertheless, they are able to understand each other, because they both thrive on mystery and deep, secretive things. However their way of functioning is completely different. The parent doesn't really fathom how the child operates and his/her way of not being affected or moved by anything. While one is very respectful of laws and regulations, the other couldn't care less.

Parent 8 and child 7: The relationship is a little difficult, in that the child requires more structure and must be taught how to be less gullible. The child struggles to understand the rules and the way things work around her/him. Yet the parent is unable to explain such, to the point where, over time, the parent may ask the child for advice on how to regulate her/his own life. This may result in an upside down type of relationship. The parent acts through instinct and alternative ways, and is therefore not very interested in accumulating experience or education. This does not suit the child, who hopes to be reassured with safe and settled views. The parent is pragmatic, attached to immediate pleasures and as such is able to face life's difficulties and changes with a certain peace of mind. This is why s/he will eventually be able to help the child understand that s/he should not live on hypothetical visions and beliefs. The parent motto is: "live your life, seize the moment and you will see what happens after".

Associates 7 and 8: Although they are very different in the way they go about life, they are both very attracted to financial and material gain. Sevens are canny visionaries who are able to weigh the pros and cons with care, even in situations of dire straits. Eights are opportunists who search by whatever means to take advantage of what falls into their hands, refusing to take into account the possible consequences. This being said, they can be extremely lucky. They also bring each other a great deal of profit in several fields, provided Eights manage to overcome their immoral ways which respectful law-abiding Sevens just cannot accept. This being said, the too confident and naïve Eights can easily swindle their partners. In turn, if things go too far, Sevens may become less ethical and give Eights a hard time.

Love relationship between 7 and 8: Romantic and sentimental Sevens have a hard time with Eights who cannot be bothered with fuss and convention, preferring to go straight to the point. If Sevens expect their partner to recite poems or play the guitar under their windows, they can wait a long time... But this doesn't mean that they don't have a love life, on the contrary. Sevens like adventure too and for that matter, their partner is ideal as far as discovering illicit experiences are concerned. They are both attracted to money and aim to lead comfortable lives, so as to be able to escape society's pressures. Sevens tend to worry a lot about petty things, unlike Eights who trust more in life and are therefore able to face adversity with a certain peace of mind. They share a love of stories, imagination, and fictitious worlds; and should therefore refrain from getting too involved and carried away as this would distance them too much from society.

7 with 9

General aspect: This association is either religious or pure business. They share a quest for peace, harmony and shared faith. Everyday life is regarded as spiritual. Material comfort and diplomacy are also present. Yet, they should not indulge in laziness, or an artificial paradise. There is a need to self-impose rigor and discipline in their life.

Parent 7 and child 9: The parent must be attentive to the child, who is not grounded in the daily world. They can understand each other, for they both are visionaries and tend to live in a dimension which is beyond so called apparent reality. This being said, the parent tries to shape and structure the child, who is a bit lazy. Fortunately, the child appreciates the parent's efforts to help her/him succeed, although s/he does not appreciate being pushed around or forced. The child enjoys peace and quiet and cannot understand why the parent disturbs her/his dream world and meditations with such demands. However, the parent is sensitive to the child's sweetness, even if s/he doesn't necessarily understand her/his inner mechanisms. The parent will eventually respect the child's need for privacy.

Parent 9 and child 7: The child is blessed to have such a sweet, flexible and attentive parent. However, the child needs to express her/his deep nature and will not always feel understood by the parent who is unable to express her/his own inner self. The parent will only be able to connect with the child's inner universe through intuition and empathy, without the child needing to explicitly ask for it. This will not necessarily help the child express her/himself, in that s/he will be tempted to think that everybody will react like her/his parent does. The child makes up stories and lives in fantasy worlds: so requires to be given a framework in order to give shape to his thoughts. And the parent finds it difficult to pass on educational imperatives. This being said, the child will always cherish the parent's sweet understanding.

Associates 7 and 9: They get along well, with regards to education, insurance, business and religion. Sevens will want to know why their partner acts like s/he does, but this will never happen, which is likely to result in frustration and dissatisfaction. Sevens also want to know who they are dealing with, and unfortunately, Nines are difficult to decipher. This being said, although they may be a little lazy, Nines are helpful and devoted. They are also playful, and will often be amused by their partner's self-imposed responsibilities. They can bring a lot to each other, with regards to setting up safe projects and protecting themselves from the hardships of life. Relationships abroad and travels are also favored, as well as being near water.

Love relationship between 7 and 9: Romance, sweetness and feelings are present in this relationship that is rooted in tenderness and a shared desire to enjoy life's pleasures. Nevertheless, Sevens would love to know their partner's inner and metaphysical world better, and Nines will not allow such. Sevens need to be reassured, loved and cared for. They will have to learn to be conscious of their partner's daily affectionate gestures, instead of expecting soothing words. If not and they force Nines into talking, Nines will be tempted to run away, for they hate nothing more than being told what to do. As it stands, Sevens in love tend to offer a lot of presents to their loved ones, and Nines will definitely enjoy this.

7 with 11

General aspect: They look as if they share the same objectives but they actually differ widely in their idealistic views and in the way they express and attain them. Both of them are willing to go beyond pre-established ideas. They have a real capacity to develop all sorts of projects. Sevens can support Elevens' initiatives and Elevens can help Sevens to implement their aspirations. Yet, the relationship is not necessarily smooth.

Parent 7 and child 11: Although the parent is patient, s/he will have a hard time with such a boisterous child who wants to constantly explore the world and have non-stop adventures. The parent keeps calling for caution and is seldom listened to, although in the long run, prudence will be taken into account. The child's thirst for knowledge will eventually be satisfied, although s/he finds the parent's teaching too dogmatic and cumbersome. The child needs to be structured and the parent serves this purpose. However, arguments must be expected, as well as challenges and rebellious questioning. The parent needs to be more moderate and avoid getting upset by the child's unruly behavior. As time goes by, the child will appreciate the parent's principles, even if s/he disagrees with their method.

Parent 11 and child 7: The child is liable to feel upset and overwhelmed by this parent who is at times far too impulsive, angry and intolerant. The child needs to structure and analyze the world around her/him, which the parent doesn't understand. Yet, the parent helps the child, in relentlessly driving her/him to express her/himself, thus forcing her/him out of her/his introverted shell, so as to be more spontaneous when wanting something. Luckily, the child's natural charm will calm the parent, even if the child's sweetness is not always without a reason. In the long run, despite the resentments, the child will eventually benefit a lot from this dynamic and decisive parent.

Associates 7 and 11: Putting together a fine calculator who is convinced in knowing right from wrong in order to reach goals with a wild, reactive pioneer who cannot be disciplined is a true challenge! If the one keeps scouting, researching and exploring, while the other takes care of the stability of the business, everything will go just fine. However, it is imperative that they trust each other and keep to their respective domains and skills, otherwise open conflicts are bound to happen. Sevens need to protect themselves and will take advantage of any weakness they might spot in their partners. Their feelings are easily hurt. Sevens attempt to improve her/his safety, finances and knowledge, whereas Elevens cannot stand losing face. Elevens need to calm down and listen to their partner's wise advice. Moreover, Sevens should try to be more daring. In short, the relationship is far from being smooth.

Love relationship between 7 and 11: Romantic Sevens need to admire the person they are in love with. They need to be able to share their partner's future hopes, while giving life to their own. This is why here they have found the ideal partner whom they will be able to support, help and give advice. They not only share love, but also a mutual passion for their common goals. Sevens know how to turn their savings into gold, and will therefore ensure their lives are comfortable. Elevens must admit that Sevens are truly reliable and trustworthy, and need to show how grateful they are to Sevens, who need acknowledgment. Although Elevens' natural authority isn't challenged, idealistic Sevens might be tempted to leave if their partner becomes too self-centered.

7 with 22

General aspect: The association is constructive in the long term. They make an effort not to oppose each other. They both search for peace and quiet and would rather live in a natural unaffected environment. Twenty-twos consistently protect Sevens, who in turn, give Twenty-twos substantial support and unconditional love. Family life and children's education are highlighted. However, because they are great searchers of truth, Sevens can prove a little intrusive at times and must therefore be careful not to get in the way of Twenty-twos' need for material comforts.

Parent 7 and child 22: The child seems to be cold and distant but is in fact very shy, which is why s/he will appreciate the parent's warmth, attention and support for success. The child has nothing to fear from the parent who truly appreciates the child's solid reserve. Even if the parent is a visionary loner who tends to live in her/his own world, while attempting to push the child to do likewise, s/he does not necessarily understand why the child enjoys solitude so much. The parent is driven by faith and would love to share it with the child who is too pragmatic to be sensitive to such. Actually, the child does not wish to be taken away from his down-to-earth views into what s/he regards as pure invention. Indeed, the parent genuinely appreciates and admires the child's calm steady ways and the ability to face adversity with cool determination. The parent will nevertheless eventually succeed in teaching the child to open up and be more casual and communicative.

Parent 22 and child 7: While the child deeply appreciates the parent, who is reliable, safe and able to face adversity with determination, she/he would also like the parent to be a little more expressive, lighter and happier. The parent is a serious person and emphasizes long term creations, having no interest in trivial games and gossip. This is why the parent finds it difficult to enter the child's theatrical realm and answer constant questioning. Investing the energy needed to step into the child's imagination would be like turning a black and white film into a color one. Nonetheless, the parent will provide solid support to the child and meet her/his basic needs. Despite their many differences, as time goes by, the child will come to admire her/his trustworthy parent.

Associates 7 and 22: They share many similarities. Twenty-twos are stable and reliable, and can therefore ensure their partner evolves in a peaceful environment. In turn, Sevens can make valuable contributions to the efficiency of their business. Having nothing to fear, they can act freely, relying on their partner's capacity to organize projects. Moreover, Sevens give wise advice and Twenty-twos will be inspired to listen. This will prevent her/him from wasting energy while fighting against adversity alone. Twenty-twos try to make it on their own, even in rough terrain. They are fierce warriors and know it. Therefore they will not let anyone fight on their behalf, although their exaggerated ego might be their downfall.

Love relationship between 7 and 22: Sevens enjoy aesthetics, life's pleasures and sweetness, while Twenty-twos prefer austerity. Yet, love can grow, for Sevens have nothing to fear from stable and safe Twenty-twos. As a matter of fact, Sevens truly regard their partner as ideal, for they greatly appreciate being with a reliable person they can completely trust. Moreover, Sevens' significant warmth partly makes up for Twenty-twos' aloofness. This being said, Twenty-twos should not force Sevens to live in a cold and dull environment or they might well run away, no matter how honest and reliable they are. Together, they search for a natural unaffected life, away from constraints, although they might get involved in charity work and humanitarian projects. A large family, children and animals are definitely on the agenda.

8 with 8

General aspect: With such an association it is all – or nothing. Respect and mistrust are present, as both them are perfectly aware of the strengths and weaknesses of each other. Their union is based on the pleasures of life and material interests. Destruction or sublimation. Capital success or critical failure. Being flexible is required, as their covert quest for power may turn out to be fatal. Who is best suited to correct the other's antics?

Parent 8 and child 8: Communication and dialogue are definitely not their cups of tea! They strive to keep their inner world secret and jealously prevent anyone from entering, except for the very few people they trust. The parent is not particularly perturbed by the hardships of life and will therefore be able to teach the child from an early age how to deal with obstacles. And the child will have no problems understanding, because this is exactly how s/he operates anyway. Both of them are authoritative and quick-tempered, which is precisely what they need to work on, so as to learn to be calmer and gentler. Because they are so deeply conscious of their immoral ways, they neither fear excess or abuse. As a matter of fact, they consider their extreme reactions as normal and nothing to worry about. They actually have a problem with being too naive and gullible. How can a naive parent teach a child to be more rational? They both thrive on the magical and extraordinary, and constantly seek the mysteries of the unknown. As Eights are the number that refers to good luck and opportunities, the parent will easily be able to teach the child how to benefit from life, without worrying too much.

Associates 8: Both of them thrive on similar ambitions, all to do with money, power and pleasure in material goods. They can bring each other a great deal, because they certainly know how to make their investments profitable. This being said, they possess an extremely powerful and potentially destructive power, which is liable to end up ruining their common interests. Yet, they will understand each other perfectly well and business will run smoothly, as long as they stay concentrated on their goals. As soon as they begin to mistrust each other and compete for power, there will be no turning back, for both know how deep their own instinctive distrust can become. Will they be able to overcome this lack of trust? They are constantly defending their interests, fearing that someone might do them wrong. They need to eradicate these feelings of paranoia, all the more so as they are aware of being too gullible and naive. Moreover, they should refrain from mixing sex and business.

8 in love with another 8: What an agenda! Not only are they strongly attracted to one another, they constantly explore their delight of being in love, by pushing the limits even further. They can get along very well, as they both enjoy life's pleasures and understand each other's need for escapades. They are mischievous and naughty, and don't mind sharing their partner with another. Nighttime is their favorite moment. They thrive on wealth. In addition, they fiercely face adversity and possess great resources of energy with which to reach their goals. Yet, they do preserve their secret inner world, to which no one is allowed access, particularly those who are close and who would be very surprised by what they would discover...

8 with 9

General aspect: They share a common taste for earthly pleasures and material goods. They get along very well. Their understanding may reach the point of becoming mystical. Nines are able to soothe and inspire Eights, by opening them up to a more spiritual way. Eights, through their achievement and success, are able to provide protection to Nines.

Parent 8 and child 9: Such a parent will certainly not diminish the child's imagination. As a matter of fact, because the parent's tolerance is imbued with a deep thirst for mystery and secret phenomena, s/he will easily accept that the child may need to live in other spiritual worlds. However, the parent is pragmatic, whereas the child is a dreamer. This is why the parent will be able to teach the child how to face adversity, handle obstacles and follow her/his own way towards success, at all costs. This will definitely help the child not give in to her/his natural trend of escaping into other worlds. The parent will also teach the child how not to run away from reality, when life becomes difficult. The parent may have to rant and rave, in order to bring the child back down on earth. Yet despite the occasional disagreement, they both love to live in peace, which for the most part is how they will live together.

Parent 9 and child 8: Such a parent is well able to understand the child's mysterious worlds, thanks to her/his natural empathy. Over time, her/his admirable patience and capacity to deal with life's blows will enable her/him to soothe the child's often frequent fits of anger and accept their need for withdrawal. With their finely tuned perceptivity, the parent is able to see and understand why the child behaves in such ways. In turn, the child will learn to deeply trust their parent who has no intention of harming her/him. As time goes by, the child's reactions will be less intense. While the child may think their parent is not aware enough of material needs and issues, s/he will be highly grateful that the parent was always supportive. As parents, Nines are better counselors than sergeants.

Associates 8 and 9: Here we have a high potential for success, thanks to Eights' natural abilities and Nines' flexible nature. Nines are easygoing and diplomatic enough to be able to handle her/his partner's aggressiveness. As a matter of fact, Eights can prove somewhat brutal and when they explode, they do so without taking into account the impact of their behavior. When this happens Nines are able to wait until their partner calms down. But should this occur too frequently, Nines are also able to simply walk away, leaving Eights speechless. Eights can be extremely annoyed with Nines' hesitation, lack of interest and seemingly impassive reactions. Eights need to deal with down-to-earth dynamics, not fleeting perspectives. They also need to feel their efforts will not prove useless, and Nines' transient ways fail to calm and reassure them. Eight are so attached to material goods that they can become easily mistrustful and suspicious.

Love relationship between 8 and 9: Eights can be a little aggressive sometimes and this does not go well with Nines, who search for calm and tranquility. This does not necessarily mean they are unable to love each other, but unless Eights succeed in being more romantic and sentimental, they will not be able meet Nines' needs. Nines are not insensitive to sex, but they need to be approached in a certain way. Unless Eights work on their foreplay approach, they are likely to find Nine's door closed. Nines need to dream and fantasize about love, unlike Eights who prefer to get straight to the point. However, they can find common ground, providing both are willing to put in a lot of effort. They enjoy living peacefully, away from the hardships of life. This being said, Nines are flexible and understanding enough to accept some infidelity from their partners, particularly if this allows them to maintain peace and quiet. Nines never contradict anyone, and will definitely not start doing so with Eights.

8 with 11

General aspect: The association is productive but gives rise to possible conflict. Here we have two strong personalities. Elevens' independent spirit is not suitable with Eights' need for control and authority. Yet, they can get along, providing both subdue their egos. Eights are able to bring into being Elevens' projects, as long as they play fair. The relationship can be passionate but fleeting.

Parent 8 and child 11: The parent is pragmatic and efficient, and will have a lot of work with this child s/he finds too idealistic and not focused enough on carrying out projects to the end. Parents Eight are very understanding, but cannot fathom why their child keeps talking about ideas without considering the significant consequences. Actually, two different worlds oppose. The child is set on going beyond the limits and exploring new horizons, whereas the parent requires down-to-earth results, even while being aware that true reality is much more than what one sees. Yet, the parent is not satisfied with pure ideals, s/he needs facts and will therefore teach the child how to give shape and structure to their projects. However, because neither of them is very diplomatic, fits of anger and frustration can be expected. Despite all odds, they do admire and give each other recognition because in this relationship both are direct and play fair.

Parent 11 and child 8: The parent is likely to manhandle this child, whose vast and secret universe s/he is unable to grasp. And this will deeply upset the child. Such a parent is too boisterous and tends to push everyone around. S/he is faced here with a child who remains impassive, and whose inertia s/he is unable to understand. The child certainly needs structure, but refuses to be coerced and controlled. The parent will succeed in opening the child up to outside relationships and therefore inspire her/him with a zest for life, thereby preventing her/him from withdrawing from the world. Yet, the parent needs to learn that the child requires going into his inner quiet world, as this is part of her/his deep nature. If the parent wants the relationship to last, s/he will have to be more gentle, flexible and patient. If not, Elevens' legendary brusqueness is liable to fuel the child's rebellion and make her/him run away.

Associates 8 and 11: Everything is fine, as long as Elevens go conquer the world and their path to success, while leaving Eights to manage the financial and material aspects at large. But as soon as one steps on the other's toes, argues over their next direction to take, or tries to impose their own authority, conflict will arise. Their common goals need to be shaped and structured, so as to generate material success. Under no circumstances should their objectives remain as ideas, which Eights cannot accept. In turn, idealistic Elevens are strongly driven by their urge to move away from constraints, and are not as attached to material gain. If Elevens aren't allowed their ideals, they will be tempted to walk away and look for other prospects. Arguments are to be expected. Both will have to show a great deal of compromise, in order to carry out their common goals. This being said, suspicious Eights cannot accuse Elevens for not being honest, true and loyal. Unlike Elevens, Eights are calculating.

Love relationship between 8 and 11: A tumultuous relationship with ups and downs. Elevens' exhilarating and adventurous side are certainly capable of seducing Eights, but it won't be lasting. Eights need to live passionately and completely with all their senses, whereas Elevens fail to understand their partners' desires and needs. Elevens do not have the same appetites as Eights. Elevens need to dream and immerse themselves in spiritual realms, unlike Eights who need facts and figures. Under such circumstances, a loving relationship will certainly not be easy, and may give rise to a great deal of misunderstanding. This being said, if what they want to live a boxing-ring type relationship with sexual feats, they have found the perfect partner to do so.

8 with 22

General aspect: This is the ideal association to create, carry out and achieve. They share a common taste for the material world and the pleasures of life. One condition must be met, though: Eights must be completely honest and flexible with Twenty-twos, who are often shy and tense. Together they are able to create an enjoyable and stable family life. Even though conflicts of egos may arise, the association is a very powerful one.

Parent 8 and child 22: The parent's nature is not very open, smiling and spontaneous as s/he doesn't easily express their deep feelings. The child is also indirect, not very smiling and open. S/he keeps to her/himself. Although they are able to share and understand each other without always needing to talk, they leave little room for joy and enthusiasm. They are not especially morose, for they do enjoy life; it is just that they just don't see why they should express themselves so effusively. The parent is pragmatic and willing to protect the child and support her/him in any of her/his desires, which are peace, calm and quiet. The parent has faith in the child's abilities and skills and will therefore never attempt to push or force her/him away from her/his secret world. The parent will be patient with the child's slow and timid ways; and will know how to make compromises.

Parent 22 and child 8: The parent is extremely protective and will do everything to provide the child with safety, peace and quiet. The child needs such an environment, in order to live her/his deep inner world. The parent has natural parental authority and is attached to principles, order and respect. S/he is certainly able to teach their mischievous child some rules, because s/he remains steadfast and unmoved by the child's disruptive angry behavior. The parent has long-term objectives and will eventually succeed in bringing the child back on the right path. It will not be easy, for the parent might not be very assertive and self-confident, which could prevent the parent from seeing the child as s/he truly is. Yet, the child will end up learning to be more honest and direct over time.

Associates 8 and 22: Can honesty and mischief get along? Twenty-twos act as honest knights, relentlessly trying to prove how true they are. They are intent on building their goals over time, making sure they do nothing they can be blamed for. They are serious, trustworthy and will never attempt to wrong anyone nor take advantage of anything they shouldn't. However, Eights are less scrupulous. While they are not gangsters, they don't pay too much attention to the means they use to what they want. Under such circumstances, one may wonder how this association can work. And yet it does, as both of them are attracted to the material world. In this respect, they can bring a lot to each other. Eights completely trust their associate, and admire their capacity to face adversity with persistence, as they themselves are strong when faced with opposition. Provided Twenty-twos accept their partner's flaws, they can prove very efficient together. Eights need instant gratification of their goals, whereas twenty-twos are famous for their patience. This is why they should tune their pace.

Love relationship between 8 and 22: Both of them are grounded in what is material and concrete. They love enjoying life and are always willing to try out new pleasures. While Eights can be expeditious and lack romanticism, this seems to suit their partner. They will therefore get along extremely well as far as their sex life is concerned, in addition to the management of their common possessions and interests. They can have many children. They may also share secrets. Twenty-twos will protect and build, thus helping reassure and calm their partner, even if Eights decide to explore other horizons. Twenty-twos are liable to behave pragmatically, by protecting their loved ones and focusing on family life. A life close to nature is advised.

9 with 9

General aspect: They get along very well, seeking harmony, peace and comfort. They give priority to leisure and well-being. They love traveling. They are always available for helping others. Their intuition enables them to understand each other without needing to communicate verbally. They share common dreams. However, their attraction to spirituality may lead them to disconnect from reality.

Parent 9 and child 9: There is no conflict here, as they both enjoy tranquility and harmony. They have a peaceful relationship. They are a little shy however, even sometimes lazy but will never attempt to overshadow one another. As a result, parents Nines are unwilling to force their child to be tidy, efficient and accurate. However, the parent is aware of her/his own issues with order and organization, and will try to prevent the child from behaving likewise. The parent will wisely advise the child and watch over her/his education. They are tender and affectionate with each other. However, because the parent is too liberal and therefore unable to teach how to deal with the hardships of life, the child is likely to lack energy when faced with adversity.

Associates 9: As long as they work for social causes, teaching, volunteering for charities, arts or local business, everything will go fine. But they lack persistence and energy to fight when needed. They only do what they want, cannot bear being told what to do and hate any type of restraint that hinders their projects. Their main objective is to create a peaceful aura around them at all times. They understand each other completely. They are very intuitive and can bring a lot to one another, provided they do not attempt to avoid real life's problems. By refusing to look at difficulties and details, procrastinating the solving of problems when they come up, they might be faced with unsettled troubles. They are trying to escape reality by not facing it and pretending there is nothing to worry about. Is this the right solution? A connection with foreign business is likely.

9 in love with another 9: Tenderness, sentimental feelings and gentleness are present. Why ask for more? Both of them are determined to live a peaceful life of harmony and aim to satisfy each other's needs. Nevertheless, their innate shyness and passivity may lead to a certain lack of communication. They are too focused on not creating any trouble whatsoever. They are attentive to the world's suffering around them and might set up shelters for destitute humans or animals. In doing so, they should be very careful to not let themselves become overwhelmed by their hypersensitivity. They love beautiful things, the arts and music in general and will therefore want to create a nice and cozy environment for themselves. They enjoy telling stories and discussing world issues. They are fond of travel, preferably near water.

9 with 11

General aspect: This association does not operate smoothly. It requires a great deal of mutual understanding, for each of them live in different spheres. Yet, they are brought together by their common interest in humanitarian and progressive ideas. Nines are able to subdue and pacify Elevens' restless bustle, while Elevens are able to boost and fuel Nines' energy.

Parent 9 and child 11: This parent has a lot of work with such a boisterous child, who just won't leave her/him alone. The parent finds the child much too nervous and therefore refrains from addressing controversial issues, as s/he expends much effort on avoiding life's possible traps. Adversely, the child finds the parent much too cautious and intends to experience precisely that which is forbidden, without taking any advice into consideration. Under such circumstances, will the parent manage to make the child aware that s/he is not invincible, without smothering her/his spontaneity? This is the question[4].

----

[4] If 20 is found among the other sub-numbers of this Eleven, the child will be more attentive.

Parent 11 and child 9: The parent keeps pushing the child, as s/he finds her/him too impassive and inert. However, all of this bustle is in vain, as the child has her/his own dreams and cannot be disturbed by the parent's hectic behavior. This is why the parent must learn to be more patient and quit resorting to anger which never works. The child will be much more attentive to what is explained calmly and gently. S/he cannot handle violence or aggression, which drives her/him to withdraw into her/himself. The parent will eventually learn to be diplomatic and come to accept the idleness s/he takes for inertia. Yet, the parent should not give up trying to boost the child to accept challenges and take initiative[5].

Associates 9 and 11: Nines' legendary diplomacy will be needed here, to subdue and curb Elevens' restless quest for new adventures. Although they have the necessary skills to soothe difficult relationships, this will be difficult for Nines. Nines are cautious, whereas Elevens are not. This is why both must take a step forward to meeting each other halfway, so as to be able to come together. Nines are extremely sensitive. They are visionaries, at times intangible, whereas Elevens are efficient, active and fast. As a result, they do not move at the same pace. However, they can pursue similar goals and get along, despite the fact that Elevens have a difficult time getting a hold on their partner's fleeting world. If they succeed in doing this (this will be made easier in the case of 20 being part of the theme), they will discover a brand new world and will able to take advantage of it for their common goals. One thing is certain: Elevens who struggle with Nines, blaming them for all sorts of things, will eventually understand that Nines are harmless. In turn, Nines must learn to express themselves and explain why they act in certain ways, otherwise there will be misunderstandings. In addition, Nines should not always try to escape from what they don't like, as they usually do.

---

[5] This will be all the more emphasized if 20 is found among the sub-numbers of the theme.

Love relationship between 9 and 11: Paradoxically enough, these two beings can get along perfectly well, even though they operate in different ways. As restless as Elevens may appear, they are daring enough to be able to crack through Nines legendary innate shyness. As a matter of fact, Nines will find it very amusing, to be pursued by this kind of lover. They will love feeling wanted and desired. Elevens, who are always looking for challenges and conquests, have found here a worthy chase. This being said, they will need to learn telepathy, if they want to understand their partner's desires. Unlike Nines, who can easily perceive their partner's needs, through their empathetic sensitivity to the world around them. Elevens are adventurers, whereas Nines are dreamers. Let's hope that Elevens will be able to carry out and shape the projects and visions that Nines may have. One thing is certain; Nines' pacifying temperament will never be too much for Elevens.

9 with 22

General aspect: Their association is constructive and positive, thanks to their genuine complementary nature. Twenty-twos want a life built on sound and solid foundations, which suits Nines, perfectly well, as they look for calm and safety. Nines uphold faith in life. Therefore their sweet trust in the universe will calm and reassure Twenty-twos in their undertakings. They share many ideals which may come to fruition, thanks to their mutual respect.

Parent 9 and child 22: This parent is over-protective and tries to prevent the child from encountering danger. S/he will be surprised to realize how well the child can actually handle life's problems on her/his own. The latter is determined and knows, deep down, that s/he will reach her/his goals one day. As a consequence, the child tries to put across that what s/he needs is support and not warnings, but the parent will not listen. The parent is highly sensitive, and will be startled by such a child, who behaves as if s/he doesn't feel anything at all. Both of them appreciate a calm and peaceful life, but for different reasons. The parent struggles to protect her/himself from everything, whereas the child persistently pursues her/his ambitions, without taking emotions into account. Nevertheless, their relationship is a smooth one. Luckily, they are able to understand each other without needing much explanation, as neither is skilled at endless speeches.

Parent 22 and child 9: The parent's legendary strength of character and caustic attitude are liable to hurt the child's somewhat excessive sensitivity. The parent never shows much endearment, even though this is exactly what the child wants. As a matter of fact, the child finds the parent abrupt, even though the parent helps and supports her/him in difficult situations. It is obvious that with such a parent, the child will learn how to toughen up from an early age, although this may trigger frustration and a lack of communication. As a result, the child might compensate her/his need for affection with other family members or pets. The parent just cannot understand nor accept what s/he regards as whining and complaining. Despite this, the parent would never close the door on their child and is always willing to support her/him whatever the circumstances may be.

Associates 9 and 22: They can get very well along, particularly when it comes to business, dealings in real estate, material goods and luxury items. Twenty-twos need to carry their projects through to the final stage, and hate nothing more than feeling they are building on slippery sand. Nines love nothing more than to feel safe, so as to avoid hardship. As long as they find a common goal which will benefit them both, the association will be very positive. Should this not be the case, they will not be able to share anything. Both of them are very shy and too attached to their inner worlds. This is why there may be blockages when it comes to them communicating their objectives. They tend to leave things too late and/or to address problems at the very last minute, blaming one another for not taking the lead. They would be well advised to choose activities linked with nature.

Love relationship between 9 and 22: Things will never become an open conflict or turn into a serious crisis with smashing plates. On the contrary, they are very much attached to peace and quiet in the home. They are able to build a little nest, away from the tumultuous world and ideal for their children's well-being. Both of them enjoy silence and can't handle noise, upheavals or turmoil. Nines show a lot of love to their partners, but while Twenty-twos enjoy the affection they are much less demonstrative. Nines are not particularly disturbed by this, in that they know, through their natural empathy, that they can rely on their partners, no matter what. As a matter of fact, Nines aim to maintain their peace and quiet at any cost, and will therefore, accept and forgive their partner's possible occasional dishonesty.

General aspect: How can they possibly get along? This association is not likely to work, unless they succeed in sharing their common goals seriously through the long term. We have here two very distinct strong egos, thus triggering a great likelihood of confrontations. Both of them need to feel reassured that they have not been ripped off in any way. Also, their need for acknowledgement means that the outcome of their actions must be evenly and fairly distributed.[6]

Parent 11 and child 11: They are both enthusiastic and need to feel they can conquer the world. The parent is delighted to have a child who is so similar to her/himself, i.e. interested in her/his views on life. Many exchanges take place in this spontaneous, direct and sometimes explosive relationship. Neither of them wants to yield or to admit they are wrong. The child needs to be nurtured by new experiences, to push limits further and explore. In this, the parent is very supportive. Yet, caution and a certain form of wisdom are needed and must be taught at an early age. Such a parent might not be able to do this. As a matter of fact, in this case the parent-child relationship is more of a buddy-buddy friendship. Since Elevens love making friends, a great number of people, of all ages and walks of life, are expected to show up in the home.

Two associates 11: As long as they pursue common goals based on innovation, self-fulfillment, exploration, uprising and transformation, they have found the right partner. Providing they are able to move in the same direction with regard their common goals, they have nothing to fear. However, as soon as one of them is intent on proving to the other that she/he is right, the fragile balance can tip and result in direct confrontation. Both are extremely impulsive and reactive, which means that whenever they disagree, their egos get in the way. Neither is willing to make the

---

[6] This aspect must however be put in perspective, in case the sub-number 20 is present among Elevens' sub-numbers, in each respective chart.

first step towards peace. Let us hope their friendly and eccentric nature will enable them to solve their issues.

11 in love with another 11: They are more interested in genuine friendship than in passionate love. They both need to communicate a lot, so as to unite and come together. They do want to experience passion, but their natures operate in such a way that they require numerous exchanges so as to understand and accept each other. They need to feel they belong together, before they can truly appreciate each other in their respective fields. We are in presence of two original beings who are deeply attached to their independence. They need to devote more time and space to their relationship and less to their friends (unless they have friends in common), otherwise it will be to the detriment of their relationship. In addition, they are subconsciously driven to compete with one another and this is liable to give rise to much conflict. They are not driven by an intense desire to have children.

11 with 22

General aspect: Conflict over authority. They have diametrically opposed ways of operating. Elevens are builders who need immediate and visible results, whereas Twenty-twos discreetly build over the long term, with cautious reserve. They both search for fulfillment but considerable compromise will be needed to succeed in common goals. Yet, if Elevens manage to inspire Twenty-twos, they will be able to accomplish projects of remarkable skill and quality.

Parent 11 and child 22: This parent enjoys transforming and radically changing her/his environment. However, s/he will be very annoyed with their child who opposes with great passivity and apathy. As a matter of fact, the child will refuse to immediately obey; instead he/she will take their time when faced with what s/he considers as useless agitation. This being said, s/he will end up wisely complying with the rules, as giving in will allow her/him more space and quiet. In any case, s/he is concerned with avoiding conflict and carefully avoids anything that would disturb her/his peace or oblige her/him to justify her/himself. S/he therefore accepts the rules set by the parent out of reason, rather than acceptance of their parent's beliefs. Parent 11 finds it very difficult to understand how the child operates psychologically. Such a parent desperately expects some kind of reaction or answer, and this is not going to happen. The quiet strength of Twenty-two opposes the impulsive Eleven.

Parent 22 and child 11: Although the parent manages to calm the child's nervous excitability, s/he doesn't seem to do well with communicating. The parent is pragmatic and strong enough to face life's hardships, without much worry. The child rebels and expresses anger, while the parent lets things be. The parent's famous patience will definitely be required, to temper the child's curt and excessive personality. Fortunately, the parent is resistant and protective, and therefore will not be overwhelmed by the child's demands. In turn, the child will learn s/he must look to other sources of inspiration, to quench her/his thirst for knowledge.

Associates 11 and 22: The foundation of this collaboration depends mainly on Twenty-twos, and will be fructuous as long as they accept being pushed around. If not, there will be stormy conflicts. Elevens are turned towards that which is exterior, driven by discovery and finding new paths. Yet, they must listen to their collaborator Twenty-two's wise advice, instead of complaining that their joint projects are progressing too slowly. If this is not the case, calm Twenty-twos will only see their Eleven partner from time to time, as Elevens are often too busy running after their many other projects. Although Elevens are often irritated and angry, they will soon realize the futility of such excessive behavior. They will end up learning how to be more impassive and constructive. Elevens are extroverts, whereas Twenty-twos are introverts. Can the two meet halfway? It is certainly possible, providing they share the same level of confidence in their common goals.

Love relationship between 11 and 22: Twenty-twos are not willing to sacrifice themselves for an affair they consider as speculative or vague. They need a quiet and stable life, based on dependable regularity. And this is not at all what Elevens are looking for. If one is ready to stay home while the other is out exploring, all is fine. If this is not the case, conflict and arguments are likely to arise. Both of them are extremely independent, each in their individual way, which is not always conducive to them having sincere communication. Twenty-twos may at first appreciate their outgoing companion, but as time goes by, they might lose interest, especially if Elevens don't carry through their common goals. Elevens don't understand when Twenty-twos withdraw into themselves. They must learn to be more patient and listen more carefully. They mustn't get annoyed and angry as soon as they feel Twenty-twos are being lethargic. As we all know being in love can help transcend anything...

22 with 22

General aspect: The association is beneficial, as they share similar goals. While elation and enthusiasm are not expressed, long term construction definitely is. It would help them to inject a little more joy and lightness, so as to avoid becoming too stern and austere. This is a solid rather than dynamic relationship.

Parent 22 with child 22: If you happen to like a silent and calm home where peace and quiet prevails, this is the ideal home. Both get along extremely well, for they are able to understand each other without having to say anything. The parent would never dare disturb the child. Both of them are hard-working and enjoy what is down to earth and hands-on. They understand each other all the more when they are engaged in serious work. They are not particularly keen on deep exchanges about complex psychological and philosophical topics. They love nature and animals.

Associates 22: If they intend to live in a monastery, the countryside or any place where peace and quiet take precedence, they have found the right partner. What's more, should one of these criteria be absent, they would nevertheless succeed in building a calm environment which meets their needs, thanks to their strong determination and commitment. Both of them are pragmatic and must carry out that which they feel is worthwhile. Even if they lack poetic sense and embellishment, they are hard-working and dependable. This is why they will manage to implement their projects very successfully.

22 in love with another 22: They tend to live a practical and functional life. They will be tempted to settle in a nice and quiet comfortable home, within a natural environment, if possible. They love being surrounded by many children and animals. Both appreciate good food and physical pleasures. In other words, they particularly enjoy life's delights. They might seem cold and shy to the outside world, but this is only because of the distance they put, against what they regard as vulgar or improper. The relationship is liable to last in the long term, as they are willing to put in a great deal of energy to preserve it.

CHAPTER IV

Aspects between Life Paths

"No wind ever favors he who knows not where he is sailing to."
                                          Seneca (latin philosopher)

Definition: The Life Path is calculated from the date of birth, and therefore embodies essential data in the theme. On the one hand it refers to our inner nature, the aspects of our being which we will have to face and interact with through the people we meet (or meet again) along the way. On the other hand it refers to our environment. It is in this way that the compatibility between two Life Paths significantly highlights how two persons are likely to get along.

Within the concept of inner nature (Life Path) lies the idea that life drives the person to encounter resistance and adversity if one is inappropriately using his/her abilities. This differs from the Expression number, which will be studied further on and refers to the energy used so as to evolve and grow.

How it is calculated: There are three ways to calculate the Life Path number. All three calculations must be done, in order to know which sub-numbers are sitting behind, especially if your Life Path is

2, 4, 11 or 22. In both of these cases, you must check to see if your Life Path is more 2 than 11, more 4 or 22 - or the other way around.

Note that we use the European format dd/mm/yyyy.

First method: add all the figures of the date of birth and reduce the result.
Example:
16/10/1965 → 1+6+1+(0)+1+9+6+5 = 29 → 2+9 = 11

Second method: add the day, month and year of birth, and then reduce the result.

Example:
16/10/1965 → 16+10+1965 = 1991 → 1+9+9+1 = 20
20 → 2+0 = 2

Third method: add day, month and year, after having reduced them to a simple number (except if the result is 11 or 22), and then reduce the final result.

Example: day 16 is reduced as 1+6 = 7, month 10 makes 1+0 = 1, year 1965 makes 1+9+6+5 = 21 → 2+1 = 3 (in the case where the reduction comes to 11 or 22, keep that number as such, for a master number cannot be reduced).
Add 7 (reduced day) + 1 (reduced month) + 3 (reduced year) = 11

In our example, two methods result in 11, while the third method results in 2. This is therefore a person whose inner nature is 11/2, with a dominant 11.

Please note: Sub-numbers are dealt with in the last chapter of this book.

Life Path 1

A person whose Life Path is 1 refers to a determined and headstrong character, who is attached to his or her ego, through achievements and self-image. There is no room for doubt or hesitation, given that their entire and very direct nature doesn't allow such feelings which are regarded as negative.

These individuals are not bad people. They don't hassle or destroy for the sake of it; they merely put aside that which gets in their way. They lack consideration and are often thoughtless. They seriously need to learn how to collaborate, to listen more to others and stop believing as if they are the only ones who exist. Such individuals are entrepreneurs and creators (in most cases very efficient ones).

They will have to accept other people's ideas and desires, in other words to be a little more human. All the partner of this number asks, of this great and powerful being, is to be a little more tolerant, which he/she has within their abilities.

Shared Life Path 1

Both have a gigantic ego, are adamant and do not accept compromise, simpering ways or hesitation. They will both have to calm down, unless they want to kill each other. They have an identical way of working, are interested in the same things and are both aware of the impact they have on others, thanks to their strong personalities.

Both are leaders, and consider life as a battlefield devoid of any rules. There are no limits in this type of association. It can be either 100 % positive or 100% negative. The rest of the theme must be looked into, for what has just been said might only deal with certain particular points.

They can double their legendary strength so as to unite against the adversity their destiny often forces them to face. However, they must understand that power struggles should not exist merely for the sake of it.

Life Path 1 vs. Life Path 2

Their true natures are diametrically opposed, yet a long intimate relationship might enable them to reveal and learn to accept their differences. The sticking point that life brings these individuals differs, in that they can be the one who represents the other's sticking point. In other words, the obstacles that 1 will face are those caused by 2, and vice versa: the fears that 2 will have might drive 1 crazy. Therefore, while they are not on the same wavelength, they might provide each other with what each of them needs. This relationship is obviously not a smooth one and conflicts are bound to happen. The rest of the theme will show if this association is likely to last or not.

Life Path 1 vs. Life Path 3

Their true inner natures are very different and therefore all is not perfect here. Life Path 1 truly requires to push aside whatever gets in the way of his/her undertakings and that which hinders inspirations and ambitions. Whereas Life Path 3 needs to compare, analyze, study and poke into things. The latter is more of an intellectual, who finds number 1's creativity hard to follow. He/she needs more details to make decisions, and is aware of the danger of impulsive action. Fortunately, both are intelligent enough to find a comprise, so as to combine two seemingly opposed forces. Number 3 can become a wise adviser, able to manage and operate the energy provided by 1. Yet, violent arguments are likely to occur along the way.

Life Path 1 vs. Life Path 4

The main obstacle for number 1's fire is number 4's passivity. The latter needs a safe environment and is unwilling to explore new horizons. This association can be explosive, but nevertheless, it can give number 4 the opportunity to overcome his/her usual daily routine, in order to have new experiences and make number 1 happy. However, this is providing number 1 learns to behave more quietly, as 1's wild energy and selfishness can make number 4 very nervous.

Life Path 1 vs. Life Path 5

This association, chaotic as it may be, can prove very constructive, as long as both succeed in calming their egos. Both have tremendous energy. Number 1's energy is focused on personal fulfillment, whereas number 5 needs to share their energy with her/his close circle of friends and loved ones. However, finding a way to agree will be necessary and therefore both will have to learn how to compromise. Life path 1 may be too direct and domineering for Life Path 5, while 1 blames 5 for being too carefree, caustic and offhand.

Life Path 1 vs. Life Path 6

Number 1 and number 6 are bound to generate great struggle and conflict, for they have completely opposite views. Ones focus on their instincts and undertakings, and can't be bothered with how sixes plan ahead. They actually consider sixes as being incapable of making decisions and taking action. Number 6 will have a hard time letting go of their desire for perfection. They require more certainties which make them feel safe in what they intend to do. This association is nonetheless feasible, provided 1 accepts being criticized while 6 puts up with finishing what 1 has started.

Life Path 1 vs. Life Path 7

These two natures are very complementary. Both are driven by "a fire in the belly" and are able to blend together easily and in harmony. The 1 creator will be happily supported by 7 who is often searching for an initiator and leader. Number 1 will listen to the wise advice of 7, proud to be backed by such a lucid, observant and profound person, providing 7 doesn't keep criticizing 1. Number 7 requires someone charismatic enough to represent his/her idealistic views and that's what 1 does here. Yet, 7 needs to be absolutely sure before committing, and will be deeply disappointed if 1 doesn't comply. As soon as 7 stops admiring 1, he/she will go and find another partner.

Life Path 1 vs. Life Path 8

It is all – or nothing. The energies can either blend or oppose, to the extent that both yearn for power and do not hesitate to resort to any available means to reach their goals. Yet, they choose to do so in very different ways. Number 1 operates in the open, and claims what he/she wants face to face, whereas number 8 remains hidden in the dark, sometimes using unscrupulous means to meet his/her needs. If they manage to come to an agreement, they will be a winning team. On the contrary, if one of them fails to respect the terms of the agreement, direct conflicts will be triggered as number 1 will consider that number 8 has tried to take advantage of the situation (which 8 does very well!). Or it may be that number 8 considers 1 is being too arrogant!

Life Path 1 vs. Life Path 9

This is an association in which the two protagonists do not try to harm each other, even if they can't really understand each other. They're simply not on the same route. Number 1 considers that success can only be reached through strength, whereas 9 emphasizes aspirations, intuition and the secret mystical side of life. There is neither conflict nor aggressiveness, yet they have opposing views on life. Can they get along? Yes, provided neither 9 nor 1 (especially 1) tries to impose his/her views on the other. Life Path 9 is wise enough to know that number 1's constant restlessness stems from his/her ego's need of acknowledgement, which couldn't be further from 9's own concerns. Yet, 9 should follow the example set by 1, who expends a lot of energy in initiating and carrying out his humanitarian endeavors.

Life Path 1 vs. Life Path 11

The association between these two numbers is difficult to manage. Number 1 characterizes great vitality, initiative and success. Number 11 has similar qualities with double the ego, but can have strong emotions (in the case where there is sub-number 20 in the theme's calculations). The true nature of 11 is difficult to understand: they strive to transcend their lives towards and for the collective. In function with the sub-numbers found (see the last chapter), especially if 2 is very present, emotions might be overwhelming. A "pure" 11 will happily blend with 1, because they will find common interests. But if 2 is too present and prevents the person from handling his/her emotions well, then number 1 will not be able to cope (as in 1 with 2). An impulsive and emotional 11 who keeps bypassing the limits is not appreciated by 1 who finds him/her too idealistic.

Life Path 1 vs. Life Path 22

This association brings conflict. Their views are diametrically opposed, as well as their respective arrogance! Whereas number 1 is ready to immediately break through any barrier, without listening to anyone, number 22 is determined to methodically build in the long term. Without forcing his/her views on anyone, 22 pursues the same goal as 1, namely having control of the situation, which doesn't please impulsive 1. Both strive for power, though they have chosen different ways to obtain it. At first glance, they are likely to encounter many difficulties in understanding and appreciating each other. They will both have to make considerable effort to discover what one can bring to the other and vice versa: 1 provides the energy and will power, 22 supports long term vision, constructive efficiency, fair play and structure.

Life Path 2

Those whose Life Path is 2 search for happiness through their relationships, from the perspective of the couple, the family or community (be it political, social or collective movements...) These individuals are very connected to children and/or any defenseless beings (such as animals, victims...) who they strive to protect. Twos emphasize the domestic environment, comfort and harmony in the home, as well as clothing and arts. Yet, they might prove immature at times, for they can be imprisoned by irrational fears and inhibitions. The more they are offered what they most lack, namely protection, safety and harmony, the more these individuals will acquiesce to their partner. If necessary, Twos will not hesitate to use their greatest traits of charm and charisma. Their psyche is moody, inconstant and unpredictable, due to being overwhelmed by their emotions they can't control.

Throughout their existence, they will come across many people who will offer them help to overcome their weaknesses and to not give in to their oversensitivity. Life Paths 2 need to toughen up and face obstacles, by letting go of egoistical tendencies and infantile moody behaviors.

Shared Life Path 2

This association should lead to a calm, quiet and happy life, unless uncontrolled emotions on both sides get in the way and cause strife. The waves they both try not to make come from their need to avoid obstacles and the harsh reality of life. This results in them using their significant ability to create a peaceful environment, in keeping with their aspirations. On the other hand, they may be unable to fight against obstacles when needed. If they fail to overcome their shy nature and difficulty expressing their deep thoughts, they may end up as to two solitary human beings who are unable communicate in a reasonable way. By pursuing a common goal to use their hospitality to welcome, help and protect others they will be motivated to go beyond their tendency to otherwise close themselves off from the world.

Life Path 2 vs. Life Path 3

No particular obstacles prevent these two numbers from getting along, as number 2 thrives on the skills that number 3 has of accuracy, efficiency, order and organization. Number 3 also loves the skills that number 2 has of gentleness, sweetness and desire for harmony. Threes enjoy talking with people, communicating, and expressing their ideas through a certain methodology. Thanks to an open ear, they can help number 2 express his/her feelings and inner nature, while being amused by the childish aspects of their partner (who must not be mocked, even lightly). Number 3 can be an excellent spokesperson and protector on behalf of number 2. This will succeed in calming 2 while alleviating number 3's impulsive and unpredictable ways, through a maternal kind of love. Yet, there remains a big discrepancy between number 2's stay-at-home spirit and number 3's urge to be on the move.

Life Path 2 vs. Life Path 4

These two numbers are an excellent combination. Number 4 brings material and financial security that number 2 needs, as well as a smooth and quiet life. Number 4 appreciates the human qualities of number 2's genuine nature. Fours like building on firm ground and are fond of down-to-earth things and not being noticed. They don't enjoy saying what they think or decide. They communicate only when they feel safe and surrounded by reliable and trustworthy people, such as number 2. They will have to make sure their lives don't turn into a monotonous routine which could cut them off from the rest of the world.

Life Path 2 vs. Life Path 5

This association is very peculiar. They belong to such different worlds that they could easily be unaware of each other. Only the magnetic charm of Number 2 can help slow down number 5's need for a frantic life, who is always eager to explore and discover, whereas number 2 can't be bothered. Number 2 can calm number 5 down, by soothing and curbing his nervousness and restlessness. Nevertheless, number 5, who is likely to find twos too quiet and introverted, will try to push them. What can we say about such a relationship? Although neither of them intends to hurt their partner, both of them may end up going in opposite directions.

Life Path 2 vs. Life Path 6

Such a team is extremely positive, thanks to a true symbiotic relationship. Each of them is dedicated to creating an encouraging and peaceful environment for their partner. They are considerate and thoughtful towards each other and would never try to harm their relationship. Sixes, who endeavor to lead a happy emotional life, will find that twos are perfectly able to give them the loving care they need. Likewise, twos truly appreciate sixes' dedication to inspiring and encouraging them to enjoy life while showing them a lot of new horizons. However, Number 6 can be very critical at times. They have a nose for discovering what is wrong, which enables them to analyze their partner quite accurately. Yet, they must be careful not to be judgmental. As for number 2, he/she should learn not to take number 6's scornful observations too personally. Number 2 will help sixes to express their emotions more freely and thus let go of their excessive mental activity.

Life Path 2 vs. Life Path 7

Even though both are very different, this association can be very beneficial as they have similar ways of being. They both have an extremely fertile imagination. Introverted number 2 strives to protect his/her family, home and close environment, as does number 7. Yet, they achieve this through different means. Number 2 hates conflict and will do anything to avoid it, whereas number 7 will never hesitate to fight, if need be. Both share the need to have their cupboards well stocked, so as to feel safe and secure. Number 7 acts as protector to number 2, who in turn shows great tenderness and care.

Life Path 2 vs. Life Path 8

This peculiar combination is not as strange as it looks. Mysterious, complex, unpredictable number 8 can easily get along with Twos, whom they see as individuals they can mold to the way they'd like them to be. Number 8 is searching for power and money and has a very strong will power, which enables him/her to successfully face adversity when needed, thus assuring number 2's basic needs. It can take number 2 a long time to understand who number 8 truly is. Both of them are naive and gullible to the point of falling into each other's trap. Nevertheless, number 2 is able to efficiently support their companion, by meeting his/her needs. In return, eights will open 2s to new and sometimes mysterious worlds, which will fuel their imagination as they thrive on exploration. What's more, number 8 is generous enough so as to satisfy number 2's whims and demands.

Life Path 2 vs. Life Path 9

This is a peaceful, quiet and happy association. Neither of them tries to overshadow the other. Both are sensitive, well-intentioned individuals. Number 2 holds on to his/her dreams, desires and demands, whereas number 9 has much wider views. Number 2 works hard at creating comfortable living conditions and avoiding whatever gets in the way of this. This is not what nines are after. Nines tend to avoid what they regard as materialistic fancies, but will do so without expressing their exasperation or discontent. Number 9's universe is not easily understood by the sometimes selfish number 2. Therefore, they both need to work hard at making each other understood: Two must pacify his/her emotions, while Nine needs to come back down to earth.

Life Path 2 vs. Life Path 11

In the instance of 2 and 11/2, (as in the case of two Life Paths 2 together) this association gives promise to a quiet and happy life, providing stormy emotions on both sides are controlled. Unless they manage to deeply express their inner feelings, thus overcoming their natural shyness and inhibitions, they could well end up as total strangers, unable to communicate, especially if number 11/2 can't subdue his/her emotions by removing himself from an environment he finds too restrictive or stifling. By setting a common goal to help, welcome and protect others, they will find the motivation to move out of their small inner world, which they may otherwise find themselves enclosed.

The waves that number 2 constantly tries not to make and her/his strong emotions that stem from a desire not to face life's hardships, can actually fuel a storm, in the case of a "pure" 11. Number 11 never feels sorry. This might result in a difficult relationship, even though they share similar goals. Number 2 doesn't like to step out of her/his usual circle, while number 11 wants to go beyond the limits. They both yearn to live in keeping with their deep inner nature - namely in harmony with their loved ones, yet the ways they choose to reach this goal differ. Number 11 is much more outgoing and daring than number 2. It is true that while 11 can come across as conciliatory and easy-going, he/she can also be very unpredictable.

Life Path 2 vs. Life Path 22

Although they function differently, they can get along very well, therefore proving this to be a beneficial and constructive association. Twenty-twos relentlessly keep moving towards their goals, without allowing anyone to distract them. Time is on their side, for they have sufficient self-confidence and persistence in mastering their life. Number 22 is enduring and assertive. They will not let adversity have the last word. These characteristics are likely to reassure number 2's needs for protection and support. Yet, number 2 is very emotional, nervous and outgoing; unlike number 22 who is the complete opposite. The latter will therefore have to make a great effort to express his/her true nature, which is not easy. He/she must stop being so excessively serious, pessimistic and sermonizing, so as to be able to fit in with number 2's foibles and help him/her gain in wisdom and self-confidence. If they succeed in meeting half way, they will succeed in creating a nice and safe environment. Living near to nature is advised.

Life Path 3

A person whose life Path is 3 is open, critical and sometimes skeptical. They are available and enjoy contact and communication. They are also very useful and dedicated, especially when circumstances require it. Their creative energy is intensified when in a competitive and challenging environment.

Such a person only acts after having weighed the pros and cons and having planned ahead the consequences of his/her acts. They have great organizational skills that sometimes come across as militant. People usually love following in their wake, for there is no one like them. They can at times be childish and very eccentric. Through fear and/or insecurity, they have a constant need to be in contact with others, which is aimed at hiding their true nature, flaws and bodily imperfections.

They have a keen sense of humor and like what is linked to studies, research and knowledge. They must be careful not to be too superficial, critical or rhetoric. Verbal jousting must also be avoided. Their skill in comparing, analyzing and studying is fine, as long as it's not excessive.

Relationships with brothers and sisters and children play an important role, whether or not the person wants it. The biggest task this person has is to learn how to relax and to free him/herself from the restraints and responsibilities that they have placed on themselves. This person has an inner adolescent spirit that needs to be freed and expressed. Practicing sports is a good way to rest their intellect and chill out.

Shared Life Path 3

We have here two dual personality characters. Two different aspects, which are sometimes completely opposed, must be taken into account. There is on the one hand, a juvenile and carefree personality; and on the other, a personality who strives to analyze and structure everything. Therefore giving rise to either two immature teenagers or two hardworking intellectuals intent on structuring their lives based on their analyses. Such an association will lead to constant exchanges, dialogues, communication and sharing. This kind of challenge is not easy for the people around them to put up with, but the couple in question finds it very natural. They can bring each other a lot, even though there is little interest in exploring human biological nature. In other words, this may be an asexual relationship. Provided they find common topics of discussion, the relationship can work, but if not...

Life Path 3 vs. Life Path 4

Nothing runs smoothly in this difficult association, as each individual functions very differently. Number 3 uses his/her analytical mind which keeps conflicting with number 4's pragmatic and reserved way of being. Number 4 needs things to be established in a down-to-earth way and isn't interested in number 3's constant hypothesizes and advice. Number 4 is likely to feel annoyed, disturbed or even upset by 3's behavior. Number 3's persistent need for exchange and communication will not help them feel satisfied with a 4. Yet, number 3 can be a good spokesperson for number 4, provided he/she understands what number 3 is after. As for fours, they can be inspired by number 3's lucid ideas, even if their prolific concepts stem from a hyperactive mind, making them nervous and preventing them from having the peace they need to be happy. In turn, number 4 may be too slow and not flexible enough to satisfy number 3's need for fast action. Fours prefer quiet accomplishments.

Life Path 3 vs. Life Path 5

Although this association is not a smooth one, agreement can be found. Number 3 is wise but can be very critical and does not refrain from expressing his/her disapproval of what he/she deems as too independent or nonconformist in Five. Yet, number 3 also has an adventurous side and enjoys discovering and challenging things. They will therefore be easily inspired by fives who keep exploring new horizons. However, number 3 won't hesitate to point out when number 5 is lacking in consistency and persistence, as they find Fives too versatile and idealistic. In turn, number 3's bitter criticism tends to annoy number 5 who feels his/her freedom is being hindered. If they find a common goal on which to unify their efforts towards the same aim of conquering the world, all will be well. Otherwise, some conflict, at times violent, may arise. Nevertheless, both are intelligent and aware that direct confrontation is not the solution; and that comprise and agreements are necessary for reaching harmony. Number 3 can either prove very inspiring in his/her way of communicating - or completely debilitating. In the latter case Number 5, who is not very patient, may well end the relationship bluntly.

Life Path 3 vs. Life Path 6

There is no major opposition here, as both individuals are similar, even though they function differently. Number 6 accepts number 3's advice and complies with his/her life values and organizational skills, for he/she also enjoys order. Communication and exchanges are favored. Number 6 brings a touch of tenderness to number 3 but should be careful not to become too dependent. Number 6's quest for perfection is likely to annoy number 3 whose criticisms often lack justification and show a discrepancy between what is said and what is done. This is all the more paradoxical in that number 3 is also a perfectionist, yet less persistent than number 6. However, agreement can be found, provided threes accept to minimize their criticisms and carry through with their ideas.

Despite number 6's love for order and precision, he/she won't care much for number 3's verbal frenzy. In the end, it will be 3 who eventually acknowledge that number 6 is the master of 3's predilection: perfection.

Life Path 3 vs. Life Path 7

Communication and teaching are favored through this association, in spite of their very different views. Threes' spontaneous minds enable them to express their criticisms and ideas, sometimes in a superficial or over-synthetic way; whereas sevens endeavor to express their views with profound and well-thought out argument. They hate nothing more than fast thinking. Seven's legendary introspection and observation skills spot the flaws and are in complete opposition to Three's active mind. While number 7 strives to control and possess, without ever disclosing his/her strategy to do so, number 3 does exactly the opposite!

Both are very curious and fond of what's new, thus proving they can be a productive team. Number 3 can be an excellent spokesperson for number 7. Order and efficiency are values they share, although number 7 is always ahead of number 3, due to his/her strategic mind. They can bring a lot to each other and create a positive and productive life. Number 7 is likely to carry out number 3's ideas, providing his/her introverted ways and absences don't put off outgoing number 3. This association also promises prolific creativity.

Life Path 3 vs. Life Path 8

These two natures are miles apart; they do not live in the same world. Number 3's need for communication doesn't suit number 8 who is not so fond of dialogue. Will number 3 be able to uncover number 8's mysterious world? Will he/she eventually see through number 8's deep motivations, thanks to his/her considerable clear-sightedness?

Trying to match these very different personalities is not easy, but this challenge will appeal to number 3. Eights do not appreciate number 3's restless and nervous ways, as they hate what is superficial and whatever obliges them to unveil their true nature. Number 3 tends to think that number 8 keeps responsibilities at bay. Number 8, who relies on his/her ability to work out life's issues, doesn't care much for the petty details number 3 fights over. Agreement can be found if number 3 understands and accepts that number 8's universe is out of their reach. As for the latter, he/she must make an effort to communicate more and comply with number 3's life principles and values; otherwise they may end up ignoring each other.

Life Path 3 vs. Life Path 9

This union is possible, as number 9, through his/her considerable empathy and diplomacy, is able to understand and accept number 3's nonstop talking and criticisms. Number 9's universe emphasizes meditation, contemplation and feelings, and therefore doesn't pay much attention to whether his/her environment matches his/her desires or not, which is not at all the case of number 3. Moreover, nines never try to challenge their partners, unlike number 3, who tends to be annoyed by number 9's docile and languid personality! Yet, both of them are interested in the psyche and psychological. Both are willing to help each other. Number 9 doesn't see why he/she shouldn't let number 3 take over organizing their life. Number 3 has found the ideal partner he/she can advise, support and encourage. Nevertheless, let us not forget that number 9 is a dreamer and a poet, which might not suit number 3's rational mind. Number 9 is of a non-violent, shy and fearful nature, whereas number 3 is daunting and loves nothing more than to challenge.

Life Path 3 vs. Life Path 11

The partnership can be very positive. Both persons encourage and inspire each other, for they share the same spirit of competition and a strong determination to achieve and be fulfilled. The means they have chosen to reach their goals are not the same, yet they are not opposed. Both are communicative and love to express their feelings and claim their rights. Number 3 strives to express him/herself, organize and expand on how he/she will go about reaching their goal. Elevens are more likely to work on their own and will serve their own interests before those of their partners. This association is therefore not as smooth as it seems, for we are dealing with two very strong personalities. Although number 11 tends to be selfish and finds it difficult to accept number 3's criticisms, he/she might suffer from a lack of recognition from number 3. Nevertheless, 3 easily accepts and will support 11's initiatives, as long as they are going in the right direction towards a common good. Number 3 can be too down-to-earth, unlike number 11, who is motivated by more idealistic values.

Note: in the case where there is a 20 in the different sub-numbers of Life Path 11, also refer to Life Path 2 vs. Life Path 3.

Life Path 3 vs. Life Path 22

This association is particularly beneficial because both aim to make their goals a reality, even if threes might appear slightly too agitated for twenty-twos, who enjoy building in the long term. Twenty-two's love of authority is a deep part of her/his nature and thus lends them a very strong will power. They will not be deterred by number 3's criticisms and opposing views. Threes have found their ideal partner who gives them the comforting and trustworthy support they need. Anxious number 3 always requires being reassured so as to feel safe, and number 22 can give them this. Although they both enjoy being the boss, their ways are very different. Threes use speech and communication, whereas twenty-twos act. By Twenty-two's side, number 3 will feel less restless and nervous and will calm down. He/she will love supporting, helping and taking part in number 22's productive actions, as a spokesperson or strategist. Number 22, who is undeterred by criticism and overall agitation, will not be irritated by number 3's constant talking. The couple can however lack in joy, enthusiasm and zest for life.

Note: A pure Life Path 22 seldom occurs. Sub-numbers referring to a 4 often occur in the different calculations of this Life Path, in which case, see Life Path 4 vs. Life Path 3.

Life Path 4

A person whose life path is 4 emphasizes regularity, efficiency and persistence, especially in the socio-professional fields. Everything this person carries out has to result in tangible outcome, and couldn't be further from imaginary fantasies. This does not mean to say that fours don't like dreaming. According to them, dreaming is fine as long as it doesn't overshadow common sense and pragmatism.

Fours like to feel safe; they therefore strive to protect themselves from any hardships that might occur, and they do so through purchasing and preserving what is essential to their lives, no matter how much effort this takes. These individuals are not slowed down by hesitation or obstacles. They consider that time is on their side, and thanks to their persistence, that which cannot be done today will be achieved later.

Fours are ready to do just about anything to preserve what they have. They can also be too materialistic. This aspect of their true inner nature drives them to think things through and over-analyze, cutting them off from their environment and their loved ones.

Everything to do with family ancestry and genetic heritage is of great importance, on the material level as well as that of their ascendants. They will have to learn how to lift the burden of their ancestry from their shoulders, and break away from the transgenerational family patterns that don't belong to them. Fours have incarnated so as to learn that they are not responsible for what took place before they were born. Because they can be so easily settled in a comfortable routine, they tend to have difficulty in widening their horizons.

Though hardworking, they also tend to sink into laziness and daydreaming. Fours need to learn to be more joyful, relaxed and more in contact with other people. They can't stand people who are nervous, intrusive or talk too much, who they consider as troublemakers. Fours must overcome their tendency to be possessive and jealous.

Shared Life Path 4

There is no blatant opposition between the two but life tends to be monotonous. Both of them try to protect themselves against any odds, through an emphasis on work and purchasing material goods. They are driven by regularity and everyday routine, for they search comfort and tranquility. Their loved ones might find such a life too dull. As long as they share a common goal, everything will be fine. Thanks to their quiet nature, little conflict will occur. Yet, argument over material issues might come about if ever one of them feels that the other one is attempting to take something away from them. Despite their shy nature, they will have a rich sexual life.

Life Path 4 vs. Life Path 5

In this particular case, number 5's restlessness will get in the way of fours' quiet routine, and make them very nervous. Yet, they might like it, for Five brings an unusual touch to their life, providing things don't get out of control! On the other hand, fives are not excessively bothered by their partner's calmness, which might even soothe them.

Nevertheless, things will become difficult where projects are concerned. Adventurous 5 does not suit quiet 4. They will have to make a real effort in order to come to agreement. Fives will have to calm down and fours need to accept to change their ways, and not be afraid if he/she has the impression of losing their bearings. Harmony is achievable through communicating with each other. Fours are slow to fathom things, unlike fives, who will in turn have to be patient and give fours time. There is a very strong opposition between fours' materialistic nature and fives' carefree personality.

Life Path 4 vs. Life Path 6

This association brings about positive, enriching and trustworthy collaboration in the long term. There is no blatant opposition between the two, as both look for persistence, efficiency and regularity. Their union is a perfect one as each innately has what the other searches for, with fours who favor a life of comfort and sixes who favor peace. Sixes particularly appreciate how fours are skilled at obtaining material things, for they are also attached to a nice lifestyle. Number 6's critical mind is likely to be less acerbic than usual, for number 4's legendary inertia easily lets it wash over him/her like water off a duck's back. Fours are particularly good at not being hurt by criticism. Sixes find a willing listener and advisor in Fours. As sixes can be at times too cerebral and analytical, they will benefit from sensual fours.

Life Path 4 vs. Life Path 7

Sevens are idealistic people. They are moved by their profound faith and strive to act in accordance with their beliefs. Above all, they act for the good of everyone, or at least for the good of their loved ones. They are attached to success, material goods and financial comfort. All this is fine with their partners, who see what sevens can bring them in the way of protection and everyday life. Even though they are very independent and act accordingly, sevens appreciate the stability, quiet and peacefulness of fours. Fours are reassuring, because they are predictable, especially for sevens who keep wondering about the deep motivations of those around them (they need to know if they can rely on people or not). If both make the effort to communicate this union will be a profitable and positive one - providing number 7 doesn't suddenly go on a crusade somewhere far away from the small universe that suits number 4. This is a successful association.

Life Path 4 vs. Life Path 8

This association is one of two diametrically opposed natures. Although they mutually enjoy acquiring material goods and the pleasures that life can offer, they use very different means to reach the same goal. Fours patiently attempt to obtain what they desire and reassure them, whereas eights will use whatever means they can, sometimes in a corrupt way, to get what they want. Both of them agree that material comfort is important, even if it means being selfish at times. Yet, there is a great gap between them due to number 4's inability to understand number 8's mysterious world, which stems from number 4's innate shyness. Eights can get along very well with timid fours, whereas fours will never know exactly whose these enigmatic eights they're living with are. Unconventional Eights will topple fours' quiet ways, which is a positive thing. In turn, fours will inspire eights to enjoy daily work, persistence and to appreciate completed projects.

Life Path 4 vs. Life Path 9

This association is gentle and enjoyable, for neither of these two genuine natures' attempt to harm the other. Both of them are quiet, sweet and peaceful. They look to create a life of harmony and peace so as to be sheltered from life's ups and downs. Fours bring persistence and determination to nines who tend to be more carefree about everyday matters. With their legendary patience, fours will need to bring nines back to reality, for the latter often prefers to keep away from earthly concerns. Nevertheless, nines enjoy being supported and encouraged by gentle fours, as they feel that fours are genuinely by their side. The goals of these two can be very different one from another: fours aim for that which is concrete, whereas nines aim for what is universal. They are both discreet and hate noise. Provided they don't fall into a deep lethargy, they will manage to achieve their goals, hand in hand, with a view to helping the world. They share a love of music, art interior design and beauty.

Life Path 4 vs. Life Path 11

This is an association of two completely different natures, except where there is a 20 (as in a sub-number to 11). Fours, who search for peace and quiet, will feel that hyperactive elevens push them around too much. They don't see life the same way. Their abilities to implement their plans are also not the same. Fours create in the long term, whereas elevens react in the present and want everything immediately. Elevens therefore will be very annoyed by fours' lack of reactivity: they will not understand why their partners procrastinate on all that could be done today. This collaboration is not one of the best, for they do not acknowledge each other's fine points. Elevens will have to be very patient and accept that fours need time. While fours are attracted to elevens' strength and spirit of initiative, they are not likely to be offended by Elevens, and will continue their own quiet way. They will see each other periodically.

Note: If sub-number 20 is found behind number 11, the association will be much smoother. Number 2 (2+0) pacifies number 11. See Life Paths 2 and 4.

Life Path 4 vs. Life Path 22

Because both are driven by a motivation to do well, with a great emphasis on material comfort, they will be willing to help each other. Long term projects don't frighten them. On the contrary, Twenty-twos are very stable and are seldom unbalanced by life's hardships: they will therefore provide trust and support to fours who need more confidence. Fours might nevertheless blame twenty-twos for their lack of gentleness and delicateness. Moreover, twenty-twos' ambitiousness might be a problem, inasmuch as they are often far from home. Fours ask twenty-twos for care and attention, but twenty-twos are too busy to notice. Fours are torn between their desire for a closer relationship and their need for security. Twenty-twos will particularly appreciate a four who is able to force them out of their habitual environment. No conflict is to be expected in this area of their life.

Note: Life Paths which are completely 4 or 22 are rare. There is often a sub-number 22 behind a Life Path 4. In which case, one must look at two Life Paths 4.

Life Path 5

A person whose life path is 5 has an open, free and outgoing nature. They are optimistic. Nothing (or almost nothing) frightens them, for they are unaware of danger. They keep trying to push the limits even further, so as to overcome them and free themselves from what hinders, discourages or slows them down. They love communicating, are fond of novelties and love exploring all sorts of new fields. They're always up for new adventures and whatever takes them away from burdensome routine. Above all, they appreciate their freedom and independence, for they are idealists. They can be very restless, excited, adamant and even angry. They will have to learn to be more patient and to listen more to others, which is difficult for them. Nevertheless, they do have altruistic views and care a lot about people. The problem is that, although they think they rapidly understand others, they often miss the ins and outs of each situation.

Fives are revolutionaries and therefore create dynamic movement among the people around them, especially when they feel they are being useful to others. Paradoxically, although they love motivating people, they don't like being taken by surprise. They should therefore learn not to do to others what they wouldn't like to be done to themselves. They live unchained and free, but paradoxically can't live without being surrounded by other people. The obstacles that are likely to rise, will serve to teach them patience. Travels and adventures are fine, but a rolling stone is unable to build anything.

Shared Life Path 5

This dynamic association can prove restless, as both of them keep pushing the limits even further, in any given field. This is a good friendship which enables them to give their life meaning, even though it might prove a little unrealistic. The relationship is based on friendship that they work at hard to maintain, as they do their freedom. Both have brilliant minds and are unconventional. Who will be the first to settle down? The rest of the theme will tell. Provided they manage not to let inadvisable friendships invade their space, they can accomplish great things. Otherwise, conflict is to be expected. They love exchanging their points of view and giving speeches, but this will not nourish them. They need to find common avant-garde activities (i.e. Show business, clubs, travels …) they can share together. Otherwise they won't be able to lead a life together and will only see each other from time to time.

Life Path 5 vs. Life Path 6

Such a relationship is one that is based on the mind and intellect, for each is very cerebral. Yet, this is not the perfect association, as their inner natures are very different. Sixes love to arrange, tidy up and plan, whereas fives take life as it is. Yet, both of them are intelligent and enjoy their genuine exchanges that keep them together. As long as number 6 accepts number 5's excesses, everything will be fine. If not, number 5 is likely to flee because he/she will feel trapped. Sixes have nevertheless a lot to bring to fives, in that they can pacify them and give them a structure. In return, fives bring stamina to sixes' lives. Sarcastic humor is highlighted.

Life Path 5 vs. Life Path 7

This is an interesting relationship. The ideals these two share are identical, unconventional and transcend all limits. But they do not express themselves in the same way. Both sevens and fives search for knowledge and experience. They love to create their own experiences, in independent ways. But this is where their similarities end. Sevens are structured, methodical, and idealistic, a bit guru-like; whereas fives are free spirits and totally unpredictable. If they wish, they can gain significant knowledge about life in general, but they will use such in very different ways. Sevens endeavor to turn what they invest in, for that which is lucrative, tangible and profitable; unlike fives who regard each step as an additional adventure, nothing more. Fives don't try to gain money from their experiences; they simply want their knowledge and awareness to give them more freedom. This difficult association can however bring a lot to each of them: namely knowledge and mutual respect.

Life Path 5 vs. Life Path 8

How to join the dark with the light? This association is contradictory and unconventional. There is a risk of them not paying much attention to each other, except in particular instances. However, they share the same spirit of independence and freedom. This being said, the bright side of five is incompatible with the dark side of eight. Fives easily reveal their plans and who they truly are but show little hesitation to whatever comes their way. Whereas eights, who intuitively know everyone's true inner natures, don't always reveal their plans and will use their instincts to get what they want. They are very determined and don't bother with niceties to reach their goals. Fives have scruples, particularly when they feel they are not following their true inner nature; unlike eights, who aren't bothered and have no qualms. As a matter of fact, eights are not always conscious of their underhandness, which comes natural to them. They are likely to use uncertain (at times dishonest) ploys to prove their rights. Because fives and eights live in such diverse worlds, imagination is required to envisage a marriage between the Moon and the Sun. When they are together, one eclipses the other. Yet, if they manage to find a common goal, which isn't impossible, they can be a formidable force and achieve much together.

Life Path 5 vs. Life Path 9

Thanks to nines' empathy, much agreement can be found, due to their innate gentleness, diplomacy, loving and quiet nature. In exchange, fives can bring their companions the pep and stamina they need to discover new horizons. Yet, fives must be careful not to push nines too far, otherwise they might run away. Fives will find good listeners in nines, and will therefore be able to confide their adventures, secrets and failures, realizing they have found their ideal companion. Nines are dreamers, unlike fives, who have an ability to carry out their dreams, except if they lose themselves in their dream world. There is no aggressivity in this relationship, for they are both humanitarian and possess an irrational side that can take them far from everyday reality. Nines are exceptional advisors and will be able to tell fives their weaknesses and advise how they can correct them to be more successful. Strong sensuality can be born between these two.

Life Path 5 vs. Life Path 11

These two paths come together to move beyond the limits of everyday life towards all that is universal. But the similarities stop here. Unlike fives, « pure » elevens have a strong and domineering ego, which might cause trouble. They both have similar views, but fives hate to feel dominated and will never accept what they consider as being "bossed around". In the case where a sub-number 20 is also present within their Life Path, elevens will tend to be more conciliatory, cooperative, and giving.

Both personalities are strong, but common goals might smooth things out. Elevens definitely bring fives the necessary skills to carry out an idea to the end, instead of squandering their energy in endless adventures. Equally important, elevens can encourage their partner to implement their numerous sources of inspiration, thanks to their determination. In turn, fives can teach elevens how not to take things too seriously. They can understand each other very well, for their true natures share the same essential value: to free themselves from everyday routine. The question is: will they manage to tame their egos? What will save them are friendship, humor and playful games.

Life Path 5 vs. Life Path 22

A partnership between these two is very unlikely, for they function completely differently. How can fives, who thrive on adventure and freedom, get along with twenty-twos, who insist on structure and discipline? How can twenty-twos, who are attached to a constant, regular and productive life, get along with fives, who are so versatile? They are both intelligent, and are able to understand each other, but where the one is outgoing, the other one is reclusive. One keeps talking, while the other keeps silent. One cares about circumstances, the other doesn't. One advocates for justice and equality, always searching for revolution, whereas the other one claims ancestral values, even if they are out of date. They blame each other for being wide off the mark and missing the point. Yet, an association is possible, provided a great deal of effort is made to get along.

Life Path 6

The persons whose Life Path is 6 endeavor to stand up to their responsibilities and build a perfect, regular and ideal life. They strive to be impeccable and don't accept criticism but disapprove of those who don't agree with them. They are reliable, trustworthy and won't walk away, in other words they work hard to create a perfect living environment.

They should, however, learn not to impose their points of views on others and stop stressing over events that don't live up to their expectations. Their critical mind can go against them and be the cause of them being misunderstood by people around them who feel judged. On the other hand, they are excellent advisors, when they calm down and are flexible.

They need to admit they also make mistakes, which are not necessarily catastrophic. They deeply desire to help and collaborate. The perfection they are searching for is meant for the good of all. Love, friendship, devotion and commitment are part of their inner nature. They know how to be useful and need to be careful not to focus on that which displeases them if they don't want to become too rigid.

Shared Life Path 6

This association is feasible in that their inner natures lead them to do things well, for both are perfectionists who work hard to build an ideal life. They can bring a lot to each other, for they will quickly understand that their inner motivations are identical. Everything will go well, provided they share the same tastes. If not, criticism and confrontations are to be expected, which will result in casting judgments that will make them both angry and even more inhibited. In spite of this, sixes' conciliatory and pragmatic nature pushes them to find peace and harmony. As time goes by, they will learn how to compromise. They can be libertine and gourmand, as they are fond of all the refined pleasures life can offer. They will however need to refrain from living only for the ultimate.

Life Path 6 vs. Life Path 7

This partnership suffers from an obvious incompatibility between how the two function, as they hold very different views on life. Both seem driven by a common motivation to achieve things accurately and efficiently, but in fact the processes they use to reach this goal are different. This is a crucial problem. Sixes are pragmatic and keep trying to make their life better, through harmony and beauty. They are only satisfied once they have found how to implement their precise ideas. Sevens also search for perfection, but they tend to idealize it and expand on it, trusting in their faith as much as in their actual projects. Sevens regard life as sacred. They don't necessarily need to trust in the immediate feasibility of their plans, for they know they will make it one day, somehow, sooner or later. Sixes on the other hand organize, using whatever they can to reach their goals as quick as possible. « Here and now » is their motto. They don't need hypothetical visions. As a matter of fact, sixes consider sevens as dreamers, idealists and story-tellers... and do not want to take part in such ways. On the other hand, sevens might become impatient when sixes hesitate about whether a plan is worthwhile or not. They don't understand why sixes limit themselves. Sixes carry out, whereas sevens dream. This doesn't mean that sevens are inefficient or unproductive, just that this is how sixes perceive them. What's more, sixes don't appreciate sevens' adventurous side. Nevertheless, they do agree on hygiene, order and structure.

Life Path 6 vs. Life Path 8

The relationship is not a calm one. Honest and irreproachable Sixes will have a difficult time in the beginning, accepting eights' limitless ways of behaving. Sixes are pragmatic and like order, efficiency and detail. In other words, perfection and this is not what eights can offer them. Eights want to satisfy their thirst of pleasure and desire by any means it takes, without anyone knowing their deep motivations. An association is however possible... providing they manage to understand each other. Sixes keep pointing out eights' imperfections, even though their conciliatory nature does help them to understand their partners. Eights strive to escape intrusive sixes who are excellent at spotting flaws. Yet, they can bring each other a lot; eights find easy solutions to success while sixes bring implementation. Eights' position is more awkward though, in that they feel spied on far more than they can put up with. Sixes can bring a certain morality and honesty to eights. Moreover, they are aware of the significant energy and will-power that eights invest in their business. Sixes will therefore have to up with eights' moodiness, while eights will have to accept sixes' meticulousness.

Life Path 6 vs. Life Path 9

This association is not easy, for we are dealing with two opposing natures. Sixes endeavor to manage and organize their lives according to very specific criteria, whereas nines live through their aspirations, intuitions and visions. Nines don't care much about social organization nor feel they have to comply with rigid rules. They'd rather be in their own universe, which is regarded as fantastical and idealistic. Sixes can become exasperated when seeing how nines operate in such a seemingly disorganized way which doesn't rely on a sound foundation.

Yet, these two individuals do have something in common: they are both attached to serving others and are dedicated, though not in the same way. Sixes are disciplined and will attempt to push those who want to help them, to follow their views in a somewhat strict way. Whereas nines tend to help people unconditionally, which in some cases cause them to be exploited. Sixes do help, but they will always make sure that their rules are followed, so that no problems arise. Nines also help, but they act in the present, without trying to organize their own lives or that of others'. What fortunately saves this relationship is their humanity. They are very sensitive to other people's problems and are able to act together to give a helping hand.

If they do reach mutual understanding, they can bring a lot to each other. Nines will tone down sixes' organized nature, and sixes will plan and manage nines' sometimes chaotic life. They will also bring logic which will help nines overcome their fears. Nines are idealists who live beyond time and space and could do with a bit of sixes' pragmatism. Sixes will also teach nines how not to systematically run away when faced with obstacles.

Life Path 6 vs. Life Path 11

This association is not a restful one, particularly with regard to couple troubles. Sixes are pragmatic organizers and may not understand excessive elevens who are boisterous entrepreneurs. Elevens are driven by a desire to innovate and discover new worlds, which they love to share with those around them. But they are not always able to plan and organize. They want things to be new and quick, they thrive on other people's company, but are not likely to sit down and think things through. Elevens have a strong ego and tend to think: « love me or leave me ». Yet, if others don't follow them and they end up alone, they can become troubled and might lose interest in their ideas. They wish to be independent, but they are not. There is therefore a great disparity between elevens who regard sixes as nit pickers and sixes who regard elevens as dreamers, even if they do consider some of elevens' ideas as brilliant. Elevens are nonetheless more open to the world than sixes are, as they do not generally worry about protecting themselves, whereas sixes try to avoid risk.

Elevens must accept that their partners are slower than them, and sixes must give up their rigid principles that are tied to their idea of perfectionism. Sixes are intelligent and open enough to accept their companions' bright ideas, although they will ask them to be less excessive. Elevens will have more trouble understanding that sixes are harmless and only trying to protect elevens from themselves. One is a pioneer, the other is an organizer.

Life Path 6 vs. Life Path 22

This is a positive and stable association, for both persons desire to live in a structured, organized and lasting world, in keeping with their principles. There is no violent opposition, for they don't try to harm each other. Serious and strict twenty-twos appreciate efficient sixes who can support them in their goals. Sixes regard twenty-twos as trustworthy people they can rely on, although they might blame them for being a little reserved, distant, and sometimes cumbersome. Twenty-twos are helpful indeed, but they need time to achieve things. Their passivity might appear as though they are not present when you need them most. This drives sixes crazy. Sixes want efficiency and they cannot understand procrastination. Oddly enough, twenty-twos' patience is not tried when sixes keep telling them what to do, so they let sixes organize as they wish, to the smallest of details. Collaboration can come about for they are pragmatic, hardworking and solid. Moreover, they both appreciate life's pleasures.

Life Path 7

People whose Life Path is 7 give priorities to their ideals. They trust life and are confident about their undertakings. From their perspective, their goals are more important than the means. They have a "fire in the belly", are sharply intelligent and have an insatiable curiosity. They are always seeking new ways to succeed.

They are also imposing and have very set ideas. This sometimes prevents them from perceiving the duality and consequences of certain conflictual situations, which can intensely annoy and anger them. Their souls are like those of gurus who try to force their knowledge onto their disciples through their magnetic charisma. They are extremely idealistic and therefore need references, role models and icons to identify with, so as to focus on a definite goal.

Yet, success is assured and awaits them once sevens manage to trust in their own abilities and gain other people's confidence. This might not be easy for them, because, paradoxically, these independent beings hate nothing more than feeling tamed and don't know how to live on their own. They need their family, other people's presence and fans. They can be successful in many different trades, because of their perfectionism, persistence, accuracy and ambition. They become specialists in the fields they are interested in, or at least, this is what they aim for.

Sevens often need to be told what to do. They want "God" to hand them a signed document, with instructions of steps to follow. Sevens also like to be around people: they tend to join groups and elitist associations, which can at times cut them off from regular mortals.

Sevens find it difficult to accept untidy and dirty environments. They are actually obsessed with cleanliness, although they can live in perfect disorder and do not see what the problem is! They respect the laws they recognize as fair. They are not especially generous...except when they are in love. They don't often act without a motive. They are good at calculating where their interests lie and how to defend them. They are astute collectors.

Shared Life Path 7

This association is fruitful as long as both individuals share common ideals. Otherwise, conflicts will arise. They are kind and considerate and will do anything they can to help each other, to the point where the relationship may become extremely soothing and devoted. They must learn to stay grounded, so as to deal with everyday life and not to escape into imaginary or real adventures. Finances are favored, although some conflict is to be expected. There is passion, at least in the beginning of the relationship. Yet, passion must endure in the long term, if they want to share the benefits. Although they tease each other all the time, they truly admire each other.

Their lives may be focused on research, travel, sports and exploring new horizons. Their livings conditions need to be stimulating so as to allow them to fully express their aspirations. They will create a cozy, quiet, secluded nest, away from curious eyes.

Life Path 7 vs. Life Path 8

Because both of them are attached to a certain form of reserve and concealment, they naturally agree when it comes to preserving their common interests. Yet, do they understand each other? That's another story. Eights dissimulate when their ambitions and voracious earthly appetites are involved, whereas sevens dissemble when their secret intentions and objectives are involved. Their association is nevertheless compatible because they both appreciate power, money and earthly goods in general. Their appetites are powerful. If they find common ground, they can become very rich. However, eights are likely to suffer from intrusive sevens, who want to know everything. Eights will also find it difficult to understand sevens' fundamental beliefs and ambitions. Yet, eights will bring a lot to sevens, through their ability to explore clandestine worlds. In turn, sevens will know how to help eights follow more upright and straighter paths and eights will help sevens become less rigid. Financial conflicts are to be expected.

Life Path 7 vs. Life Path 9

This association can lead to a comfortable and peaceful life. They both endeavor to conceal, or at least to behave in the least conspicuous way, for they cannot stand being noticed. They will test you before letting you in. Both of them are driven by that which is spiritual and mystical.

They are very sensitive to human's most intimate nature. Through their empathy, they are able to perceive a subtle universe that most people are unaware of. They have similar views on love and feelings in general. They are more interested in emotional exchanges than in profit and benefit. This is all the more true when nines deeply trust sevens, thereby accepting to follow them. Likewise, sevens must accept their partners' slow nature, who is able to subdue and pacify them, thus enhancing their trust in Life. Sevens should listen to nines' wise advice as they can sense subtle worlds through their intuition. If sevens find nines too lethargic, problems will come about. This being said, a vast universe is within their reach, based on human relationships, trade and exchanges.

Life Path 7 vs. Life Path 11

They can bring each other a lot as long as they pursue common goals. If not, direct confrontations are to be expected. Sevens never give up. They anticipate, weigh and appraise whatever they plan. They work towards one goal at a time. Elevens are more spontaneous and direct, and cannot bear feeling restricted. They react according to their instincts, exploring all possible directions at once. Can altruistic, open elevens follow calculating sevens? What's more, elevens have a big ego and their need for recognition is as strong as the energy they invest to succeed. This leaves the door open for sevens' withering sarcasm, who has figured out their partner's true motivations. Nevertheless, sevens can be moved by elevens powerful energy, especially if they realize how they can benefit from it. In this case they will become the perfect associates, while keeping in mind their own separate interests. Even though they acknowledge their partner's intelligence and abilities, elevens will need to make a great effort to understand sevens' long term ways.

Life Path 7 vs. Life Path 22

This is a very positive association, as cautious sevens will not hesitate to rely on twenty-two's strength, even if only to be under their protection. Time is an ally for both of them. Twenty-twos have a stability and persistence that perfectly suits sevens who require solid foundations to reach their goals. Sevens will act as spokespeople for twenty-twos, whose interests they will defend, as well as explaining the ins and outs of their undertakings. They both search for a quiet, peaceful life, if possible within nature. They are likely to commit to some kind of structure (political or otherwise). As Twenty-twos need to lighten up, they will thoroughly enjoy sevens' enthusiasm.

Such a partnership is built in the long term, although it may look a little monotonous to the outside world.

And yet, both are hedonists and appreciate the pleasures of life in all senses. They are perfect hosts. They have strong personalities and are able to defend their acquisitions with determination. If they are associates, they can succeed at all their goals. But because they don't give up, if ever they are ever in opposition, they can destroy each other.

Life Path 8

People whose life path is 8 possess powerful, covert and, at times, overwhelming energies. Whether they are aware of it or not, they are deeply attached to the vital energies of creation and the occult sciences. Their mysterious and impermeable aura leaves a strong impression on people, who might feel uneasy in their presence. The dark forces at work within eights can compel them to manipulate their peers so as to possess more. Eights aim at enjoying a comfortable material life and will not hesitate to use any means to get what they want. This is why eights choose profitable professions which enable them to be leaders, although they refrain from ruling in the open, as number ones would. Number eights wear masks and act from behind the scenes. Yet, people trust them, because they are attracted by their innocence, for eights can be extremely naive.

Those who are on a life path eight have a strong personality, which can at times turn nasty. They are not frightened by the exceptional, the strange, and possibly dangerous experiences that destiny puts their way. Their path is twisted, strewn with ordeals that can be scary for some. But eights are exceptionally brave, although they are not always aware of danger. They instinctively know that they are protected by mysterious forces. Yet, they have to learn how to master and channel these secret powers. They also have to learn how to let go and moderate their appetites... One cannot consume everything! They have a strong will-power, which they can also use to serve and benefit other people. They are blessed with Luck. Despite life's tribulations, they are able to bounce back and start anew in many different fields, achieving success for themselves as well as for others around them.

Shared Life Path 8

If these two forces of nature manage to agree on a common goal, they will create a happy and fruitful life. Their life will be filled with the unexpected, without which they will annihilate each other. Eights need to be monitored and advised, for they never hesitate to explore all of life's possible experiences, including those

191

which are obscure. In such a case, we may wonder if eights are wise advisers for eights...

Two eights together are drawn to experiencing all sorts of domains without limits, from material and spiritual possessions to intense earthly pleasures. They look for enjoyment and will struggle to avoid life's hardships. Violent arguments can be expected. Everything to do with children and their education is not particularly favored.

Life Path 8 vs. Life Path 9

This association is very positive, in that eights are able to bring a great deal of energy to their partners, who tend to lack willpower. In turn, nines are able to provide gentle wisdom which eights tend to lack. Eights can at times be harsh, because they do not know how to control their feelings.

The partnership is all the more positive in that they complement one another. Eights do not regard nines as competitors and are therefore willing to protect and support them. They offer nines their shoulders to lean on and are skilled at cheering up their partner as they love to play the savior. In turn, nines are subtle and empathetic philosophers and as such, are able to find the right words and suitable tone of voice to help their partner, without offending eights' sensitive feelings. Although nines will never be fooled by eights' manipulations and appetites, they will understand and forgive them.

Life Path 8 vs. Life Path 11

This partnership is difficult, in that we have an idealistic person associated with a pragmatic person. How can revolutionary and spiritual elevens complement possessive and earthly eights? The discrepancy is huge between these beings who are likely not to understand each other at all. They both enjoy having leverage on other people, and yet they use very different means to reach their goals. Mood swings and outbursts are to be expected.

This being said, eights can prove to be excellent partners, provided they make up for elevens' lack of persistence and meet their financial needs. In turn, elevens can supervise and set rules for eights who sometimes lack virtue. However, finding common ground for exchanges and understanding involves tremendous effort from both of them. However, they do deeply admire one another, each recognizing the other's strength, provided no vital stakes are present.

Life Path 8 vs. Life Path 22

This association is both pragmatic and profitable. Neither overshadows the other. On the contrary, they help and support each other. Eights do not see twenty-twos as foes, but rather acknowledge and respect their strength and ability to create projects in the long term. This is actually the ideal framework for eights who never have their fill of power and earthly pleasures. In turn, twenty-twos have found here a reliable associate, who teaches them to discover the hidden and the ins and outs of his/her undertakings. Eights may even financially support twenty-twos, who being cautious and righteous, might not be willing to take the side routes that unscrupulous eights suggest. This being said, twenty-twos also possess a strong earthly appetite and for this they are both likely to be in agreement. Eights will disclose the mysteries and secrets to twenty-twos who will in turn give them shape and form. In addition, twenty-twos will appreciate eights' naive innocence.

Life Path 9

Those whose life path is nine tend to escape whatever disturbs their peace and quiet they love so much. The world they live in is far from reality. They live in a higher spiritual realm. Their natural empathy and ability to perceive people's subtle intentions, give them a mysterious aura and personality. They are deeply affected by human suffering and despair; and are torn between the need to escape an ugly world and their longing to offer help to those who need it. They are very sensitive to the subjective world, travel and dreams. They must learn not to run from what disturbs, upsets or stresses them, so as to confront reality and establish themselves.

They can be successful in very diverse fields, provided they have contact with other people and feel useful. They are skilled at meeting other people's needs, which is why they can be found in professions such as traders, social workers, teachers, and diplomats. Deep inside though, they love to play but must be careful not to regard everything as a game. They are particularly sensitive to the arts and music; art for them being a way to bring harmony to their environment. They are liable to be overly sensitive and extremely generous, which can indicate they may find themselves in delicate situations. This is why they need to learn how to protect themselves and not give everything away disproportionately. They must also learn how to structure their lives and take more care of what they consume. In other words: a little more discipline, so as to overcome their lethargic tendency. Water is very beneficial for them.

Their spiritual longing sometimes encourages them to behave like a guru. In such a case they must pay attention to keep their ideas clear so not to lead people into dead-ends or vague dreams. In other words: be more realistic! Overcoming their fears remains nines' most significant challenge.

Shared Life Path 9

As long as they do not sink into a dull and inconsistent life, they can benefit each other a lot. They would never harm each other, but this is precisely what can prevent them from making decisions and choices. By attempting to protect themselves from any aggressive exchanges, they risk ending up in uncommunicative silences. This being said, they are skilled at telepathically communicating and sensing what the other one does not say out loud.

They can find common ground in fields such as social work, trade or teaching. They may go through life unseen by others, as they tend to favor their personal interests and consensual relationships.

Life Path 9 vs. Life Path 11

From nines' perspective, sharing life with elevens' is not easy. Nines do understand their partner's motivations and want to support them but... they can get very upset by elevens' excessive behavior. They will however benefit from this partnership, provided they learn how to overcome their fear and accept to be shaken up. As for elevens, although they will not benefit from unswerving support by nines, if they succeed in moderating their impulsive behavior, they will gain a certain form of stability and a first step towards serenity.

With this association, the biggest risk is that nines may lose interest and be tempted to walk away. In such a case, elevens will then seek adventure elsewhere. Nevertheless, through their common goals, they are able to walk a short path together.

Note: In the case where there is a sub-number 20 on Life Path 11, the association is easier. (See also Life Path 2 and 9)

Life Path 9 vs. Life Path 22

In this association, twenty-twos prove to be excellent protectors to timid nines. Thanks to their strength, twenty-twos are able to shape life serenely and calmly: exactly what nines appreciate above all. There is nothing to be worried about, as both individuals support one another. Nines' diplomacy serve to help twenty-twos, who hate being shaken up, let go of their reserve and natural resistance. This partnership is one that is built in the long term, on solid foundations. They are both searching for an idyllic setting to live in, possibly near nature. They enjoy receiving guests and making their lives enjoyable. They are likely to volunteer and become involved in charity or social work. Their children will be blessed. Yet, they need to keep in mind not to fall into a certain lassitude nor give in to the temptation of living only in their inner world and keeping their private life hidden as this could lead to a form of withdrawal from society.

Life Path 11

Those whose Life Path is 11 strive to move beyond their limits and daily routine, so as to escape from a cumbersome life. They are fueled by a strong faith and conviction in their goals and potential. Yet, they emphasize their ideals excessively and wish everyone would embrace them as much as they do. They have a nervous and impulsive nature, which can be very tiring for those around them. They must learn how to channel their anger and rebellious feelings.

Elevens are not easy to follow. Indeed, while they strive to be nice and helpful, they quickly give in to their impulsive instincts and susceptibility, thus pushing away the very people who might have been useful in supporting and encouraging them. They are not without intelligence or abilities to succeed, but they do suffer from a terrible lack of patience.

With time, they will slowly gain in wisdom and will understand that what is important for them may not be as important for other people. In this respect, much necessary rethinking of their way of being will occur in their life. They can be attracted by many diverse fields. They are skilled at pioneering and finding new paths, paving the way for others. They actually thrive on the idea of having other people walk in their wake.

The associative fields will be more or less probable; especially if the sub-number 20 is found among the other sub-numbers of this Life Path. Elevens are not true stand-alone independent people, in that they love being free but need other people's presence.

Shared Life Path 11

Depending on whether 20 is found within the calculations of the sub-numbers or not, this association will vary. Both of them are impulsive and angry, which does not help. Nevertheless, this aspect will be considerably subdued by the presence of 20/2. Both of them are attached to common goals and ideals. Together, they strive to step out of their routine and free themselves from a limited and restrictive world. As long as they are able to understand one another and share the same goals, they will benefit from this collaboration. As soon as they stop understanding each other, violent conflicts will arise. They are set on conquering the world, transforming society and opening the eyes of their co-citizens! However, they are far too susceptible and directive to be able to share a quiet life together.

Life Path 11 vs. Life Path 22

These human beings have opposite natures. Quiet, structured and disciplined twenty-twos are unwilling to accept the turmoil elevens are liable to trigger in their lives, especially when their routine is disturbed. Twenty-twos consider that nothing worthwhile can stem from agitation. Elevens will never understand why twenty-twos won't listen to them. Please note that if sub-number 20 is found behind 11, this will then depict more favorable conditions towards compromise. i.e. 11/2 and 22 will be able to find common agreement.

Twenty-twos are as idealistic as elevens, but their methods to reach their goals are very different. Elevens are impatient, whereas twenty-twos have time on their sides. Both of them have very set personalities and strong tempers, which makes confrontations unavoidable. Once again, if sub-number 20 is found within Life Path 11, then 11 will definitely pacify 22, thus bringing about a more harmonious relationship. Please also refer to sub-numbers 4 within Life Path 22.

Life Path 22

The profound natures of those with Life Path 22 have a very ancient heritage. We are in the presence of old souls who have gained significant knowledge through their numerous past lives. Whether they are aware of this or not doesn't matter. They are wise beings who intuitively know how the laws and mechanisms of Life work. They are convinced they can achieve their aspirations thanks to their reliable ally: Time. They know the possible traps on their path to avoid.

They have a strong personality and a great ability in facing adversity. Yet, they can become paralyzed by the weight of their ancient knowledge, which may feel burdensome. They must therefore learn when to keep it at bay, as they give the impression of not being bothered with daily tasks. They also need to overcome their pessimistic tendencies which can make them appear cold, serious and austere.

Transgenerational issues are important to them. These beings are more or less marked by the footsteps of their ancestors, to the point that they may also project the same to their own descendants. They must learn to be lighter, more carefree and joyful. They emphasize all that is connected to nature and home. They need to ensure their lives are productive. They aim to leave their mark on their lineage.

Shared Life Path 22

It is relatively rare that both partners only have 22 as a final result of all the calculations in the life path. This is why one seldom comes across such an instance... These individuals will get along very well if they both aim at leading the life of a monk. They tend to worry far too much about the way things might, could or should have been. They can be great builders or politicians. If number 4 is well present, which is often the case, family matters will be particularly favored, protected and harmonious. They are also very attached to children and animals, and are likely to set up peaceful havens for them. Trade is also favored.

CHAPTER V

Aspects between the Expression Numbers

"In contemplating Love and Pity, I forgot the differences between myself and others."

Milarepa (Tibetan Yogi)

Definition: Along with the Life Path, the Expression Number is one of the most important indicators of the theme. It depicts the person's way of expressing, how they behave in front of other people and how they convey their views on Life, and their profound beliefs. It deals with the exterior aspect of the person, as is perceived by the outside world. As a matter of fact, most people only pay attention to the outward aspects. As a consequence, they are liable to confuse a person's profound inner nature with what the person shows, i.e. Life Path vs. Expression Number.

The Expression Number can be regarded as the exterior signature of a person: what does the person wish to show, when she/he addresses someone? As exterior characteristics may be very different from the person's inner nature, one should certainly not rely on superficial appearances.

How it is worked out: Reduce the addition of the value of each letter of every first name declared at birth plus the mother's birth last name.

Example: Suppose somebody has the name Peter Henry Taylor, whose mother's last name was Smith (her maiden name).

```
Peter Henry Smith
75259 85597 14928
7+5+2+5+9+8+5+5+9+7+1+4+9+2+8=86
86 → 8+6 = 14 → 1+4 = 5
```

Peter's Expression Number is 5

Expression 1

Expression Number 1 emphasizes the chauvinistic side of the person. The image of the father (or anyone who might have played that role) is very strong.

Development of one's abilities is highlighted. Intensity, natural authority, will power and courage are very present. These people aim at having leverage on the people around them. They are independent and passionate.

They are also good guides, who know how to set rules and organize things. They are initiators, who can pioneer new ways; but they often fail to finish their tasks, relying on subordinates to complete what they have launched. In extreme behavior their spontaneity can highlight theirs faults such as selfishness, being dictatory and susceptible.

Expression 1 vs. Expression 1

The sincere, direct and virile expression of these two people will only be possible if they pursue identical goals and/or if both of them have transcended their karma (see theme indicators). Provided they have freed themselves from their powerful egos, they will have a lasting relationship, as they are intelligent enough to be able to do so.

They are naturally straightforward and therefore can talk about things openly. They are able to tell each other what they truly think. Being able to hear what your partner thinks of you is certainly not easy and requires wisdom. It is imperative that neither partner tries to have ascendancy over the other. An intense and brief passion might bring them together for a short time, but a lack of common objectives can pull them apart just as quickly as it began. However, mutual pride and admiration for each other can seal their union. Progress, innovation and the spirit of adventure are favored.

Expression 1 vs. Expression 2

Expression number 2 portrays an emotional, shy and secretive personality. This is the complete opposite of Expression number 1. Twos communicate through intimate understanding. Luckily, ones can understand number 2's sensitivity thanks to their spontaneity and liveliness, although they might miss the smaller details. Ones are direct and can't be bothered with the extra details. This doesn't suit twos, who would like their partner to be more lenient and make more allowances. Nevertheless, they are likely to appreciate each other's differences.

Despite obvious differences, they can admire each other for what they do not possess, thus giving way to a beautiful complementary union. Ones stimulate Twos, by helping them not to wallow in their past, particularly their childhood. Twos acknowledge Ones' strength and support, which make them feel safe. In turn, Ones admire Twos' ability to soothe and comfort.

As long as Ones don't given in to their sometimes ruthless tendencies and accept Twos' hypersensitivity, everything is possible. If not...

Expression 1 vs. Expression 3

Such an association can be very profitable, in that both individuals are optimistic, direct and straightforward. Dialogue, communication and expression are favored. Ones respond to Threes' need for challenge. They provide them with many possibilities and opportunities to advance. Threes find Ones inspiring, in that they have the precious quality of being able to do without long analyses and excessive details. Threes can be irritating, with their need to plan and organize every single thing, and telling others what to do. They are often very skeptical and need proof. Ones should however listen to them more.

Both need to guide and direct others. This is why they will need to compromise. If not, confrontations are unavoidable.

This association can only be successful if both manage to make their goals come true, otherwise they are liable to blame each other for their own failures. Threes' bitter criticisms are likely upset egotistical Ones, but Ones are equally able to hurt Threes' feelings. Beware!

Expression 1 vs. Expression 4

Ones are outgoing, very much unlike Fours. Can this association still work? Ones' expression might seem a little too active and intrusive to Fours, who enjoy nothing more than their peace and quiet. This leads to a great deal of misunderstanding: Ones feel frustrated and blame their partner for not making enough effort. Whereas Fours consider Ones' spontaneity useless and tiring. Brave Ones with cautious Fours do not make for a smooth relationship. This being said, pragmatic Fours can help their partner calm down, and Ones may manage to push Fours to act with a little more enthusiasm.

Yet, communication problems are bound to occur. Working towards a common goal will help. Ones will have to be very patient when listening to gloomy Fours. All the more so, because if Fours feel misunderstood, they shut down.

Expression 1 vs. Expression 5

We have here two passionate beings with spontaneous and straightforward natures who are able to get along perfectly well. This association often leads to passionate though brief encounters. Fives are free, independent and communicative. They may seem carefree or superficial, but this does not bother Ones, who are also very direct and somewhat brutal in their ways of explaining things and expecting to be obeyed. Both thrive on adventure and cannot stand to stay at home. Exploring new horizons can lead to extra conjugal relationships. In keeping with their personalities they often talk more than actually do.

Because they like a certain freedom and independence, they must respect each other's privacy and not tread on each other's space. Otherwise, it will not work. As they often express themselves with humor, which is sometimes caustic, they need to be careful not to come across as superficial. If they want the relationship to work, they will have to sit down and look each other squarely in the eye and express what their souls truly feel, otherwise they risk taking each other for granted. Intimacy and home life is not their cup of tea. They need to learn to be responsible and to think in terms of the community, not just oneself. They are likely to live outside of society, but tend to meet a lot of interesting and rewarding people.

Expression 1 vs. Expression 6

Such a relationship is suffused with intelligence and courtesy which can work very well. Ones never explain much of their plans. They will learn a lot from Sixes, who are good at explaining what suits them and what doesn't and why. Ones respect their partner, who aim for perfection and never hesitate to improve the way things are. Sixes also appreciate sudden impulsive action, but are pragmatic enough to gauge the right situations. Ones can be very touchy and Sixes do not refrain from telling their partner what they think. This is why both will need to compromise, or else... This being said, Ones often look for efficient collaborators, so as to carry out their projects. They have found the ideal partner with Sixes, who are skilled and serious.

Moreover, Sixes do not merely accept vague ideas, thus obliging Ones to explain things on a deeper level. In turn, Ones will help Sixes to be a little less conformist. But be careful! This relationship might lead into a self-complacency and self-congratulatory attitude, so they need to be careful not to fall into snobbism. They must also keep in mind not to close themselves off from the outside world, thinking that their truth is worth more than the rest. This being said, their exchanges are rich and rewarding. They mutually support each other, so as to advance their limits.

Expression 1 vs. Expression 7

These personalities can get along very well. The relationship is positive, even if it can be incisive at times. Both use their sense of humor to lighten up the atmosphere and soften the differences between them. There is true respect. Nevertheless, their ways of expressing are very different, which often triggers misunderstandings. They both desire a certain form of balance, and try to create a peaceful and comfortable environment. The harmony they have managed to create will help them face any hardships coming from the outside, and benefits their mutual wellbeing. Discussions are rich and profound, even though they might not be understood by other people, as their conversations are often tinged with the obscure and mystical.

Their way of expressing is often intellectual, although the physical is not absent, as they use their body language to make themselves understood. Yet, they must be careful not to think they are above everybody else, or they might close themselves off from the outside world that they tend to scorn for being vulgar or uninteresting.

Expression 1 vs. Expression 8

Although their personalities are opposed, these two expressions are able to get along, in terms of success in business projects and attaining wealth. They are motivated by a particular desire to carry out common projects, especially those that are of an ambitious nature. Yet, opposition between them may be significant and thus result in conflict. Both of them must find agreement, otherwise they will destroy each other. The violence and rage they express in public may prove extremely difficult for the people around them.

They are often accompanied by influential (at times highly-placed) people and opportunities for success. Both have a great spirit of initiative, including for that of sexual matters. They can prove very direct and saucy, which is likely to shock certain people. They are straightforward and can't be bothered by romantic frippery. They enjoy a certain form of naughtiness and look to spice up their sex life. If they get to know each other and tame themselves a little, they can be very successful. Their relationship is one of undertakings, success and developing their mutual potential.

Expression 1 vs. Expression 9

Their individual ways of expressing themselves are very different, which results in significant opposition. They must accept each other's differences, or else, their relationship is jeopardized.

Ones are straightforward whereas Nines are obsessed with being nice and polite. Without a great effort made to accept and understand each other, the relationship is bound to fail. Without any doubts, the biggest job concerns Ones, who must learn how to subdue their aggressive nature, in order to reassure Nines, who get upset by contentious behavior.

If they manage to get along, their sex life will be harmonious and fulfilling. If not, the relationship may evolve into S&M dynamics, Ones being the active and nines the passive.

As far as finances are concerned, ups and downs are to be expected.

Unfortunately this will heighten Nines' feelings of insecurity. Ones go after ambitious personal success, whereas Nines only want a peaceful environment and happy relationships. However, the major differences in their views may act as a powerful lever to help them understand that a middle ground must be found, and that extremes are not a solution. In this sense, such a relationship favors inner transformation.

Expression 1 vs. Expression 11

The expression of such a relationship is impulsive, excitable and challenging. Both persons are determined to leave an imprint of their personality on those around them. As long as there is some agreement in their exchanges, all will go smoothly. But if this is not the case, arguments are bound to happen. The relationship can be very positive, but it certainly isn't peaceful. Each of them must make a great effort not to overshadow the other, nor to give orders to the other partner. This is especially the case with Ones, who can be very direct and adamant; whereas, Elevens are more aware of other people's needs and therefore act accordingly. As far as financial matters are concerned, ups and downs are to be expected, for while both are pioneers who are skilled at scouting, they are not very competent when it comes to completing the tasks they have started. They must learn how to be more consistent. If it is adventure they are after, they have it.

Sexually speaking, it's either everything or nothing. In other words, they may trigger fireworks at times or nothing at all because they are far too busy elsewhere.

Expression 1 vs. Expression 22

These two protagonists are diametrically opposed. Ones speak easily with open minds, whereas Twenty-twos refrain from conveying their feelings, emotions and opinions. Both of them can be very proud and domineering, although in different ways. Concerning finances, they can help each other a lot. Twenty-twos bring persistency and balance, whereas Ones bring the energy and new ideas. In other words, Ones initiate the projects that Twenty-twos then put into operation. Concerning finances, Ones can rely on their partner, to maintain what they have gained. Nevertheless, in more intimate matters, the association is awkward. Twenty-twos hate being pushed and bossed around. And Ones are likely to walk away as soon as they feel they don't get enough excitable reaction.

Concerning sexuality, they might have to schedule appointments according to their busy agendas, if they want to meet! Twenty-twos like sex, as long as it's enjoyed with care and time, whereas Ones are excessive and don't have time...

Expression 2

The personality of this number is suffused with emotion, which may cause speech difficulties. These people are searching for harmony and agreement. They do all they can to avoid conflict, thus escaping adversity. They are the perfect subordinates, being fearful and scrupulous. They may therefore come across as obliging, accommodating and available. Yet, this is not always the case. Their whimsical nature can make them selfish, eccentric and selective. But when they are searching for the ideal partner, they are unable to assert themselves and, under pressure, will tend to accept anyone. They are stay-at-home people.

Expression Two can be the rare result of the sub-number 20, in adding all the values of the letters of the first names of the person plus the mother's maiden name. Or expression Two can also come from the direct addition of Aspiration 11 (all the vowels) and Potential 9 (all the consonants), in which case we would have the following for our example: $9 + 11 = 20 -> 2$.

Expression 2 vs. Expression 2

These two identical personalities have poor energy. Their emotional natures prevent them from gaining momentum, so that often initiatives fall short. The relationship is nevertheless one of harmony, with little conflict. They both search for a peaceful environment; and want to lead lives away from aggressivity and frenzy. Regarding intimate matters, they always endeavor not to hurt each other's feelings. They act scrupulously and their sexuality is cautious. Tenderness and respect come before passion. They will have to be careful not to close themselves up in their little universe, far from the hectic world.

They are both very charitable and likely to host, protect and help other people. They also give assistance, using their financial affluence, without being excessive. Such a relationship emphasizes family and social recognition.

Expression 2 vs. Expression 3

There is a real possibility that such a relationship will lead to Eternal love, as their personalities are prone to this form of expression. Both search for contact and dialogue, and enjoy having people around them. Communicative joy is present, thanks to Threes' playful expression who doesn't regard Twos as rivals. Shy Twos will learn a lot from expressive Threes, who will teach them to be more self-confident and less fearful of the unknown. Threes must nevertheless pay attention to their sometimes lively and hurtful way of expressing themselves, which can be upsetting to emotional Twos'. Threes favor contact with the outside world which encourages intimate close relationships. Youth is emphasized, which enables them to reach out for the new and sensational, and not be encumbered by daily routine. Everything must be enjoyable, which can prevent them from taking the bull by the horns when need be. Collaboration together should not be at the top of their priorities as their ways of expressing themselves are so different. They must also be careful not to indulge too much in material acquisitions, or their finances will suffer. They will find this hard to do, as they are predisposed to enjoying life and sharing its pleasures together.

Expression 2 vs. Expression 4

As with good wine, this relationship gets better with time. Both are materialistic and protective and share a desire for a comfortable life. They are able to spend significant amounts of energy to reach this goal. However, they lack imagination and can prove too conformist at times. Their lives are overflowing with work activities. They particularly appreciate people who meet their criteria i.e. discipline, order, common sense and efficiency.

As far as sexuality is concerned, they are more sensual then sexual, preferring soft tenderness to intense sex. They avoid arguments. Their finances are bound to prosper, as they invest and save with extreme care. They can be drawn to advocate a worthy cause. Such a relationship favors a responsible and harmonious family life.

Expression 2 vs. Expression 5

These two are very drawn to one another. Fives are attracted by the charm and sensuality of Twos, whereas Twos are sensitive to the encouraging words and admiration their partners express to them. Fives drive them to try new experiences and to discover the hidden treasures of life. They enjoy a play on words and may therefore come across as two-faced. Fives' ability to speak and explain can help Twos become more outgoing and even (almost) rebellious. When they get along, they can be very eccentric, having very diversified tastes and original ways of behaving. They love to adapt to situations and people.

Fives will take their partners away with them on journeys, to discover all sorts of cultures. They have fun and appreciate entertainment. Yet, Twos must compromise, in order to put up with excitable and nervous Fives.

Sexually speaking, they get along well, provided Fives accept to calm down a little and Twos accept their partners' restlessness and somewhat intrusive friendships. They might want to search for elements to liven up their sex life.

Fives dedicate a lot of time to their outside occupations, whereas Twos are more focused on family life. Twos are likely to bring financial equilibrium to Fives. Behind a seemingly carefree surface, they are both interested in exploring the secret and profound aspects of life.

Expression 2 vs. Expression 6

The association is balanced, in spite of Twos' emotional excesses – which are often due to Sixes' criticisms. Sixes lay emphasis on appropriate language and expression. According to them, words have a meaning and they make this known. Nevertheless, they do look for harmony by avoiding conflict, which may result in a certain form of immobility or non-aggressive pact. Art is the mode of expression they prefer. They are also sensitive to their loved ones' hardships. Associations, help and support are favored. Although they don't participate in competition, they like to keep in physical shape and stay healthy. They strive to protect their privacy and only disclose their true nature to very intimate friends.

As far as sexuality is concerned, their pleasures are found in mutual respect and the desire to satisfy each other's needs. Twos' emotions can override their common sense, which is liable to upset Sixes. But as they want to avoid conflict, Sixes will accept this and place heart over reason. They express their good taste discreetly and appreciate a comfortable life, even though these are not their priorities. They are able to create a satisfying life for everyone. They are particularly sensitive to issues of justice, equality and honesty.

Expression 2 vs. Expression 7

The relationship is based on what is unsaid. They avoid insults and arguments by concentrating on their interests and peace. This does not prevent them from taking good care of one another and never missing an opportunity to please each other.

Sevens are unafraid of emotional Twos, who they don't consider as rivals. Twos can always trust in Sevens' protection. They might be disturbed though by Sevens' independent and adventurous spirit who looks to argue outside the home. They enjoy sharing their views on current issues. They are both very attached to family life and are drawn to teaching. They will in any case teach their children. They love being around educated and rewarding people, although they may feel misunderstood by their loved ones because they are so selective in their relationships.

Regarding sexuality, they love to set up scenarios and make up stories. Religion and other noble causes are likely to strengthen their connection. However, they don't understand each other's emotions very well.

They must pay attention not to always be worrying about their finances, as this will create misunderstandings over what are often imaginary frustrations. Such a relationship encourages both to develop greater empathy to better understand other people.

Expression 2 vs. Expression 8

Both express a very particular intimate sensitivity. Twos are very emotional, while Eights aim at satisfying themselves. Eights do not regard Twos as a potential source of conflict, for they are strong enough to face life on their own. Through their powerful intuition, Twos will manage to calm their companions, who may appear austere and inaccessible because they are trying to hide and protect their secret world. With time, they will reach a balance which will enable them to improve their relations which is often based on what is unsaid. Eights' skills for power and finance can make Twos feel safe and tranquil. Eights' awareness of human despair makes them want to help other people, as do Twos. They are lucky people and easily attract support from others, as well as unexpected financial profits. They are interested in money and will need to agree on how to manage it, if they want their partnership to last.

Regarding sexuality, they get along well. Twos easily comply with Eights' fantasies. Yet, problems appear when they are not in sync due to being too preoccupied with other things in their life. If Twos expect a lot of tenderness and love, they will be disappointed and their frustration may lead to major tensions. In order to maintain a united relationship, they must learn to know each other better and to accept each other's emotions.

Expression 2 vs. Expression 9

Both individuals lay great emphasis on peace and gentleness, which might lead to living in an illusion. Their obsession for unity drives them to preserve their quiet life at any cost, therefore avoiding confrontation. They are calm, quiet and diplomatic. They are sometimes regarded as non-conformist pacifists. They enjoy and aim to live a protected life in a comfortable environment.

Arts in general are favored, particularly music. They must be careful not to escape from everyday life.

They associate inspiration with sexuality, thereby finding new ways to use their combined energies subtly through innovating spiritual techniques. They will have to learn how to manage their money and be more determined and focused, and claim their rights, as money is not among their priorities.

Expression 2 vs. Expression 11

Twos' main trait is gentleness. They love to protect their loved ones and turn their world into a peaceful haven. They have no problem accepting excessive and eccentric Elevens, even if they find them a bit tiring with time. Despite their constant need to explore and feel independent and free, Elevens are very sensitive and will therefore easily get along with Twos. As it is, they agree on most things, especially if humor, kindness and tenderness are present. Twos, who search for financial and material safety above all, may find Elevens difficult to put up with, as they are not consistent in this area. Professionally speaking, Twos can manage the business, while Elevens look for clients, thanks to their numerous contacts and gift in making new ones. Twos wish for a quiet home and as long as they create one big enough to fit in all of Elevens' friends, everything will be fine. If not, elevens are likely to come home late.

Concerning sexuality, they will not necessarily explore all of Karma Sutra, but they will nevertheless be satisfied and happy. Everything will go well, provided Elevens accept Twos' desires to have children.

Expression 2 vs. Expression 22

Gentle, emotional Twos are often immature. They never face confrontation directly nor impose their points of view, as they fear harsh reality. This is exactly the opposite of Twenty-twos, who are strong and adamant when it comes to conveying what they hold true. In this sense, Twos and Twenty-twos are opposed, while paradoxically, being very complementary to each other. Twenty-twos are good advisors for fearful Twos: through their protection and strength, and will encourage them to be more self-confident. In turn, Twos will soften abrasive Twenty-twos, through their gentle ways. Money matters are particularly favored in this relationship.

Sexually speaking they get along well, despite not being very romantic. Both are very attached to family and will therefore want to have many children. They may set up refuges for people in need.

Expression 3

A charming personality marked by generosity, availability and a true gift for listening. These people enjoy livening things up, by speaking their minds, sometimes too openly. They love talking and contradicting people. They may not be very consistent, but they are easily forgiven as they are so much fun to be around! Socially speaking, they want to seduce and might therefore come across as two-faced, to the point they may end up lost in their own labyrinth.

Because they are interested in so many diverse issues, they want to explore all sorts of different domains. Their personality is witty and smart, and at times they may upset people. They must try not to criticize what they dislike, nor give their opinions when not asked. They are firebrands, preaching what is wrong in order to know what is right or to obtain information through third parties. They are dynamic, especially when they feel supported. Threes are efficient and practical, knowing how to get straight to the point. They are creative, love challenges and are skilled at getting to know people from all sorts of diverse cultures. At times they can be complacent and/or superficial.

Expression 3 vs. Expression 3

These two mischievous beings, who can at times be aggressive, are also surprising. They can agree or disagree, intensely. They obviously have a lot in common and they easily share together, like carefree teenagers. They enjoy life as much as they do competition which, if there is no contradiction, will lead them to live their goals. Their chosen field is turned towards interpersonal relationships. They have genuine capacities for exploring varied fields, such as the arts, dancing, photography, or anything related to the mind, including special techniques and teaching. Threes seldom express themselves with restraint; which is why they need to focus more, yet neither of them is able to do this. They will need to be open to outside ideas; otherwise their critical spirit may overwhelm them when there are problems. They need to be less superficial and more persistent in what they aim to achieve. Finances will go through ups and downs.

As far as sexuality is concerned, it can be everything or nothing. Either an endless discovery of each other, or disinterest due to a lack of depth and intimacy.

Expression 3 vs. Expression 4

The relationship can work as long as protective Fours do not try to limit carefree Threes too much. Although they are very rational beings, Threes hate feeling restrained. Fours will therefore find it difficult putting up with Threes' immature behavior, although they will certainly appreciate their rigorous organizational skills. Fours need to be stimulated, but not too much! They both need time to discover and learn about each other, particularly Threes who are always in a hurry. Both are searching for peace, even if Threes, because they are so straightforward, often attract opposition.

As Threes enjoy expressing themselves about everything, they don't understand their partners, who seem to prefer to linger endlessly over pointless discussions. Fours are craftspeople who like efficiency and dealing with what is down to earth. They are calm and quiet, unlike Threes, who are quick and restless. Fours are introverts whereas Threes are extroverts. Threes are not persistent where finances are concerned, but they can rely on Fours to manage money.

Sexually speaking, they aren't very compatible as Fours need to live their feelings and sensations intensely, whereas Threes are more intellectual.

Expression 3 vs. Expression 5

This relationship is not a smooth and quiet one, as they both want to express whatever they feel and think. They are very lively, love challenges and are genuinely optimistic. Yet neither of them is very stable. They are original, different and set on showing this to the world. They must try to calm their fervor and be more temperate, if they don't want to end up in permanent dispute. Their happy spirits will definitely help skirt the obstacles they are bound to face.

They can bring a lot to each other as they love to share and help each other. They will need to learn wisdom.

They can seem superficial and aloof to reality, or a little absent-minded. As far as finances are concerned, ups and downs are to be expected, as neither is able to accept advice. They prefer doing things their own way. They love to have many relationships. Their wealth comes from their experience and network of contacts. We can say that Threes are more critical, therefore wiser when it comes to action.

Regarding sexuality, they can get along, provided they arrive on time for their date and take time out for each other. They are likely to try out positions from the Kamasutra, on the back of a whale! And why not? There is always a first time for everything.

Expression 3 vs. Expression 6

This relationship may seem idyllic at first; for they both strive for perfection and aim to be excellent in whatever they do. Yet, things are not perfect, particularly when they give in to criticizing and struggle to coerce one another into complying. They deeply respect each other, but can end up becoming bored, in wanting to prove how serious they are. They need to overcome their desire for absolute perfection, or they can become paralyzed and not move forward in their evolution. They enjoy everything to do with art, decoration, and home improvement. They are intelligent, understand each other well, and aspire to make their union as perfect as possible. They are adamant about children's education and often get involved in social projects. They wish to create a perfect world, materially and financially, for they like to feel satisfied. In any case, this is what they want the world to believe. They are attentive to people's advice about avoiding hardship. Their finances are favored, as long as they accept life's constraints and setbacks.

As far as their sex life is concerned, they need to stop analyzing so much, otherwise they risk missing out on true sensual pleasure. It is advised they relax and accept that the physical body has its own needs as well as imperfections.

Expression 3 vs. Expression 7

Their ways of expressing themselves are diametrically opposed, which is why they have a lot to learn from each other. Both are very communicative, but while one is direct, straightforward and opens up easily, the other is more shy and carefully selects who he/she will talk to as well as what he/she says. The relationship is at times difficult, but is truly complementary. They are both curious, although one is happy to glide over the surface of things, while the other always looks to go deeper into an issue. If they have a common goal, they are able to put up with what annoys each about the other. They are both strategists fond of teaching, communicating and mastering all aspects of their lives. They tend to quickly criticize the details that aren't quite right. Unlike Threes, who are skeptical and rational, Sevens are attached to their faith and ideals. They will choose to explore many diverse ways and methods to achieve a comfortable life.

As far as their sex life is concerned, they need to give in to their fertile and powerful imagination, which will prevent them from ending up in a stagnant routine.

Expression 3 vs. Expression 8

The relationship is original, in that Threes are straightforward and never try to conceal anything, whereas Eights do exactly the opposite. Eights can be spontaneous too, and therefore expressive, yet they instinctively know how to keep their secrets. They have a suspicious disposition, for they know better than anyone the murky swamp of peoples' inner natures. Nevertheless, the relationship can be profitable, as Eights will feel safe with their partners, even if at times they have to accept their remarks and criticisms. Although their ways of expressing are very different, both strive to make a strong impression on the people around them. Discussions can prove very positive. Eights bring their calmness, while Threes bring their stamina. They love challenges, which explain why they are a good team, capable of facing life's obstacles. They must learn how to select their friends and relationships with care, so as to maintain their privacy. They have a lot of energy, which allows them all sorts of opportunities to be successful, particularly as they are both very pragmatic.

They also enjoy experimenting and discovering all aspects of sexuality. Yet, they must be careful their sex life doesn't become merely a sportive feat. Eights will manage to talk Threes into letting down their barriers, particularly when the latter become too cerebral.

Expression 3 vs. Expression 9

The relationship can prove very awkward, in that Threes never stop from rising to new challenges, while Nines search for quiet, peace and comfort. Nevertheless, they can get along, for Nines know how to compromise and are able to understand why their partners are so agitated. In general, Nines express themselves with care and goodwill, always careful not to hurt anyone's feelings. However, this is not the case of Threes, who are very direct and bluntly say what they think, no matter what. This being said, they can get along, providing they both make an effort to understand each other (which at first glance does not look easy).

Nines have to accept to follow restless Threes (often against their will), which will force them to show a bit more resistance. As for their partners, threes will have to calm down and be less impatient. They can do a lot together as many different domains and activities are open to them. Educational and social matters are particularly favored.

They are willing to do anything to protect themselves financially, although they consider that money exists mainly to achieve and fulfill their dreams. Friendships can be numerous and beneficial, including friendships from abroad.

As far as their sex life is concerned, the refined and romantic atmosphere provided by Nines will fully satisfy Threes, who can be a little inhibited when expressing their feelings. Threes will become more gentle.

Expression 3 vs. Expression 11

Their expression may appear over done to the point that it may come across as fake and superficial. They are likely to agree on many diverse fields where logical reasoning is involved with the need to debate and convince. As long as they are on common ground and can communicate without being too aggressive, everything will be fine. If not, the relationship is likely to generate much conflict. Both can be a little too quick and straightforward at times. If they are looking for a lasting relationship, they will need to learn to be gentler with each other and not automatically resort to being competitive.

As far as their sex life is concerned, their cerebral minds can take precedence, which is why things may become difficult. They must try to relax and let themselves express their feelings freely, instead of analyzing everything so much. To achieve this, their impulsive and youthful natures can bring this about, creating true complicity.

Expression 3 vs. Expression 22

Twenty-twos are silent most of the time. This is why they usually don't get along very well with Threes, who are direct and often intrusive. Twenty-twos do not express what they feel deep inside, nor do they tell their plans to others. They can't stand being told what to do and dislike having their privacy invaded. And this is precisely what Threes love to do! Such a relationship looks to be more of a teacher-pupil relationship, or a grandparent-grandchild relationship...

As far as their sex life is concerned, they are bound to have difficulties, in that Threes have an urge to talk things over and thrive on long exchanges, whereas Twenty-twos dislike details and prefer to go straight to the point.

Expression 4

As soon as they feel ill-at-ease, these people tend to oppose with inertia and their innate reserve. They usually don't express themselves openly, preferring to focus on work and efficiency. They feel at ease with tangible situations that they can stay in control of and master in their pragmatic way.

They are trustworthy, reliable and responsible and make a point of finishing what they have begun. They seldom take the initiative as they first need to feel safe before committing and launching any project. They listen to advice, although sometimes can be very stubborn. They appreciate their loved ones' support which is what they require before going ahead. Once they have made up their mind, they can be tremendously efficient. As their expression is deeply connected to efficiency, they are bound to succeed, even if it takes time. They must nevertheless refrain from becoming too rigid, adamant and absolute.

Expression 4 vs. Expression 4

The relationship can appear to be a good one, as they share similar ways of expressing themselves. Yet reality shows otherwise. While they both search for calm and comfort, they do so by expressing what they think as little as possible. This can lead to a lack of dynamic energy between the two.

This being said, if they have the same aspirations and if their jobs unite them, especially ones linked to trade or craftsmanship, everything will be fine. In most cases, efficiency, material achievement and enjoyment of whatever life can offer prevail. Yet, their difficulty in coming out of their reserved shell and truly expressing themselves can become a real issue. They are very attached to material and financial comfort, as well as to a peaceful and quiet family life.

As far as their sex life is concerned, they are both very committed to earthly pleasures. As a matter of fact, they enjoy all types of pleasure, not only sexual. They need to overcome their somewhat natural reserve and shyness.

Expression 4 vs. Expression 5

They are absolutely opposed in their way of expressing themselves. Fours are reserved and reticent, whereas Fives endlessly aim to go beyond the limits, to the point they might come across as superficial and indifferent. This being said, friendly Fives do enjoy teaming up with Fours, in that they particularly like their sensuality and calm quiet ways, which are a far cry from their own nervousness. Yet, Fours will need to keep in mind that Fives are fast moving and changeable at all times. They won't act covertly or refrain from saying what they think. Provided Fours manage to put up with their noisy and restless companion, everything will be fine. Otherwise, these two personalities will never get along! While Fives don't have an aggressive nature, they can be explosive at times! This is why they need to slow down a little when necessary and listen carefully to what their companion has to say.

In addition, finances and material aspects are not big priorities for Fives, unlike for Fours, who view them as essential. Here again, lengthy arguments can be expected!

As far as their sex life is concerned, the dynamics can be quite enjoyable, for Fives are extremely attracted to Fours' seductive charm. In turn, Fours love their partner's eccentricity.

Expression 4 vs. Expression 6

This promises to be an excellent relationship, as both of them enjoy pursuing their shared interests. Whether it is in a professional capacity, or at home, there are no clouds on the horizon. Fours have found here an ideal partner, who will relentlessly attempt to give form to what he/she wants to express. Not only are they deeply connected in their ways of being, they also enjoy material comfort, which is therefore likely to ensure that will have a pleasant and enjoyable life sooner or later. Because they hate nothing more than worrying about domestic issues, they tend to anticipate and manage their affairs well.

Their exchanges are respectful, benevolent and caring. Sixes love articulating their thoughts, making sure they are sensible and logical. This way of being might well put an end to Fours' continuous qualms and regrets over past and future worries. These two beings are united by a genuine quest for harmony, comfort and peace.

Sexually speaking, they get along just fine, expressing a great deal of tenderness and affection towards each other. They are likely to appreciate sensual pleasures such as massages etc...

Expression 4 vs. Expression 7

Sevens are enterprising and charming, which Fours were certainly not expecting in such abundance! Both are reserved, but each in his/her own way. They both refrain from revealing themselves, especially to people who are not part of their intimate circle. They are attracted to what is beautiful and, at times, costly. Sevens love to offer their loved ones presents, and Fours certainly appreciate this. They are therefore likely to get along very well, when it comes to expressing their needs and desires. They are looking for a nice and cozy environment, away from prying eyes. Their professional collaboration couldn't be more positive and beneficial. Sevens are wise and protective, while Fours are cautious and secular: they are therefore very complementary. The blend of Sevens' elitism and Fours' conservatism will allow them to put aside what doesn't suit them.
Sexually speaking, they both appreciate subtle and refined pleasures.

Expression 4 vs. Expression 8

Material and financial concerns are at the center of their debates. The most important thing for them is to have a certain amount of control over life's destiny. Fours strive to preserve their interests and what they own as they need to feel safe and never put blind trust in their partners. As long as suspicious Fours accept Eights' antics and refrain from interfering in their business, everything will be fine. If not, Eights are likely to feel their privacy has been violated. Neither of them actually wants to be noticed:

Fours due to their innate cautiousness, and Eights who don't want to reveal their plans (which are often shady).

As far as sexual matters are concerned, they can get along well provided Eights succeed in making Fours feel safe enough to open up. It must be noted that Fours are sensual, whereas Eights are sexual, which can cause a problem. Eights will need to be patient and understanding, if they want to explain to fours how nirvana can be reached through Kamasutra!

Expression 4 vs. Expression 9

This relationship is based on mutual understanding, thanks to Nines' innate empathy which enables them to sense what their partners need without them having to actually express it...This is perfect, as Fours don't like expressing themselves and would rather fret in silence. Fours do this so as to protect others, but they need to learn to say what they feel and think, especially when things go wrong. Fours are very sensitive to Nines' emotions and hypersensitivity, and love to protect them. They are both searching for peace and quiet, so as to preserve their common interests and their comfortable life. Nines are frightened of responsibilities, which they attempt to escape from. This is why they will be thankful to Fours, who are happy to stand up for them, particularly as far as material and financial matters are concerned. Their expression is that of sensation and feelings. They are particularly sensitive with regard to the arts. They are likely to explore decor, atmospheres and positive vibrations.

Sexually speaking, they are likely to try all sorts of pleasures, despite their inherent shyness.

Expression 4 vs. Expression 11

Fours' expression is quiet, taciturn, and introverted. This is the opposite of Elevens, who tend to be direct, straightforward and sometimes explosive. Elevens don't always know how to calm their nervousness and can be irritable and angry, while silent Fours are unable to soothe them. On the contrary, Fours will tend to think their partner is noisy and tiresome, and that their privacy is being invaded. The partnership can nevertheless be positive, provided that Elevens become more moderate and that Fours agree to at least listen to them. It is vital that Elevens understand that their partner requires long periods of tranquility. In turn, Elevens will benefit from their companion's wise advice on material and financial matters.

Regarding love and sex, they are likely to get along well, although their relationship can go through various ups and downs. They will either be intimately close or surprisingly distant from one another, depending on their ability to understand and communicate with each other.

Expression 4 vs. Expression 22

They both function in very similar ways, in that neither feels compelled to constantly express who they are and what they want. They don't like talking merely for the sake of it, as they above all want to be appreciated for their reliability and seriousness. They do not seek crowds of friends. They share a taste for the material aspects of life, which will be particularly favored in this union. However, they must pay attention not to fall into boredom or a stagnant routine, which would be detrimental to their relationship.

Yet, both of them are very balanced and skilled at discarding whatever is superfluous.

Regarding their sex life, they are likely to get along, as they love savoring the pleasures of life. They know how to surround themselves with that which is indispensable to them.

Expression 5

These people oppose all kinds of standards and norms, any type of routine and confinement. They are mobile, available and ready to take up any challenge and to explore every horizon. They need movement, activities and varied situations. They are highly excitable, revolutionary and at times too explosive. They are direct and straightforward, and likely to hurt many people's feelings, although they do not mean to. They are sometimes considered as aggressive, such is their mighty energy when expressing themselves.

Fives have an outstanding ability to adapt and adjust to life's circumstances. They can easily accept the consequences of events. They have a remarkable understanding of situations and are able to fit in and adapt to very different ones. They demand their freedom and want to be original. They can change their mind and alter their views according to those around them. They listen to advice, providing they consider it to be well-founded and astute. They are sensitive, quick and clever but can also be anxious, unreliable and excessive in their need for pleasure.

If they want to be successful, they will have to understand they won't be able to rely on the people around them, any more than they can their friends.

Expression 5 vs. Expression 5

Both of them thrive on traveling and discovering. They love expressing themselves, explaining their views and opening up to the world. Yet, this relationship is not an easy one, because they are so excessive in everything. They obviously have a lot in common, and this may be the actual problem, in that Fives want to be unique and original and therefore can't stand being in competition. Moreover, they have a great need for freedom and independence, which may not be conducive to a lasting relationship. However, they are deeply connected by their friendship and a fraternal type of love.

Financial matters are not favored in this relationship, as neither is interested in money. They are rolling stones who do not gather moss. However, they have many friends with whom they enjoy having long discussions about the state of the world. But they are often angry and adamant: so beware of arguments!

Regarding their sex life, they can be trusted to invent all sorts of tricks in this domain, for they love what is new and original. However, they are unable to differentiate true love from deep friendship.

Expression 5 vs. Expression 6

This relationship can be awkward, in that they function so differently. Whereas one is outgoing and without limits, the other is methodical, accurate and efficient. Unless they accept one another's idiosyncrasies, they are bound to disagree and argue endlessly. Fives tend to find that Sixes constantly nitpick and lack imagination. In turn, Sixes tend to think that Fives are too careless and need to be monitored and controlled. If they manage to understand each other, they will have considerable success, for Sixes have the ability to implement the ideas that Fives come up with. Sixes will support Fives sincerely and devotedly, as well as financially. Although Sixes enjoy a social life, they will have to select the real friends from the fake ones, among Fives' crowd of acquaintances. Otherwise Sixes will at times have to put up with Fives' intrusive friendships.

As far as their sexual relationship is concerned, with love and patience Fives will be able to break Sixes' protective barriers.

Expression 5 vs. Expression 7

This relationship can be positive, provided they keep in mind that neither appreciates being told what to do and can't stand being constrained and forced to act against their will. Both are independent and love exploring new ways. Yet, they do so very differently. Fives are outgoing and need to express themselves freely and naturally. They don't easily accept being contradicted. Sevens also need to assert what they believe, but they do so in a milder and much more reserved way. They will have to give each other space, so as not to trespass and intrude on the other person's privacy. Given their thirst for discovering and understanding the world, they will make an excellent team for traveling. Yet, they might disagree on relationships, in that Sevens tend to filter and select people and situations according to their elitist criteria, whereas Fives don't.

As far as finances go, Fives are better off letting Sevens taking care of this area.

As far as their sex life is concerned, they are liable to get along very well. Although Sevens love exploring all kinds of sexual delights, they do so with sentimental and romantic feelings. They don't appreciate being taken away from their usual habits and comforts. Sevens should always bear in mind that Fives are free, footloose and informal.

Expression 5 vs. Expression 8

In this relationship, it's either everything or nothing, because these two don't function in the same way at all. Fives are outgoing and never hide anything. It's a point of honor to them to prove they are honest, upright and direct, quite unlike their partner. However, if it is dirty tricks and perilous adventures they are after, then they will get along perfectly well, as neither has any boundaries. They love overcoming their own limitations. Fives can particularly benefit from such a relationship, especially in terms of financial and material matters, which are so important to Eights.

The entertainment and movie industry is favored.

To the outside world this couple comes across as original and eccentric. This being said, Eights also need to escape the uproar from time to time and have some peace and quiet. In such moments, they are therefore likely to see Fives as boisterous and disruptive.

Sexually speaking, they are liable to get along very well, as both of them thrive on exploring new and exhilarating realms.

Whether they are able to be true to one another is another question...

Expression 5 vs. Expression 9

Such a relationship may be difficult, because Fives like to express themselves openly, without any boundaries, whereas Nines are intent on not hurting anyone's feelings, and not making noise around them. Fortunately, they are both dedicated people. Their main purpose in life is to protect their environment and act accordingly. The relationship may be positive, in that they are able to understand each other without having to explain. Fives are smart and liberal; they never attempt to act covertly but can sometimes be considered as overrated. This is where Nines, through their intuition, sensitivity and empathy, will be able to sense and understand Fives' true intentions and adjust to them. They play a form of hide and seek. Thanks to their tremendous patience, Nines have the ability to calm Fives' diatribe.

Yet, they must be careful not to idealize their union and disregard earthly concerns. Despite the fact that they are truly inspired and sincere in their quest of absolute truth, they should not underestimate and set aside the material aspects of their life.

As far as sexuality is concerned, they are likely to explore subtle and varied techniques, such as massages, meditation and so on.

Expression 5 vs. Expression 11

Both these individuals express themselves in an open, expeditive and sometimes explosive way. Although neither of them actually looks for trouble, their discussions can quickly turn out of control and degenerate into unfortunate arguments, as they tend to say whatever is on their minds. Their arguments are sudden, short and violent, as well as their judgments. Moderation is definitely not on the agenda. They must learn how to reach compromise, so as to soothe and reassure their strong egos and not hurt each other's feelings. Although their spirit of initiative is outstanding, they must learn to ensure its durability as their impatient nature does not favor material and financial matters. This being said, they are able to forgive each other a great deal, as they are very tolerant.

As far as their sex life is concerned, it's either everything goes or nothing. Once the passion of the first moments has faded, they might become very busy with their respective interests, to the point of finding little time for intimacy. This relationship is more of friendship than great romantic love.

Expression 5 vs. Expression 22

Here again, we have two opposed expressions. Twenty-twos are extremely silent, while Fives are excessively noisy. Whereas Fives tend to act out their desire for conquest through the support and approval of their circle of friends, Twenty-twos, out of pragmatism tend to act on their strategies, rather than explain.

They both enjoy exploring new spheres, but do so in very different ways. Provided they manage to find agreement and a common goal, they will get along just fine. Since Twenty-twos value the material aspects of life, they are likely to support their partner in this respect and help them settle down.

As far as their sex life is concerned, it is worth noting that while talking definitely stimulates Fives, who need to express their desires; Twenty-twos can't be bothered about explanations and would rather skip the preliminaries and get on with it.

Expression 6

These people are obsessed with perfection. They never refrain from expressing their tastes or judgments on what they regard as good or bad. They find it extremely difficult to put aside what upsets their findings and observations. On the other hand, they shine when their environment is in harmony with their needs. They must learn to focus on the positive and relevant, instead of concentrating on what annoys them. This being said, they do care a great deal for the people around them and never attempt to harm anyone, on the contrary. They consider everyone should conform to their ideal. They are good advisors and of great help in decoding and deciphering what doesn't work and why. They know how to decide what should be done consequently, so as to solve any type of problem. They are often always available and have an outstanding ability to listen to others. This is why they are exceptional confidants, who can be deeply trusted. The drawback is that they can be very indecisive when it comes to making a decision about the perfect choice. They are sensitive to beauty and love to see themselves mirrored in their partner's loving eyes.

Expression 6 vs. Expression 6

Such a relationship may prove difficult, in that they both function in the same way and never refrain from telling each other what is wrong. They must learn to view life with a more positive outlook, or they may end up becoming inhibited in their communication, out of fear of hurting one another. They have a notable quality of being able to launch and carry out all sorts of common goals, as long as they see them as relevant. They express themselves in an educated, delicate way, although at times come across as a bit stiff and rigid. This is why they must learn to relax, let go and allow other people around them to express themselves as they wish. Settling into a comfortable home is one of their main objectives, as well as the desire to have children, which they will do ... perfectly well. They are also very affected by other people's suffering, which worries them deeply. As a consequence, they strive to ease others' pain. They are friendly and welcoming and therefore love to be a host to their guests, at whatever the difficulties.

As far as their sex life is concerned, they must learn to loosen up and relax in their relations; otherwise it may be pushed into the background. This doesn't mean they don't enjoy sex.

Expression 6 vs. Expression 7

They are very similar in their ways of complaining about the details which bother them. Both are perfectionists and struggle for excellence. They also aim for perfection when it comes to asserting their beliefs. This is where the comparison ends, for their personal way of functioning is very different. Whereas Sixes worry a lot and can be very anxious, Sevens puts trust in their faith and confidence. Both of them are adamant and demanding. They can benefit a lot from each other, thus becoming ideal partners one for another. Sixes are very methodical, while Sevens readily take the initiative. As a result, the association can flourish. Both strive to build a comfortable material and financial life. They know how to tackle possible problems that may occur, in order to achieve tranquility and peace. They are selective in their friendships, and as a consequence are likely to be surrounded by trustworthy people.

Sexually speaking, some frustrations may arise, due to their fear of expressing their needs and fantasies out loud. They must be careful not to close themselves off in a wall of silence.

Expression 6 vs. Expression 8

Sixes are authentic, honest and above all sincere. Eights are mystical and mysterious. This is why, at first glance, such an association is a challenge. Yet, the relationship may work, provided Eights comply with their partner's advice and criticisms. Sixes will need to put their strict ethical principles aside and be more broadminded. In spite of their obvious differences, they can benefit a great deal one from another and be very complementary.

Sixes bring rigor and efficiency, while Eights bring initiative and new opportunities. Eights explore and launch, while Sixes implement and carry out. Material and financial aspects are also favored, in that Eights are often lucky and Sixes are good at managing money. Together, they are very likely to meet all their requirements to build a comfortable life. There is nothing to prevent them creating the family environment they wish to conceive. They know how to develop a good network of contacts and friends they can rely on, in case of difficulties.

Regarding their sex life, they are liable to get along, particularly Eights who will be able to make Sixes feel at ease.

Expression 6 vs. Expression 9

Such a relationship is ambiguous, in that these two individuals express themselves in completely different ways. Sixes are often very judgmental, whereas Nines try not to hurt or harm anyone. One is accurate, efficient and hates nothing more than approximations, whereas the other easily accepts them and actually couldn't care less. Nevertheless, they can benefit a great deal from each other, as both share strong humanitarian beliefs in helping and supporting others.

Thanks to their desire for a calm and harmonious relationship and they are able to reach mutual agreement, which enables them to become closer to one another. Social and medical fields are favored, as are the arts, particularly music. This being said, they need to learn to strike a balance between their idealistic views and reality. They also need to compromise with a society they don't always understand and appreciate. With time and patience, material and financial aspects will turn out well and result in tangible and concrete achievement. Friendships are also favored.

As far as their sex life goes, they get along well. Nines' tenderness and sweetness will dissolve Sixes' anxiety and tenseness.

Expression 6 vs. Expression 11

Sixes express themselves in an accurate, efficient and rigorous way. Whereas, Elevens tend to be playful, carefree and less methodical which means they sometimes tackle issues too quickly, burning bridges along the way. They can however get along, providing they succeed in moderating their ways of expressing themselves. Sixes need to be less analytical and adamant, while Elevens need to be more patient and less excitable.

As far as their sex life goes, finicky Sixes are much more sensitive to atmospheres. When faced with spontaneous Elevens, Sixes tend to close up. Such a relationship is obviously not an easy one. Mutual effort is required, if they wish to have a lasting relationship. However, intellectual exchanges are particularly favored through a healthy rivalry between the two.

Expression 6 vs. Expression 22

Such a relationship can be very productive, as the methodical and efficient ways of Sixes perfectly suit Twenty-twos, who are attached to structure and roots. Both need to show how serious they are (sometimes too much). They exchange and talk a lot about the projects they share in common, and are likely to carry through to the end. They must be careful not to settle into a stagnant routine, as out of not wanting to ruin such perfect harmony, both refrain from expressing anything contradictory.

As far as their sex life is concerned, Twenty-twos are upright, honest and straightforward. They need to refrain from being too direct and will need to gain their partner's confidence as Sixes are a bit uptight. With time, they will create a life according to their level of standards, as both like to live away from the crowd.

Expression 7

These individuals are persistent and determined, acting according to their inspirations and the faith to which they adhere. They have a strong independent personality and like to be seen as clever and shrewd. They have remarkable abilities in understanding and assimilating the world around them. Their outstanding ability in assessing their environment may lead them to over-criticize what they dislike. Their acute analytical sense enables them to go beyond usual the boundaries and see beneath trivial appearances. They always aim to understand the situations they face. They are quick-witted and aware of what is developing. They seek perfection and love learning and teaching. They are attracted to books, documents, art work, teaching, drama and religion. They would make very efficient attorneys.

Sevens thrive on collections with a touch of vintage. They express themselves keenly and can be curt with those who exasperate them. They can also be incisive, inquisitive and unpleasant.

Expression 7 vs. Expression 7

Such a relationship can be extremely dynamic, in that they are both driven by the same inspirations and possess the same sense of superiority with the belief they are different. They both have an analytical mind and truly enjoy exchanging their points of view, as well as their elitist tastes. They look to join that which is in keeping with their aspirations, and do everything to keep their secrets private. They would never disclose their ambitions or quests. They preserve their privacy. Yet, they are insecure about themselves, which is why they are prone to testing (either directly or indirectly) how much their partner truly appreciates them. With time, this sort of spying will become wearying. This is why they must stop being so overly critical towards one another as their relationship can end up in bitterness and sarcasm.

Professional matters, finances and material purchases are particularly favored in this relationship. In addition, they know how to entertain their circle of friends, with whom they are likely to share deep and intimate bonds, allowing them to talk about all kinds of diverse topics, in a highly intelligent way.

As far as their sex life is concerned, they can get along extremely well, provided they succeed in creating a romantic setting in which they can express themselves freely. They are likely to produce a large family.

Expression 7 vs. Expression 8

This relationship is very positive. They both agree on the need to behave discreetly so as to reach their goals and be successful. As a result, they never reveal themselves to the outside world, let alone express themselves. Sevens and Eights are however very intrusive, poking their noses into matters that don't concern them. They never disclose their objectives or the means they use to get there. They thrive on well-kept secrets and as a result are skilled at guessing and revealing other people's secrets as well.

Yet, Eights are far more pragmatic than Sevens. As long as they act together towards a common objective, they are invincible. However, the slightest disagreement can easily turn into a violent dispute, especially if Eights feel they have been used and betrayed by their partner.

Sexually speaking, anything goes! Sevens are always up for exploring new possibilities, and will therefore accept to overcome certain taboos, in order to follow Eights, who are far more daring and uninhibited.

Expression 7 vs. Expression 9

Although these individuals are very different, the ideals they share enable their relationship to generally be very positive. They express themselves in different ways, in that Sevens are nosy while Nines are peaceful. Sevens tend to argue a lot, while Nines face their quarrelsome spirit with their legendary passiveness and patience. As a result, Sevens realize that Nines are not real opponents, and therefore give up fighting. What Sevens don't realize, is that Nines are shrewd and cunning. Behind their seemingly meek personality, lies a determination to do exactly as they want and to preserve their private interests. Flexible Nines can obtain a great deal from Sevens, as long as they are complaisant. They are better off manipulating Sevens discreetly. They actually love playing hide and seek, particularly sevens who like to play the shining knight.

They both search for a quiet peaceful life, far from noise and commotion. They are also drawn to charity work and might volunteer for tasks involving social issues. They are very good actors and can also be attracted to the artistic world.

Sexually speaking, they are romantic and sensual. As a result, they are likely to become involved in meditation, Kama Sutra or other tantric experiences.

Expression 7 vs. Expression 11

Whenever they express themselves, these individuals are driven by the need to relay messages and information so as to convince the people they're talking to. Nevertheless, they have very different ways of proving their point. Elevens are impulsive, direct and extroverted; and in some instances can become rapidly irritable and agitated. They are revolutionaries. Whereas Sevens manage to convince people much more precisely and with peaceful persuasion, which might be construed as a certain form of manipulation... Where Elevens explode, Sevens gently persuade.

As far as their sex life is concerned, they function very differently. This being said, their love of adventure will help them easily find new experiences to explore. However, Sevens need to constantly be reassured that they are appreciated and loved by their partner. Their need may even go to the extreme where they resort to a form of emotional blackmail. Elevens find this unfathomable and have no cure for this problem as they aren't like this at all.

Expression 7 vs. Expression 22

These two get along perfectly well, in that Sevens are direct, sharp and witty while Twenty-twos are creative and quiet. They truly suit each other, knowing how to stimulate one another and combine their strategies, so as to be successful. Materially speaking they are able to create an environment that complies with their deep desires.

Sexually speaking, Sevens have found here the ideal partner, in that they can only trust people who they genuinely respect and admire. While Twenty-twos may prove a little rough, they will be able to get they want from dedicated Sevens. They are likely to produce large families and might also build something for other people.

Expression 8

Eights can rely on their impressive will-power when they are facing obstacles. They are brave and persistent, especially if they feel something vital is threatened. They have a deep need to protect their own, above all else. They need to be in an environment that matches their deepest desires. These individuals are unyielding, naïve and instinctive, and as a consequence will never stop from going after what they want from life and other people. They will keep trying again and again.

They actually have a dual personality. One part of them is sincere, direct and without restraint, while the other part is obscure turned towards mediumship, hidden things and all that is to do with death (whether on a symbolic level or not). When they decide to reveal themselves, they act in such a way that doesn't go unnoticed. The energy they give off either attracts or bothers people, no one stays indifferent. Eights are obsessed with their need to dominate and coerce the people around them, in order that others comply with their desires, including sexually. They can be very naïve and blinded by what they struggle for, therefore tending to be excessive. With others, they tend to live extremes, with vertiginous ups and downs; either all white or all black.

Expression 8 vs. Expression 8

As long as they agree to unite, everything is fine. But as soon as the slightest obstacle comes up, conflicts may turn violent and war may start. They express themselves through success. They are skilled in the occult area, as well as in cinema, show business and any form of power structure. There are no safeguards in this type of relationship. As a consequence, they are likely to encourage one another to break all the rules and to disregard any limits. They must learn to behave within certain boundaries. Eights express themselves in a fiercely strong way and can in some cases prove extremely quick-tempered. Their anger frightens most people. They both enjoy having their little secret garden. But as they are aware of human nature, they'd rather close their eyes and pretend everything is fine. Money is one of their big issues, whether they have it or not.

241

They love sharing and exchanging gifts, and for this money is very useful...

As far as their sex life is concerned, everything is possible, as neither has any limitations, characterized by the desire to explore all possible and unimaginable sensations. They might collide with one another due to their mutual need to dominate the other. In this relationship there is little that encourages faithfulness.

Expression 8 vs. Expression 9

Such a relationship is positive. Indeed, Eights have nothing to fear from Nines and can therefore go on protecting their secret little garden. Although their partners are able to easily sense things through their innate intuition, they are never judgmental. Nines have a gentle nature and a remarkable sensitivity which enables them to soothe any kind of conflict and eventually find solutions.

In turn, Eights are driven by considerable energy and can consequently give shy Nines protection and support, so as to help them overcome their fears and intense emotions. They are particularly sensitive to anything connected to the occult, as well as the human psyche and never refrain from helping other people.

This being said, they are not likely to have the same profession, in that they are very different, except for commerce where they can work well together. Regarding finances, Nines are not attracted by money as such, nor ruled by material gains. Yet, they do appreciate comfort and certain advantages they may benefit from in this relationship. Unlike Eights, Nines are driven by pleasure, not by power.

As far as their sex life is concerned, they can get along very well, for Eights thrive on domination and have found the ideal partners here, in that Nines tend to be submissive.

Expression 8 vs. Expression 11

Eights express themselves in a natural, straightforward and direct way, which might sometimes be interpreted as naive. They don't see how they can be manipulated by other people, as they don't immediately pick up on what is false. Elevens are usually very lively and somewhat idealistic. They love to go on about what they intend to do, why and how. This is why they may have found the ideal partner here, with Eights who would never undermine what they say. Elevens are not manipulators as such, but they are excessive in their behavior and Eights must be careful not to get carried away by their partner's idealism. In addition, they need to learn caution and not take everything for granted. They both thrive on adventure and as a consequence get along very well. Yet, be careful not to get into trouble and avoid dubious initiatives. What's more, Eights have a darker side whereas Elevens have a brighter one.

As far as their sex life is concerned, they are bound by their mutual longing for adventure and the desire to explore all sorts of unusual experiences. This relationship is one of passion, but as we all know, passions only last for a time...

Expression 8 vs. Expression 22

Interestingly enough, they can get along extremely well, in spite of their very different ways of expressing themselves. Although Twenty-twos refrain from expressing their plans and deep desires, they are trustworthy and reliable. Eights either express themselves candidly or not at all. As Twenty-twos are more interested in action than in vain hypothesis over what might be hidden in their partners' hearts, they are likely to leave them alone. Based on this form of mutual respect, they can work together towards a common goal, in order to build a comfortable material life for themselves.

As far as their sex life is concerned, they both appreciate open and honest exchanges. Twenty-twos might prove a little shyer than Eights when it comes to exploring sexual possibilities. This being said, nothing prevents them from enjoying a happy, fulfilling family life.

Expression 9

These individuals are sensitive, friendly and idealistic. They are looking for balance, harmony and easy living. As a result, they tend to run away from whatever appears as violent or oppressive. There are likely to go off into spheres that are inaccessible to others. This is why these people may be perceived as indecisive, lethargic and not very accurate or persistent. It is difficult to know or guess what truly motivates them as they express themselves vaguely.

What's more, they are driven by noble feelings and therefore tend to idealize their relationships. They love feeling helpful and always attempt to bring that little bit more to the ones they love, to make life easier and more enjoyable. They are visionary mediums who see and perceive invisible worlds. They must be extremely cautious not to escape reality, for they can be drawn into a false paradise and/or let themselves moon about or fall into other people's deep suffering or their own.

They will need to learn very early on to trust their intuition and in particular learn to express what bothers them deeply and be more assertive. They need to understand that disagreements are part of the game and not necessarily harmful. They must express what they don't agree with, instead of turning their backs. This will enable them to tackle problems and solve them, instead of evading them. They must indeed rely on their intuition, but not confuse it with their imagination. The artistic world is ideal for them.

Expression 9 vs. Expression 9

They both get along very well. Neither of them attempts to express disagreement, because they're focused on preserving their quiet little golden universe. Yet, this might not suffice. They must be careful not to get too comfortable in expecting the other to make decisions, or else they may miss out on many opportunities. They can be given credit for making their business thrive harmoniously. Their conciliatory nature never ceases to put others at ease. They are wonderful at listening, sympathizing and being helpful. As time goes by, they are likely to communicate less with words, and more through telepathy, as their deeply empathetic natures enable them to understand and guess the other without resorting to words.

On the other hand, because Nines are not always accessible, being very independent and therefore evasive, these partners can be together a long time without ever talking.

Even though the beginning may be difficult, they will strive to build a comfortable haven for themselves and succeed in making their business proposer without harm to anyone. It is likely they feel as if they have always known each other

As far as their sex life is concerned, they are likely to explore all aspects of their legendary sensuality and discover the connection between the carnal and spiritual. If they are both available at the same time, they can count on numerous romantic evenings by the fire, lying on snug carpets...

Expression 9 vs. Expression 11

Nines' deeply understanding nature definitely benefits the relationship. Nines never look for trouble, as a matter of fact, they carefully avoid all conflict. They would rather carefully choose their words, in order to avoid harming or hurting anyone's feelings. However, Elevens are much less worried about other people's reactions. Yet, they do appreciate when their partners listen to them with sympathy and understanding. What might prove difficult is the way impetuous Elevens react, becoming irritated by peaceful Nines' diplomacy that they judge as sentimental. Elevens are likely to fly off the handle. Nevertheless, Elevens can stimulate Nines, in that they are able to force them to be more accurate and decisive, although their adamant tone might unsettle their partners.

Sexually speaking, surprising as it may seem, they can get along very well, as Nines are ready for all sorts of exotic experiments, in spite of their cautious nature. Such a relationship might very well be a lasting one, provided Elevens do not over disturb Nines' peace and quiet.

Expression 9 vs. Expression 22

Tender and easy Nines are likely to get along very well with Twenty-twos, in that Twenty-twos refrain from expressing themselves in loud and boisterous ways. As a matter of fact, Twenty-twos thrive on action, more than hypothesizing; and therefore aim to protect their partners from life's hardships. They are likely to create a nice and comfortable little world, as Twenty-twos are skilled at managing finances which results in wealth and stability.

As far as their sex life is concerned, their relationship will be sentimental and romantic, just what Nines wish for. But Twenty-twos must work at being more expressive. They need to understand they have nothing to be afraid regarding their partners, as Nines do not look for conflict in any way. Twenty-twos need to make an effort to communicate on a more intimate level, if they don't want Nines to slip through their fingers.

Expression 11

These individuals are driven by the need to show how free and independent they are with regard to the projects they plan to launch. They love showing how open-minded they are. They may even behave as revolutionaries, as they enjoy nothing more than bringing about people's awareness. They often feel the need to be helpful, supportive and are very communicative to others. They are ethical people, who work tirelessly at elevating their level of consciousness. Their sense of humor is one of their favorite weapons.

In spite of all of this, they are extremely unpredictable, to the point they can even be amazed at themselves, for having so little control over their emotions.

They struggle to set goals for themselves, especially in the beginning of their lives, as they are interested in so many diverse (at times too many) things. They need to learn to become more selective so as to choose and focus on the essential. They are basically rebels, which is why they loathe being told what to do and hate feeling forced and compelled to do anything. They become outraged when things don't go the way they want. They must learn how to control their nervousness and anger when this pattern comes up.

They love exploring beyond the normal boundaries and experiencing all sorts of situations with their innate sense of innovation. They have the genuine ability to explore and pioneer new perspectives, and can be a lot of fun as well.

Nevertheless, they must be careful not to be too idealistic. Their lack of discipline might deter them from calling themselves into question.

Expression 11 vs. Expression 11

A relationship between these two who are very lively, impulsive and direct is almost impossible to understand. They both lack patience and intend to lead and prove how right they are. This is likely to therefore cause great explosions, unless they learn to seriously calm and moderate their blunt ways. They are actually intelligent enough to refrain from being too impulsive and quick-tempered. In other words, they must understand that it is worth being more pragmatic than idealistic, at times. They must realize that implementing what they have always considered as trivial can also be very rewarding. Taking care of things that are usually regarded as minor can enable these individuals to be materially successful, as financial matters are not usually favored in this regard.

As far as sexuality is concerned, they are liable to have plenty of opportunities to enjoy the pleasures of life, because they are such ardent beings. Provided they focus a little more on each other, and a little less on their wide field of activities which often keep them apart, they will have a fulfilling sex life. Otherwise, they are more likely to become like two good buddies who have a lot to tell each other, than real intimate partners.

Expression 11 vs. Expression 22

In this association everything goes against them. Happy, lively Elevens are likely to explode when faced with slow, placid Twenty-twos. This will arouse frustrations, unnecessary agitation and even anger. Twenty-twos are not insensitive to Elevens' idealistic views, but they do not have faith in them as they need to see what is down-to-earth with their own eyes. Elevens can easily get carried away into idealistic discussions, whereas Twenty-twos prefer reasoning what is rational. Yet, if they can become close, they will both benefit immensely. Elevens are outgoing and look to discover the world and conquer it, whereas Twenty-twos are introverted and only want to build. The more Twenty-twos are involved in their joint financial and material matters, the better.

Sexually speaking, Elevens' humanitarian and sensitive nature can obviously benefit the relationship. Yet, Elevens tend to be overreaching and out of touch with reality for Twenty-twos, who need to live situations on a more profound level. Elevens are never where you expect them to be, as they are so impulsive and commanding, unlike Twenty-twos, who are persistent, determined and focused on what they are searching. Will they succeed in settling their discord? It is a mystery...

Expression 22

From the very early stages of their lives, these people are conscious of their power and strength. As a result, this very awareness can make them seem very serious. They are liable to impose their outlook on life on the people around them. They have an extremely pragmatic way of creating, elaborating and making people aware of their views. With their natural expression being based on pride and honor, they tend to instill respect from the people who surround them.

They express their steady presence through reserve, a certain form of distance and the ability to keep petty concerns at bay. They pursue their long term projects with persistence, efficiency and determination. They are driven by their powerful resolve and can seem cold and determined. Yet, they can be overwhelmed by their pessimism, particularly in the case where events don't turn out as expected. In which case, they must then strive not to behave in a misogynistic or antisocial manner, whether against women or mankind as a whole. With their disconcerting and intransigent nature they must learn to not to let it get out of control, in forcing others to submit to them whenever they are focused on a specific objective.

Expression 22 vs. Expression 22

This is the perfect association as neither of them tries to dominate one another. This does not mean that they can't have their own opinions and particular views, just that they just don't deem it necessary to systematically force them on their partner. They are liable to come to a quiet, peaceful and productive agreement which enables them to carry out their projects and meet their needs. Still, they need to express themselves more, and in a lighter way, otherwise the atmosphere may turn a little grim. A touch of joy and laughter would be most welcome!

Material and financial matters are favored, as well as long term goals. Contact with nature and family matters are also favored.

As far as their sex life is concerned, they are happy and satisfied with their direct and natural way. No need for fancy embellishment. On the contrary, they prefer and enjoy regularity and efficiency. On the other hand, as time goes by, they may feel they haven't seized enough opportunities in the past and therefore might yearn for their youthful days.

CHAPTER VI

Aspects between the Aspiration Numbers

"Reason is immortal, all else mortal."

Pythagoras

Definition: The Aspiration number determines how people desire to be fulfilled in their lives (through being, having and doing). It indicates what urges them to act in such or such way. It also defines the nature this mysterious force drives us to adopt such or such strategies so as to meet our souls' aspirations.

This number tells us about the soul's aspiration on a spiritual evolution level. The soul interacts instinctively and unpredictably within the true inner nature of the person, thus enabling them to find opportunities which will help them. The soul's aspiration helps the individual overcome their deep nature (Life Path). In order to achieve this, the energy of the soul pushes us to develop bonds which will enable us to discover ourselves through other beings. This is called "the mirror effect". For example: an Aspiration 6 will often urge the person to connect with other people whose Life Path is 6.

This is therefore a very important and relevant detail to take into account when you are establishing a theme of how two individuals are likely to get along. When two people are attracted to each other, it is particularly interesting to see if the creative energies stemming from their respective desires are attuned.

Calculation method: reduction of the addition of the value of each vowel of the first name of the person and his/her mother's birth name

Example: let's add the value of each vowel of Peter John, whose mother's name at birth was Dugal (her maiden name)

```
Peter John Dugal
 5 5   6    6 1
5+5+6+6+1 = 23 → 2+3 =56
```

Peter's Aspiration Number is 5.

Tip: For further information on aspects regarding the Aspiration number, refer to chapter IX.

Aspiration 1

Aspiration 1 vs. Aspiration 1

If they share the same desires, their aspiration will enable them to exchange their views very easily. If this is not the case, frustrations and unease are likely to arise, whether they are actually expressed or not. Their common desire for spontaneity and openness will prove beneficial assets in helping them overcome any antagonism. However, a hierarchy in their values needs to be established. In other words, if what is important to one person is only secondary to the other, and vice versa, misunderstandings will occur, bringing about deep resentment and open conflict.

Aspiration 1 vs. Aspiration 2

Number 2 searches for peace and calm, whereas number 1 dreams of conquering the world. While one person aspires for harmony, thus emphasizing all kinds of partnerships, the other person wishes to rule and coerce. Although this type of association may not seem right at first glance, it is possible to find consensus. Number 2 can easily comply with number One's wishes, in spite of the lack of sensitivity they blame Ones for and which triggers a certain amount of frustration.

Number Twos are considered as overly emotional by number Ones, who are easily annoyed by this. Yet, Ones do not dwell on unhappy thoughts for long, which is why they will overcome any negative feelings. As long as Ones refrain from judging their partner as too sentimental, the association can be harmonious. If not, a chasm of misunderstanding can come between them.

Because we are dealing with mutual aspirations, all this might not be visible or as apparent as one would like. That which is unexpressed is like the submerged part of an iceberg, and can cause discomfort within each individual's heart. Their dreams are diametrically opposed.

Aspiration 1 vs. Aspiration 3

They share a common aspiration to assert their views about life. Yet, they use very different means to reach the same objective. Number Ones need to live freely and independently, whereas number Threes are skeptical and aware of their limits, and therefore attempt to be as accurate, efficient and methodical as possible. Both of them wish to set up and organize their lives in their own individual way, although their deep motivations differ dramatically. Ones are driven, and don't let petty details deter them, unlike Threes.

Aspiration 1 vs. Aspiration 4

Number Ones look to prove they are the best, no matter what, whereas number Fours merely want to enjoy a fulfilled and comfortable material life. Number Ones' pioneering spirit need to conquer the world, and will therefore oppose number Fours' calm and reserved nature, whether they like it or not.

Aspiration 1 vs. Aspiration 5

Their aspirations meet on one point: they both aim to go beyond the limits of this world that they often consider as too small. But this is the only mutual point of agreement. Number Ones want to force their views on their partners, whereas number Fives want their partners to support their revolutionary ideas. Arguments are to be expected.

Aspiration 1 vs. Aspiration 6

Number Ones' aspirations are far too aggressive for number Sixes, who are pragmatic and analytical. They are extremely different, in that number Ones express themselves directly and abruptly, unlike number Sixes, who tend to think everything over twice, before making decisions.

Aspiration 1 vs. Aspiration 7

Sevens are much less expressive than Ones. They like to keep things discreet, and refrain from sharing their aspirations, whereas Ones systematically advertise themselves! This being said, they make a good team, in that Sevens are very admiring and supportive of Ones' strong impulses.

Aspiration 1 vs. Aspiration 8

They both have the same aspirations, in that they want to dominate and coerce, but the similarity ends here. Number Ones clearly and intelligently express their desires, whereas number Eights merely search the quickest route to realize their goals.

Aspiration 1 vs. Aspiration 9

Number Nines are eager to find agreement, to compromise and make things work at all costs and avoid conflict; whereas number Ones do the exact opposite, being focused on implementing their desires with their strong will and determination.

Aspiration 1 vs. Aspiration 11

If you were to put two impulsive jokers together, there is no doubt that explosions would occur. Both of them have assertive, direct and spontaneous goals and won't tolerate any delays. Provided they share the same ambitions, everything will be fine. Otherwise...

Aspiration 1 vs. Aspiration 22

Number Ones tend to overshadow everyone else around them. Number Twenty-twos tend to slow everything down. Therefore, direct, impulsive and instinctive Ones diametrically oppose slow, wary and quiet Twenty-twos.

Aspiration 2

Aspiration 2 vs. Aspiration 2

Before making any decisions, they will share their emotions and explore them together. But what if one person systematically takes into account what the other one wants before acting, who is then going to act?

Aspiration 2 vs. Aspiration 3

Number Threes criticize, analyze and weigh up everything. This is not easy for number Twos, who go with feelings and emotions, while Threes go by facts and figures.

Aspiration 2 vs. Aspiration 4

These two aspirations get along particularly well, for neither one wants to hurt anyone's feelings. Number Fours get the most benefit from this, as they hate being told what they should or shouldn't do. Moreover, they are discreet about what they plan to do. Their partner is not likely to disturb them except when Twos are unable to control their emotions.

Aspiration 2 vs. Aspiration 5

Number Fives' aspirations are vast and unpredictable. They constantly call into question that which is fixed and complete, without taking into account the consequences of their actions on those around them. Whereas number Twos strive to protect and support those around them; they can nevertheless meet on one point: they are both driven by humanitarian values.

Aspiration 2 vs. Aspiration 6

Number Sixes strive to accomplish everything they do, in a perfect and efficient way, without paying too much attention to their emotions. They are liable to get along well, provided number Twos manage to keep their overwhelming emotions at bay.

Aspiration 2 vs. Aspiration 7

Number Sevens' aspirations seem limitless but are fixed on a sacred and impossible quest, urging them to overcome their inner boundaries. All this is far from number Twos' worries. Nevertheless, they both share a common goal: taking care of their own little world.

Aspiration 2 vs. Aspiration 8

Number Eights are often driven by an aspiration which urges them to seize any possible opportunities, putting aside all bias and details. Eights also tend to act alone, which does not suit number Twos at all.

Aspiration 2 vs. Aspiration 9

Both of these aspirations are based on compassion, and the wish to act selflessly. Nines tend to shun life's issues, by avoiding obligations and pressure. Number Twos should therefore not force anything on Nines, "for their own good"...

Aspiration 2 vs. Aspiration 11

Number Elevens have powerful impulses, which do not suit number Two's calm and quiet aspirations. Elevens' nervous, irritable and at times aggressive behavior can upset number Twos.

Twos wish to express their love and care more, but Elevens are not receptive.

Aspiration 2 vs. Aspiration 22

Number Twos characterize friendly aspirations, in keeping with their desire to please and support those around them. This suits Twenty-twos perfectly, in that they also wish to enjoy a happy and simple life.

Aspiration 3

Aspiration 3 vs. Aspiration 3

This combination is like a contest of who comes up with the best ideas. Both of them are intent on proving to the other that they are the better qualified, in every respect. Criticisms are to be expected.

Aspiration 3 vs. Aspiration 4

This relationship is not a smooth one. Number Threes, who rely mostly on their analytical brain, seem to highlight Fours supposed lack of drive. While Number Fours' aspirations consist in carrying out their projects discreetly without anyone noticing, Threes are much more cerebral and talkative.

Aspiration 3 vs. Aspiration 5

Number Fives' aspirations are based on impulse and unpredictability, rather than on the thorough analysis demanded by number Threes. Indeed, they do not get along, as one aspires to experiment, while the other one aspires to ponder.

Aspiration 3 vs. Aspiration 6

They agree on one point: they both aspire to analyze and rationalize all of their thoughts and deeds. While perfectionist they may be, they should nevertheless stop focusing merely on what they consider as drawbacks or flaws in their partners.

Aspiration 3 vs. Aspiration 7

Number Threes' aspiration is to put forward their strategies and their way of organizing their plans. This is in complete opposition to Sevens, who prefer not to disclose their ways. Sevens do have their plans, but their deep aspiration drives them to first calculate and work out precisely where the next step will be.

Aspiration 3 vs. Aspiration 8

Number Eights aspire to put aside the details and not pay attention to their emotions. This does not suit number Threes, who end up being obliged to analyze and dissect how things go and why.

Aspiration 3 vs. Aspiration 9

Number Nines' aspiration drives them to be nice, friendly and to comply with the people around them. They look to compromise, whereas Threes point out all the faulty details and will spend hours analyzing them.

Aspiration 3 vs. Aspiration 11

Number Elevens aspire to explore their environment endlessly, thus getting involved in all sorts of different projects without creating any real bond with Threes. Such an aspiration is difficult for number Threes, who are far more critical and wary of the outside world.

Aspiration 3 vs. Aspiration 22

Number twenty-twos aspire for peace and quiet. They do not want to be focused on, nor do they want to disturb anyone and will express this by a certain form of passiveness. Twenty-two's way of searching for peace doesn't at all correspond with Three's incisive impulses and desire for competition.

Aspiration 4

Aspiration 4 vs. Aspiration 4

They both aspire to carry out the deep desires that dwell within them, without disturbing anyone around them. They are extremely attentive to the pace they use to reach their aims. Let's hope they find the same rhythm.

Aspiration 4 vs. Aspiration 5

Number Fours aspire to a quiet life that lets them create what they wish for, step by step. Whereas, number Fives aspire to constantly explore the world without any boundaries or consideration of the consequences of their actions. Such a relationship is therefore awkward

Aspiration 4 vs. Aspiration 6

Number Sixes aspire for perfection and harmony with other people. This quest is liable to suit number Fours, who aspire to keep things as they are. Therefore, as surprising as it may be, Sixes are sensitive to Fours pragmatic vision.

Aspiration 4 vs. Aspiration 7

Number Fours' aspirations do not oppose those of number Sevens, as they are both focused on keeping what they own. Their impulses do not lead to self-sabotage.

Aspiration 4 vs. Aspiration 8

They both share a common aspiration of owning and enjoying what they have. Although they share the same goal, the means they use to succeed are very different. In addition, number Eights' aspirations are not always clear, which can be very difficult for number Fours.

Aspiration 4 vs. Aspiration 9

Number Fours aspire to act hands-on, in a down-to-earth way, so as to create tangible and material results. This is not at all how number Nines operate as they prefer to use their famous diplomatic skills. Yet, they are not unmoved by Fours' peaceful method.

Aspiration 4 vs. Aspiration 11

Don't ever ask number Fours to understand number Elevens' aspirations! Elevens know no boundaries, unlike Fours who thrive on structure and limitation. Nervous and impulsive Elevens tend to annoy Fours, whose aim is to keep any type of irritation at bay.

Aspiration 4 vs. Aspiration 22

They share the same aspiration to establish and carry out what they deeply desire. Should their motivations be similar, they will be driven towards the same goals. If not, they will find it very difficult to understand each other, all the more so in that they refrain from expressing themselves out loud.

Aspiration 5

Aspiration 5 vs. Aspiration 5

Because they both are driven by the same aspiration to explore the world around them, they might very well end up being caught in a competition as to who will be the first to find the Holy Grail. Their impulsiveness leaves little room for diplomacy.

Aspiration 5 vs. Aspiration 6

Number Fives aspire to go beyond their limitations. This does not always suit number Sixes, who struggle to structure and discipline their desires. The unpredictable passions of number Five make number Six very uncomfortable.

Aspiration 5 vs. Aspiration 7

They have trouble understanding each other, because they not express their aspirations in the same way. Although they are both eager to discover, inform and educate themselves, they do not use the same means to get there. Fives tend to form quick overviews, unlike Sevens like to methodically look deeper within.

Aspiration 5 vs. Aspiration 8

Although they are both driven by strong and sometimes unpredictable impulses, the resulting outcomes are very different. Number Fives wish to share their motivations from the start with the people around them; whereas number Eights do everything they can to hide them. While one prefers open action, the other prefers covert action.

Aspiration 5 vs. Aspiration 9

Their aspirations only meet on one common point: they are both intent on freeing themselves from social structures and rules. Yet, their deep motivations are different. Number Fives keep pushing their limits even further, and do not control their impulsiveness. Number Nines push their limits further as well, but they do so in their own way, by taking refuge in a world which is intangible.

Aspiration 5 vs. Aspiration 11

This association brings together two explosive aspirations which are incompatible. The main obstacle lies in number Elevens who force their views and deep motivations on other people, whereas number Fives can't be bothered. Elevens' act individualistically, while Fives act collectively.

Aspiration 5 vs. Aspiration 22

Number Twenty-twos aspire to structure, implement and establish. This does not suit number Fives, who aren't interested in material matters. Number twenty-twos wish to immobilize things in time and place, whereas number Fives main wish is to be free from the material world.

Aspiration 6

Aspiration 6 vs. Aspiration 6

At first glance, this association looks ideal as they both aspire to similar things. Their aspirations stem more from their instincts, than reason. This means they need to be tuned in and synchronized with each other if they want it to work. As long as they want the same thing at the same time, everything will go well. If this is not the case, arguments are to be expected; due to their feeling of being judged.

Aspiration 6 vs. Aspiration 7

These two intuitive ways of being are very different from one another, but can nevertheless bring each other a lot. Number Sevens are inspired to know what they should focus on, and what strategies should be adopted to carry out their desires. In turn, number Sixes are intuitively able to spot the details which need to be worked on.

Aspiration 6 vs. Aspiration 8

Number Eights' touchy feelings are likely to be very hurt by Sixes' unpredictable and sharp observations, who don't control their tongue nor understand why they can't refrain from criticizing their partners. This may drive Eights to use questionable means, which number Sixes disapprove of.

Aspiration 6 vs. Aspiration 9

Although these two aspirations are in opposition, they are however linked by a common will to serve and help other people. They really need to find a way to talk and understand each other. If this is not the case, number Nines will never see how number Sixes

266

are good at organizing things and, in turn, number Sixes will never accept the sacrifices number Nines are ready to make to protect themselves.

Aspiration 6 vs. Aspiration 11

Number Sixes' aspirations do not suit number Elevens, in that Sixes need to structure their actions, whereas Elevens don't. Elevens are more spontaneous and can't be bothered by formalities. In turn, Sixes are more wary and find it hard to put up with Elevens' unrestrained motivations.

Aspiration 6 vs. Aspiration 22

This is the perfect match, with number Twenty-twos, who aspire to establish and give form to things, and number Sixes who aspire to regulate. Sixes will be most happy to see that their desires materialize and come true, due to Twenty-twos' efficiency.

Aspiration 7

Aspiration 7 vs. Aspiration 7

The relationship is positive, as long as neither loses sight of their common goals. Should this not be the case, violent conflicts are likely to happen. Fortunately, both of them are smart enough to manage and control their urges.

Aspiration 7 vs. Aspiration 8

Number Sevens' aspirations may prove very profitable for number Eights. Sevens are able to advise Eights at the right moment, as Eights don't always notice danger. On the other hand, Eights' self-interested aspirations are likely to fuel Sevens' legendary appetite for worldly goods.

Aspiration 7 vs. Aspiration 9

Their aspirations meet on one particular point: reaching their goals, whether they are true or imaginary ones. Their perception is exquisite with a touch of the mystical. They must however be careful not to fall into illusions or delude each other.

Aspiration 7 vs. Aspiration 11

Both of them idealize their desires with the need to avoid restrictive surroundings. Yet, they do not perceive the outcome in the same way. Number Sevens like to calculate and plan, unlike number Elevens. This is precisely where opposition may arise. Elevens' aspirations are far less self-centered than those of number Sevens.

Aspiration 7 vs. Aspiration 22

Their aspirations are suited to each other, in that number Sevens are adamant in carrying out their desires and number Twenty-twos are there to fulfill them. Twenty-twos are wise and accept to be advised and supervised by their companions, whose motivations they appreciate.

Aspiration 8

Aspiration 8 vs. Aspiration 8

There is no way for either of them to possess the other. By definition, their aspirations are spontaneous and unpredictable, and in this case, there are no boundaries whatsoever. They should avoid constant competition which will only result in a negative outcome. Provided they avoid the trap of resorting to untruthful and disloyal behavior, they will manage to find a way to get along.

Aspiration 8 vs. Aspiration 9

These aspirations are very different. Number Nines do not expect a fair compensation for their commitments, unlike number Eights, who want their efforts to be recognized financially. They will struggle to understand each other's respective desires.

Aspiration 8 vs. Aspiration 11

Anger and confrontations are likely to arise, as both of them are driven by dominating, impulsive instincts, which they fail to control. Number Eights consider their own interests first and therefore view number Elevens' aspirations as unrealistic and idealistic. Adversely, Elevens judge Eights as being too selfish.

Aspiration 8 vs. Aspiration 22

This association can work as both aspire to carry out and achieve material projects. Provided their interests go in the same direction, everything will be fine. If not, it may be difficult.

Aspiration 9

Aspiration 9 vs. Aspiration 9

Here we have two poets who aspire to a life of harmony and fulfillment... Let's hope they do not get carried away by their desires and retain some realistic views. If not, their aspirations will not prosper and could even become prejudicial to their interests.

Aspiration 9 vs. Aspiration 11

This association is awkward in that Nines who mainly aspire to peace and calm are joined with Elevens who are not particularly quiet and serene when they go after what they want. However, Nines' gentle aspirations will soothe Elevens, who appreciate not having to face obstacles all the time.

Aspiration 9 vs. Aspiration 22

Number Nines' aspirations do not suit number Twenty-twos at all. Twenty-twos need to implement what they envision and are pushed to act on, whereas Nines would rather let go of their desires if these hinder the harmony they need.

Aspiration 11

Aspiration 11 vs. Aspiration 11

Provided they share their common aspirations, to launch innovations and revolution, everything will go fine. However if this isn't the case, their extremely idealistic views and need for freedom and independence will cause conflict. Unless they find a way to control their urges, they will end up arguing all day.

Aspiration 11 vs. Aspiration 22

These two aspirations are too different from one another to ever reach harmony. Number Twenty-twos aspire to settle down and fulfill themselves by imposing their own views, whereas number Elevens look to free themselves free from any established, closed or rigid structures.

Aspiration 22

Aspiration 22 vs. Aspiration 22

They have identical aspirations, which if they manage to synchronize at the same time and place, they will definitely achieve in succeeding at. However, long periods of silence are to be expected.

CHAPTER VII

Aspects between the Potential Numbers

"Better to have listened to a string that broke than to never have stretched a bow."»

Verner von Heidenstam

Definition: This number expresses the person's potentials. It deals with the person's latent abilities, what their know-how might bring about and, consciously or not, sooner or later, what they are able to achieve.

Calculation method: reduction of the added values of each consonant of the first name of the person and his/her mother's birth name

Example: let's add the value of each consonant of Peter John, whose mother was given the name Dugal at birth (her maiden name)

P̲eter̲ John̲ D̲ug̲al̲
7 2 9 1 85 4 7 3
7+2+9+1+8+5+4+7+3 =46 → 4+6 =10 → 1
Peter's Potential Number is 1.

Unlike the Aspiration number, which refers to deep impulses and the forces which drive us to undertake certain initiatives, (at times pushing us against our will) the Potential number refers to a potential we can firmly master. Whether we actually do so or not, is up to us.

Comparing the Potential numbers of two people, so as to know if they can get along, is particularly relevant regarding socio-professional relationships. This number is also useful in better understanding one's children, in regard to their professional career choices. This is less so in the feelings and attitudes of a person. After all, it is entirely possible to love one another, without doing the same type of job and having the same abilities.

To know how two Potentials interact, you might want to refer to the previous chapter (Aspects between Aspiration Numbers), go over what has been explained and adjust it accordingly. With a bit of intellectual gymnastics, that which has been explained regarding Aspiration can be converted to Potential, namely capacities.

Example: Suppose you want to know the aspects between a Potential 1 and a Potential 4. Go back to the text on Aspiration 1 and Aspiration 4, and consider we are not dealing with hidden impulses, but with actual capacities which are bound to be expressed and manifested.

Aspiration 1 vs. Aspiration 4
Number Ones look to prove they are the best, no matter what, whereas number Fours merely want to enjoy a fulfilled and comfortable material life. Number Ones' pioneering spirit need to conquer the world, and will therefore oppose number Fours' calm and reserved nature, whether they like it or not.

Becomes:

Potential 1 vs. Potential 4

Number Ones have the ability to prove they are the best, no matter what other people think. Number Fours have the ability to enjoy the comfortable material pleasures a fulfilling life can offer.

Fours will therefore emphasize their calm and reserved nature and oppose One's struggle for power and pioneering initiative with certain form of passivity.

Once again, The Aspiration reveals the powerful desires of the soul, whereas the Potential features the applications of the person's true capacities.

Here is another example. Suppose you want to compare a Potential 3 with a Potential 8. The interpretation of Aspiration 3 and Aspiration 8, adapted to the person's Potential can be rephrased as follows:

With an aspiration 8, the subject tends to ignore the details. His moods are not an obstacle for him/her. Whereas a person with an aspiration 3 is more or less forced to analyze and weigh up the pros and cons.

According to Potential 3 and Potential 8, we can conclude the following: Number Eights' powerful Potential indicates they go straight to the point and never beat about the bush, whereas number Threes tend to analyze and dwell on things. The individuals, when they are together, have genuine abilities to succeed. This is not to do with the desires or the state of the soul, but rather the true hands-on know-how.

CHAPTER VIII

Taking Active Numbers into consideration

"Rest, knowing you have done well, and let others talk of you as they will."
Pythagoras

Definition: Active Numbers refer to how people instinctively behave. This is usually deeply ingrained in such a way that is spontaneous. Therefore people can't always differentiate from their deep nature (Life path) from the triggering factors of their actions (Active Number).

Let's take an example. By definition, Life Path 1 depicts an active, determined and enterprising person. But if her/his active number is 9, she/he will need a little time before she/he actually launches her/his actions. On the contrary, quiet and moderate people, such as life path 2 or 4, will instinctively react quickly to begin with, if their active number is 1, and then return to settle within their own true nature.

There is no denying that the more a Life Path opposes an Active Number, the more the person's actions are difficult to understand and the more they will surprise the people around them. Imagine someone with a Life Path and an Expression 4, who suddenly loses it, because her/his Active Number 11 made her/him fly off the handle!

Generally speaking, a great deal of the misunderstandings we have with other people around us stems from this first impulse, which is seldom taken into consideration. This is why it is necessary to expand on this.

How to work it out: Add the value of all the letters of the first and middle names given at birth, and then reduce the result.

Example: Take Peter John Dugal. We will only consider his first names, as officially declared at birth: Peter John. (If there are 2, we will take two into consideration, if 3, then 3 and so on...)

```
Peter John
75259 1685
7+5+2+5+9+1+6+8+5 = 48 → 4+8 = 12 → 1+2 = 3
```

Peter's Active Number is 3.

In the case where the Active Number is the same as the Life Path, the persons are likely to more easily carry out what they plan, as this is part of their very nature. If the Active Number is the same as the Aspiration Number, the urges and impulses of the persons are multiplied and emphasized in the persons' lives. If the Active Number is the same as the Expression Number, it will drive the persons to highly express and manifest this aspect in their lives. And to finish, if the Active Number is the same as the Potential Number, the persons are very self-confident and will easily implement their abilities.

It is clear that in the case where the Active Number is the same as one, two or even three of the above key numbers, the given aspect is all the more highlighted. Everything works as if coefficients have been applied.

Let's take the example of a person whose Life Path is 6, whose Expression is 9, and Potential 4. Let's consider her/his Aspiration is 5, as her/his Active Number. In this specific case, the Active Number 5 significantly boosts the aspiration 5, to a degree that will dim her/his quiet potential 4 and curb her/his sweet expression 9, to a point that might surprise the person her/himself, as well as the people around her/him.

How Active Numbers affect personalities

Active Number 1: Number Ones tend to act immediately, with delays, and never procrastinate. Their mode is adamant and unpredictable, for Ones find it hard to accept not to be leaders and pioneers.

Active Number 2: Twos usually act so as to protect their own: themselves, their families and their loved ones. This might reach a point where they act like a mother. Twos react with their emotions and tend to withdraw into their own little world.

Active Number 3: Threes are quick and flexible. They easily adjust to new environments, while re-organizing everything. They don't take action unless communication has been established. They react with humor and irony.

Active Number 4: Fours are determined in their undertakings. They do not compromise and will express considerable inertia to any projects they oppose. Their actions can spread out and linger. They react through silence and open disapproval.

Active Number 5: Fives act through their instincts. They are driven by impatience and will keep pushing their limits and boundaries ever further. In some ways they are revolutionaries. They react through anger and the wish to drop everything and start anew.

Active Number 6: They are disciplined, methodical, accurate and efficient. They plan their actions to the smallest single detail, so that all is perfect. They react with cutting criticism.

Active Number 7: Sevens act with incisive, precise and motivated intentions. They will use any possible means to get what they desire. They idealize their activities, which they want to be useful. They can be very touchy, and if attacked, will attempt to prove they are right, by searching the validity and soundness of their reasons and actions.

Active Number 8: Eights act according to the elements they have at hand. They are very practical and direct. They act through their instincts, more than through their reasoning. Their reactions can be very angry and destructive.

Active Number 9: They require much time before they can actually make decisions and act, as they contemplate and ponder over things a lot. They need to know where they are going. They will react by pretending nothing happened or by slipping away.

Active Number 11/2: These people act in an eccentric way: their actions may appear irrational, original and unpredictable. They react strongly, because their impulses are so entrenched in their emotions.

Active Number 11: They act in an innovating, excitable and impulsive way. Their ways can be disconcerting because they are so abrupt. They react out of frustration in not being able to understand or fathom what is happening.

Active Number 22: They are level-headed people. Their actions are efficient, firm and long-lasting. They have a visible impact on the environment. Their reactions are also firm, and can sometimes surprise the people around them by what is unsaid. They keep their anger within.

In the various relationships between one number and another, it becomes easy to compare their different ways of functioning.

Example: Let's take an active Number 1 with an active Number 9. Number One will coerce number 9 to comply with their rules. Number 9 if they don't agree will often give in.

CHAPTER IX

To go further...

"Cherish and serve your fellow people, by taking care of them as best you can. In any undertaking look first to your conscience."
                                            Joseph Balsamo (Count Cagliostro)

It is possible to expand on the different aspects we have just studied, thus giving even more information.

11/2: a particular case

In the various ways of calculating Life Paths, sub-numbers 20 may be found in the Expression, Aspiration, Potential or Active Number, along with 29 or 38.

To work out the Expression number, we have seen that the value of each letter in the first names of the individual's and in the their mother's maiden name need to be reduced. This is the proper way to do it.

BUT another way of calculating is possible: individually reduce the value of all the first names of the individual, and the individual's mother's maiden name and then add the two results. This might give different conclusions: for example 20 with one method, and 29 with the other!

The theosophical reduction of 29 is 11 (2+9), as in all the other sub-numbers of 11, namely 38, 47, 56, 65, 74, 83, 92. On the other hand, 20 indicates 2 (2+0).

Whenever calculations result in 11 and 2, the indicated numbers feature a powerful duality in the individual, in that both energies reside within them; while by definition 11 and 2 convey totally opposing energies. In the case where a person's Expression is both 11 and 2, it is necessary to combine these two numbers, as follows:

Definition of Expression 11/2

The expression of these individuals is ambiguous, in that they are torn between a strong desire for independence and freedom on the one hand, and a powerful need for relationships on the other.

They struggle to strike a balance between these two dynamics. They need a partner to launch their projects with, but simultaneously, they want to be left alone and able to do exactly what they have in mind. Is such a balance possible? They do have a great virtue, in that they want to free themselves from a limited world, and encourage other people to do the same. They usually have the uncomfortable feeling of having to choose between two conflicting possibilities: either express their longing for conquest and self-fulfillment or compromise with their partners.

Blending these two extremes requires them to be more patient, less excessive, and take their loved ones more into account. They can be compared to a doodlebug in love with freedom, flying to the light with a string attached to their leg. This example is for those who played with such insects when they were children...

Therefore with the analysis of those who have 11/2 as their Expression number, you need to incorporate both the aspects of 11 and 2 with the Expression number of their partner. Repeat the same procedure for the other numbers.

Example: If you have 11/2 as the Aspiration number and the partner has Aspiration 3, you have to study first the aspect Aspiration 11/Aspiration 3, then Aspiration 2/Aspiration 3, because both are equally true.

Study the analysis of Aspiration 11/2 with all other numbers. Feel free to adapt the analysis so as to be able to include the interactions of 11/2 with any other data (Expression, Potential, Active number...).

Aspiration 1 vs. Aspiration 11/2

It is generally agreed that 11 is driven by passion and enthusiasm while 2 expends a lot of energy trying to please other people and take their wishes into consideration. The relationship with 1 is therefore very ambiguous, in that 11/2 will either want the same thing as 1, such as forcing their wishes on somebody else (influence of 11), or attempting to comply with other people's wishes (influence of 2).

Aspiration 2 vs. Aspiration 11/2

What brings them together is their consideration for each other while wanting to achieve their own fulfillment. Yet, 11/2 gives off a particular energy, which can surprise and be disconcerting for their partner 2 who are so used to their humdrum routine.

Aspiration 3 vs. Aspiration 11/2

Apart from the inertia that 2 expresses in 11/2, their relationship is one of open conflict and far from peace and harmony.

Aspiration 4 vs. Aspiration 11/2

What mostly differentiates these two individuals is that Fours don't always explain what motivates them to act in such or such way. They'd rather just act it out, whereas 11/2 need to share what motivates them with the people around them. Fortunately, number 2 calms the impulsiveness of number 11, which results in a positive outcome for Fours.

Aspiration 5 vs. Aspiration 11/2

Fortunately, number 2 curbs the impulsiveness of number 11 within 11/2, because the aspirations of 5 and of 11 are very similar to the analysis of 5/11 studied in chapter VI.

Aspiration 6 vs. Aspiration 11/2

The relationship can go either way, depending on whether 11 or 2 prevails within those born 11/2. Sixes are skilled organizers, and will therefore help number 2 who couldn't ask for more. Nevertheless, in doing so, they might disturb the number 11 part of their partner who can't stand being advised nor, even worse, supervised and told what to do. Sixes love Twos' sweetness but find Elevens' restlessness difficult to cope with. Elevens tend to take everything for granted.

Aspiration 7 vs. Aspiration 11/2

Sevens' aspirations are wise, but never completely without self-interest, and are therefore in perfect keeping with Twos, who look for protection. However, Sevens' aspirations are in complete opposition to those of idealistic Elevens who are not particularly wise nor interested in their motivations.

Aspiration 8 vs. Aspiration 11/2

Everything will be fine, providing Eights' aspirations are of an altruistic nature. If this is not the case, 11/2 will never accept giving up their wishes. Actually, 11/2 wants to be free from everyday hardships and mishaps; while Eights aren't bothered.

Aspiration 9 vs. Aspiration 11/2

Nines mostly aspire for peace and harmony. They are genuinely searching for a humanitarian world. And this is in perfect keeping with the wishes of 11/2, who are also very much aware of other people's plights. Furthermore, adamant impulsive Elevens will be soothed by Nines' empathy.

Aspiration 11/2 vs. Aspiration 11/2

Their aspirations are identical and can therefore prove very constructive if they go in the same direction. If not, they will prevent each other from going anywhere. This is not a smooth relationship, in that Twos' aspirations are linked to intimate feelings, protection and tranquility; very unlike Elevens'. This being said, two Elevens together are likely to struggle and two Twos together are likely to fall asleep. Don't forget that Twos aspire for material comfort and protection of their loved ones. It is a question of how much and when. In other words, it is important to know whether at any given moment if these individuals are more influenced by Two or by Eleven.

Aspiration 11/2 vs. Aspiration 11

In this particular case, the Two part of 11/2 will mean they are looking to protect their interests and possessions, as their aspirations are more self-centered than Elevens' who aren't bothered.

Aspiration 11/2 vs. Aspiration 22

Twenty-Twos can bring a great deal to 11/2, providing 11/2 can become less eccentric and more realistic in their aspirations. If this is not the case, they may completely misunderstand each other.

The influence of First and Middle Names

We all have one or several first names. The numerological value of each of these first names refers to a particular domain, as has been explained by the French numerologist Françoise Daviet that we summarize as follows.

The First Name

The first name value refers to the way we live on an everyday basis, the qualities we express at work and the type of energy that we use when we carry out our daily tasks.

Therefore, comparing the value of the first names of two people will enable you to understand how they harmonize (or not) their energies on a daily basis and face their responsibilities and obligations.

You may want to refer back to the definitions of the aspects between Potential numbers, as well as those of the Expression numbers and adjust them accordingly.

The first Middle Name.

When there is this name, it exists to highlight our relationships with other people, be they friends or foes, or both, according to our moods.

Comparing two first middle names gives a wealth of information about love relationships, business partnerships and all other relationships: such as a parent and child, a therapist and patient, a teacher and pupil, a salesperson and customer and so on...

Focus on the aspects between Expression numbers and adjust accordingly. Pay particular attention to the paragraph that deals with love relationships. When studying these aspects, first compare the Expressions of the two persons, then the numerological value of their first middle names, if they have any.

Example: Peter has an Expression 5 and his companion Mary has an Expression 8. First check out the general aspect between Expression 5 and Expression 8, then compare the numerological value of their second middle names. Let's imagine Peter's first middle name is Henry and Mary's is Patricia.

```
Henry
85597 → 8+5+5+9+7 = 34 → 3+4 = 7

Patricia
71299391 → 7+1+2+9+9+3+9+1 = 41 → 4+1 = 5
```

Now study the aspect of Expression 7 with Expression 5 in chapter V and adapt it to their love relationship.

The second Middle Name

This reveals the person's sentimental relationships. The numerological value of this name enables us to understand the nature of the energy of the individuals when they enjoy life's pleasures in general. It also explains the nature of the bond between the person and their children.

For instance, suppose the value of the second Middle Name of a person is worth 3 and the value of the second Middle Name of his/her partner is 11. Adjust according to what is said about Expression 3 and Expression 11.

The influence of sub-numbers

Numbers are not isolated. When you work out an Expression number, it results from adding other numbers up. These other numbers take part in the final Expression too (refer to "Inclusion" in the first volume of this book). In numerology, any key number is the result of an array of different influences. In other words, the color green may stem from many different possibilities, each resulting from numerous hues.

This explains why, at a higher degree of analysis, we can say that although two persons share the same Expression number, this number is not exactly the same, if it results from the additions of different sub-numbers. Expression 6 shared by two persons might come from the sub-number 24 (2+4) for one partner, or from 51 (5+1) for the other. In the first case, the Expression 6 features more passivity because 2 and 4 emphasize the need for reconciliation and peace. In the second case, 5 and 1 are more active and thus boost the given dynamics.

Different intensities

This is an essential tool with which to further analyze numbers, although it is too often forgotten. Along with the sub-numbers that have previously been studied, we will now deal with the most represented numbers in the Expression, Potential, Aspiration and Active numbers.

As an example, let's consider the Active numbers of Daniel and Judith, who both have no middle names. When we add the value of each letter of their first names, we realize that not only do they have the identical Active number 9, but that this Active number results from the same sub-number 27! Is this supposed to mean that Daniel and Judith always react exactly in the same way? In fact, Daniel's Nine (27) comes from letters featuring 1 (A), 3 (L), 4 (D), 5+5 (N and E) and 9 (I). His Active Number therefore has an intensity of 5, as 5 is represented twice by the letters N and E. Have a look at Judith's Active number and you will see that neither the components nor the proportions are exactly the same; since there is no number more represented than another (each letter J U D I T H vibrates a different value). All these differences must be taken into account.

This is true for any key number. This being said, intensities must be calculated only with vowels as far as the Aspiration numbers are concerned, and only with consonants as far as Potential numbers are concerned.

Aspects between different key numbers

Two different key numbers can be compared, such as the Expression number of a person with the Life Path of his/her partner. Let's consider the aspects between Aspirations numbers, as studied in chapter VI. Bear in mind that aspirations act as impulses of the soul, stemming from our deep nature. Since personalities don't rely merely on this number, it is interesting to compare Aspirations and Life Paths for instance. You should then regard the aspirations of the person as his/her deep nature (life path), and not only as an impulse.

Example: Compare Aspiration 1 with Aspiration 2 in chapter VI. With a little imagination, you can now compare Aspiration 1 with Life Path 2, considering the comments on Aspiration 2 as comments on Life Path 2, keeping in mind that in the first case, we are dealing with the person's impulses, whereas in the second case, we are dealing with the person's true nature.

Such comparisons involve a little brain gymnastics, which will prove very useful and necessary if you want to seriously commit to numerology and go into deeper analysis.

All things considered, it is never possible to draw final conclusions in numerology. We have studied the main aspects of key numbers, so as to give a panoramic view of the different features. Yet, all this can be even further analyzed, through the interaction of the different key numbers as well as the elements at the basis of the calculations, i.e. such as the letters of the different first names, the numbers of the year of birth and so on... As well as a great many elements that very likely remain to be discovered...

Getting along with your own self...

The last key of this book enables you to use it not only to see how you get along with a particular person, but also how you get along with yourself. Nobody is a sole number. Everybody partakes of numerous influences, as represented by the energies of numbers.

Compare the subtle analysis of two different key numbers and apply it to yourself, so as to fathom better how different forces act, react and interact within your own self.

Example: You have a Life Path 2 with an Aspiration 1. Taking into account that Aspiration 2 is regarded as Life Path 2, consider the aspect between Aspiration 1 and Aspiration 2, as follows (refer to the suitable chapter):

Number 2 searches for peace and calm, whereas number 1 dreams of conquering the world. While one person aspires for harmony, thus emphasizing all kinds of partnerships, the other person wishes to rule and coerce. Although this type of association may not seem right at first glance, it is possible to find consensus. Number 2 can easily comply with number One's wishes, in spite of the lack of sensitivity they blame Ones for and which triggers a certain amount of frustration. Number Twos are considered as overly emotional by number Ones, who are easily annoyed by this. Yet, Ones do not dwell on unhappy thoughts for long, which is why they will overcome any negative feelings. As long as Ones refrain from judging their partner as too sentimental, the association can be harmonious. If not, a chasm of misunderstanding can come between them.

Because we are dealing with mutual aspirations, all this might not be visible or as apparent as one would like. That which is unexpressed is like the submerged part of an iceberg, and can cause discomfort within each individual's heart. Their dreams are diametrically opposed.

Keeping in mind that Aspiration 2 is your own Life Path 2, this aspect can therefore be interpreted as follows:

Although I am searching for peace and calm, and despite the fact that my destiny drives me to experience an ideal couple relationship, an uncontrollable force urges me to go beyond my limited boundaries and to conquer and explore something different. I must strike a balance between these two opposing forces within me, by giving this enterprising aspiration a direction. This will then enable me to create a nice comfortable life. I will have to accept that this instinctive and impulsive drive of mine must be expressed, even though it is bound to upset my need for intimacy and privacy.

I must find a compromise within myself between these contradictions.

APPENDIX 1

THE PRINCIPAL LATIN ALPHABETS
AND THEIR LETTER/VALUE CORRESPONDING TABLE

English/French Alphabet								
1	**2**	**3**	**4**	**5**	**6**	**7**	**8**	**9**
A	B	C	D	E	F	G	H	I
J	K (11)	L	M	N	O	P	Q	R
S	T	U	V (22)	W	X	Y	Z	

Spanish Alphabet								
Traditional classification before 1994								
1	**2**	**3**	**4**	**5**	**6**	**7**	**8**	**9**
A	B	C	CH	D	E	F	G	H
I	J (11)	K	L	LL	M	N	Ñ	O
P	Q	R	S (22)	T	U	V	W	X
Y	Z							
Since 1994								
1	**2**	**3**	**4**	**5**	**6**	**7**	**8**	**9**
A	B	C	D	E	F	G	H	I
J	K (11)	L	M	N	Ñ	O	P	Q
R	S	T	U (22)	V	W	X	Y	Z

Italian Alphabet								
1	**2**	**3**	**4**	**5**	**6**	**7**	**8**	**9**
A	B	C	D	E	F	G	H	I
L	M (11)	N	O	P	Q	R	S	T
U	V	Z						

Portuguese Alphabet								
1	**2**	**3**	**4**	**5**	**6**	**7**	**8**	**9**
A	B	C	D	E	F	G	H	I
J	L (11)	M	N	O	P	Q	R	S
T	U	V	X (22)	Z	K?	W?	Y?	

Note: Since December 16, 1990, K, W and Y have been included following an international agreement between the Portuguese-speaking countries. If they are added at the end, K (worth 6), W (worth 7) and Y (worth 8) they have the same value as in English, so you would then use the English Alphabet.

German like the English Alphabet with Ä Ö Ü ß at the end of the alphabet								
1	**2**	**3**	**4**	**5**	**6**	**7**	**8**	**9**
A	B	C	D	E	F	G	H	I
J	K (11)	L	M	N	O	P	Q	R
S	T	U	V	W	X	Y	Z	Ä
Ö	Ü	ß						

Another way to calculate the German Alphabet...								
1	**2**	**3**	**4**	**5**	**6**	**7**	**8**	**9**
A	Ä	B	C	D	E	F	G	H
I	J (11)	K	L	M	N	O	Ö	P
Q	R	S	ß	T	U	Ü	V	W
X	Y	Z						

In the case where you think Ä, Ö, Ü and ß have this placement
Otherwise, if you consider that umlauts have been formed by the merger with the vowel E you can define as follows:

$$Ä \rightarrow AE \rightarrow 1+5 = 6$$
$$Ö \rightarrow OE \rightarrow 6+5 = 11$$
$$Ü \rightarrow UE \rightarrow 3+5 = 8$$
$$ß \rightarrow SZ \rightarrow 1+8 = 9 \text{ or } ß \rightarrow SS \rightarrow 1+1...$$

Dutch Alphabet								
1	**2**	**3**	**4**	**5**	**6**	**7**	**8**	**9**
A	B	C	D	E	F	G	H	I
J	K (11)	L	M	N	O	P	Q	R
S	T	U	V (22)	W	X	Y or IJ	Z	

Fill in the table if you use a different alphabet

.... Alphabet								
1	**2**	**3**	**4**	**5**	**6**	**7**	**8**	**9**
	(11)							
			(22)					

.... Alphabet								
1	**2**	**3**	**4**	**5**	**6**	**7**	**8**	**9**
	(11)							
			(22)					

APPENDIX 2

Feel free to photocopy these pages, so as to work out all the necessary calculations. Please also see our on-line application: online-numerology.com

CALCULATING LIFE PATH NUMBERS

Work out your Life Paths, through your own date of birth and that of your partner's. (You must use all three methods of calculations, as described at the beginning of chapter IV). Note every sub-number, as well as the final reduced number.

YOUR LIFE PATH

By adding all the figures of the date of birth and reduce the result.

Example: $15/08/1971 \rightarrow 1+5+8+1+9+7+1 = 32 \rightarrow 3+2 = 5$

___ ___ _____ → _____ = __ → _____ = __

By adding day, month & year of birth, and then reducing the result.

$15+8+1971=1994 \rightarrow 1+9+9+4=23 \rightarrow 2+3=5$

_____ = _____ → _____ = ___ → _____ = __

By adding reduced day, month & year (except if result is 11 or 22)

Day$\rightarrow$6 + Month$\rightarrow$8 Year$\rightarrow$9 = 23 → 2+3=5

Day→___ + Month→___ + Year→___ = __ → _____ = _

HER / HIS LIFE PATH

By adding all the figures of the date of birth and reduce the result.

___ ___ _____ → _____ = __ → _____ = __

By adding day, month & year of birth, and then reducing the result.

_____ = _____ → _____ = ___ → _____ = __

By adding reduced day, month & year (except if result is 11 or 22)

Day→___ + Month→___ + Year→___ = __ → _____ = _

Go to Chapter IV for the interpretation of what is being said taking into account the type of relationship (parent/child, love relationships/ associates) as defined in chapter III.

CALCULATING EXPRESSION NUMBERS

Add the value of every letter present in your mother's maiden last name (leave her first name out) and in all of your first names. Then repeat the operation with all of your partner's first names and her/his mother's maiden last name. Reduce each result until you get a number included between 1 and 9, or 11 or 22.

```
LINDA NANCY WILSON
39541 51537 593165
SUM OF LETTERS = 72 → 7+2 = 9
```

YOUR EXPRESSION NUMBER

_____

SUM OF LETTERS ____ → _____ = ____

HER / HIS EXPRESSION NUMBER

_____

SUM OF LETTERS ____ → _____ = ____

Go to Chapter V for the interpretation of what is being said taking into account the type of relationship (parent/child, love relationships/associates) as defined in chapter III.

Verify your calculations at www.numerology-unveiled.com

CALCULATING ASPIRATION NUMBERS

Add the value of every vowel present in your mother's maiden name and in all of your first names. Then repeat the same with all your partner's first names and her/his mother's maiden last name. Reduce each result until you get a number included between 1 and 9, or 11 or 22.

```
LINDA NANCY WILSON
-9--1 -1--7 -9--6-
SUM OF VOWELS = 33 → 3+3 = 6
```

YOUR ASPIRATION NUMBER (Soul Urge)

_____

SUM OF VOWELS ____ → _____ = ____

HER / HIS ASPIRATION NUMBER (Soul Urge)

_____

SUM OF VOWELS ____ → _____ = ____

See chapter VI for interpretation.

Verify your calculations at www.numerology-unveiled.com

CALCULATING POTENTIAL NUMBERS

Add the value of every consonant present in your mother's maiden name and in all of your first names. Then repeat the same with all your partner's first names and her/his mother's maiden last name. Reduce each result until you get a number included between 1 and 9, or 11 or 22.

```
LINDA NANCY WILSON
3-54- 5-53- 5-31-5
SUM OF CONSONANTS = 39 → 3+9 = 12 → 1+2 = 3
```

YOUR POTENTIAL NUMBER

_____

SUM OF CONSONANTS ____ → _____ = ____

HER / HIS POTENTIAL NUMBER

_____

SUM OF CONSONANTS ____ → _____ = ____

Refer to chapter VII to see how well you are likely to get along, according to your potential.

Verify your calculations at www.numerology-unveiled.com

CALCULATING ACTIVE NUMBERS

Add the value of every letter present in all of your first names only. Then repeat the same for your partner's first names only. Reduce each result until you get a number included between 1 and 9, or 11 or 22.

```
LINDA NANCY
39541 51537
SUM OF LETTERS = 43 → 4+3 = 7
```

YOUR ACTIVE NUMBER

_____

SUM OF LETTERS ____ → _____ = ____

HER / HIS ACTIVE NUMBER

_____

SUM OF LETTERS ____ → _____ = ____

Refer to chapter VIII to see how well you are likely to get along, as far as your actions and reactions are concerned.

Verify your calculations at www.numerology-unveiled.com

BIBLIOGRAPHY

AVERY Kevin Quinn
The Numbers of Life: The Hidden Power in Numerology / DMS / 1977

BUESS Lynn
Numerology: Nuances in Relationships / Light Technology Publications / March 1991
Numerology for the New Age / Light Technology Publications; 2nd edition / December 1978

CAMPBELL Florence
Your days are numbered / Devorss Publications / 1931 / Marina del Rey USA

DECOZ Hans with MONTE Tom
Numerology Key to your inner self / Avery Publishing Group / 1994 / USA

DUCIE Sonia
The complete illustrated Guide to Numerology / Element Books Limited /1999 / USA

GOODWIN O. Matthew
Numerology The Complete Guide (Volume 1: The personality reading) / 1981 / Newcastle Publishing Company, INC / North Hollywood, California
Numerology The Complete Guide (Volume 2: Advanced personality analysis and reading the Past, Present , and Future) / 1981 / Newcastle Publishing Company, INC / North Hollywood, California

MILLMAN Dan
The Life You Were Born to Live: A Guide to Finding Your Life Purpose / HJ Kramer / 1993

POCHAT Wilfrid & PIRMAÏER Michel
The Unveiled Numerology (Volume 1: You do not necessarily carry the name you think) / Nostredame Publishing / 2011

TABLE OF CONTENTS

www.ingramcontent.com/pod-product-compliance
Lightning Source LLC
Chambersburg PA
CBHW071407090426
42737CB00011B/1384